Daughters
of the
Island

About the Cover

The cover reflects both tradition and modernity in the lives of Chamorro women. Francisco Garcia describes a female ritual at a fiesta where in twelve or thirteen women join in a circle singing histories and legends accompanied by movements of the hands. This is done in perfect time and causes no little admiration. The rhythm continues through the generations in this drawing by Hannah Torres Gutierrez and Erin Souder Freitas, nieces of the author, who have taken a glimmer from the past and made it present for us through their eyes. Fragility and hope flow from its lines.

MARC Monograph Series No. 1

Daughters of the *Island*

Contemporary Chamorro Women Organizers on Guam

Second Edition

Laura Marie Torres Souder

UNIVERSITY
PRESS OF
AMERICA

Lanham • New York • London

MICRONESIAN
AREA
RESEARCH
CENTER
University of Guam

University Press of America®, Inc.

4720 Boston Way
Lanham, Maryland 20706

3 Henrietta Street
London WC2E 8LU England

Co-published by arrangement with
The Micronesian Area Research Center

Library of Congress Cataloging-in-Publication Data

Souder, Laura Marie Torres.
Daughters of the island : contemporary Chamorro women organizers
on Guam / Laura Marie Torres Souder.
p.   cm. — (MARC monograph series ;   no. 1)
Includes bibliographical references and index.
1. Women, Chamorro.   2. Women, Chamorro—Biography.
I. Title.   II. Series.
DU647.S68   1992   305.48'79921—dc20   92–3034 CIP

ISBN 0–8191–8607–4 (cloth : alk. paper)
ISBN 0–8191–8608–2 (pbk. : alk. paper)

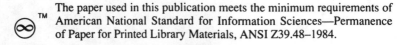

To all Chamorro Women,
Mariquita Calvo Torres Souder, my mother,
and the late Cecilia Cruz Bamba
and
to the Micronesian Area Research Center
in commemoration of 20 years of service
to the community.

TABLE OF CONTENTS

List of Illustrations:

FOREWORD

It is gratifying to me as an author that a second edition of my book is being made available to a wider readership, a wider public. This has challenged me to edit and clarify things so that people, who do not come from Guam and who are not literate about the Guam experience, can better appreciate the context in which the lives of the women that are the focus of this book have been shaped and the events that they have also helped to shape. In a sense, my revisions have included expanding an understanding of the issues for those readers.

This edition really reflects subtle, yet important changes from the previous first edition. My own insights have developed further as I have listened to and read criticisms of the book. I've learned to come to terms with my own consistency as a woman, as a professional, as one who is more actively engaged in academia, and as a teacher. I appreciate and understand how the exchange of ideas, especially between an author and a readership which the author may never really encounter face to face, can be immensely valuable in sharpening one's analysis and perspectives on one's own work. My own development and growth has required that I look at issues in ways that help to put into clearer focus the significance of the lives of these women leaders operating in a particular socio-economic and political context. Part of the continuing process of reassessment and re-evaluation has included changes in my own personal life. This is reflected in my name change as I have reclaimed my own full identity. After experiencing an unbalanced relationship which lead to the dissolution of my first marriage, I have grown in personal and political consciousness about my rights and needs as a woman. I have found in my healthy balanced partnership with my new husband that men can indeed be feminist and remain consistent with their own rights and needs.

There is a Chamorro glossary as an example of another subtle yet important change. Guam has gone through many changes in the arena of resurrecting our indigenous language, perfecting it, strengthening it, and purifying it as we Chamorros have claimed our peoplehood--this we have done by claiming our language. In our language we see the way Chamorros view the world, the way we view ourselves, and the way we seek to alter and change that which might in some way threaten our existence as a people. As we are more increasingly engaged in the process of decolonization and political/economic/social self-determination particularly in relation to the land and to the struggle against investment scams from the outside that are sometimes touted as development, it is important to understand and to appreciate the way Chamorros use language to assert peoplehood. In this context, the inclusion of a Chamorro glossary is a small but significant addition.

The basic core experiences of the women who were the focus of the first edition remain as the essence of what this book is about. Elizabeth Arriola and Pilar Lujan are still in the legislature. They both won seats in the 21st Guam Legislature. Tina Blas' husband did win the Lt. Governorship in 1986 and again in 1990. Tina continues her work as a health professional. Carmen Pearson has left the Department of Public Health and Social Services and is back at her University of Guam job as coordinator of the Family Leadership Program. Annie Roberto is still working with elders but has left Interfaith Volunteer Caregivers and is now working with the Department of Public Health and Social Services as head of the Center for the Elderly in Dededo. Geri Gutierrez continues to provide the support and networks in partnership with her husband, Carl, in their joint service to the community and to the region. Tan Delgadina Hiton serves the Church and her village even into her late seventies. Ding Gould has retired from her professional work but her cartoons and her satire continue to be the only Chamorro language humor that appears in the Pacific Daily News. Cecilia Bamba has passed away.

The meaning given to the contributions and struggles of these women must continuously be re-analyzed as we move toward self-determination as a people. We are challenged as never before about what to do with the land and our rapid alienation from it. We are faced with the challenge of educating a generation of men and women who must have a sense of respect towards equal partnerships in which the code of machismo or inequality must somehow take a backseat if we are to survive with dignity and with a sense of peoplehood. We are now experiencing social chaos as the incidence of sex abuse, incest, rape, battering, child abuse and neglect, murder, drug and alcohol dependency, gambling, and abortion skyrocket. A mere glance at the pathology on the island is enough to illustrate that we are a people in crisis.

These issues require that Chamorro women organize more creatively and differently as we enter the twenty-first century to meet the challenges, some of which our people have never been confronted with before. We must be bold. The responsibility for the continuity of peoplehood is ours!

Laura M. Torres Souder
Agana, Guam
August 1991

PREFACE TO THE FIRST EDITION

The women rule here! This is the message found in the early accounts of life in the islands now called the Marianas. Women formulated decisions and exercised authority in domestic matters and far beyond. The Chamorro tradition was shaken to its roots by the advent of Spanish rule, the introduction of Christianity and the subsequent depopulation due to warfare and disease. Women took matters into their own hands and kept alive what they saw as important.

The women preserve our culture! This is the new message found in the emerging Hispanic tradition. They carefully taught their children the language and customs of the ancestors along with the tenents of Christianity. Their influence was less direct but it continued to have wide impact in domestic and church related community matters. This influence continues to the present century and day.

The modern Chamorro women, who live today in the emerging American tradition, have as their inheritance both the Chamorro and Hispanic traditions. They are deeply in contact with the latter and are recovering the former in new and innovative ways. The unique focus of this work is women as organizers in church, civic, island-wide, regional, national, and international forums. Often a need in the community served as the starting point for the organizer to create a network which would meet the challenge and successfully resolve the situation.

The women of the Western Pacific have an eloquent voice on their behalf in the person of Laura Marie Torres Souder. She has woven an impressive tapestry from traditional material but with a distinctly modern design. The women of this book will easily recognize themselves, as will their friends and neighbors on the island. Perhaps in the future they will be seen as the women who saw the need and organized!

Thomas B. McGrath, S.J.
Editor
Agana, Guam
December 1988

ACKNOWLEDGEMENTS

This book has truly been a labor of love involving many people. I am indebted to all who have contributed in some way to making this dream a reality. Although there are too many to mention by name, I would like to acknowledge the following for their patience, understanding, and determination in seeing this project through to its completion.

My parents, Paul and Mariquita, my sister Debbie and her family, my brother Paul and his family, my staff Tessie Ramez, Katrina Perez, and Alice Taijeron have given so generously of their love, encouragement, and support. Their willingness to lend a hand, whatever the need, can never be properly recognized. My nieces, Erin Souder Freitas and Hannah Torres Gutierrez, deserve special thanks for their artistic contribution to the cover.

Without the total commitment and dedication of my most able assistant, Palauan sister, and dearest friend Elfrieda Koshiba, I would not have managed this second edition. Sulang Elfrie!

I owe deeply felt gratitude to my doctoral committee members and to my Guam advisor who guided me throughout the research and writing of my dissertation, which provides the substance of this work.

I also wish to extend my warmest appreciation to the staff of the Nieves M. Flores Memorial Library and the Guam Museum, especially Mr. William Hernandez for providing historical photographs; to Mrs. Rosa Palomo and the Chamorro Language Commission for reviewing the text for orthographic consistency; to Dr. Robert Underwood for his insights; and to the director and staff of the Micronesian Are Research Center (MARC) who have so generously assisted in the production of this edition--particularly Mrs. Rosita D. Tosco who went way beyond the call of duty in preparing the manuscript for publication.

I would like to express a "dangkulu na si Yu'os maase" to the Chamorro women organizers who participated in this study. No words can adequately convey the esteem and gratitude I hold for them and for all other Chamorro women who have inspired me to document part of our Chamorro story.

Finally, I wish to express my most heartfelt "muchas gracias" to my very best friend, kindred spirit, colleague and husband, Dr. Samuel Betances, for being, in the truest sense, an extension of my best self.

CHAPTER I

IN PURSUIT OF HERSTORY

Recovering the Forgotten Ones

"How did Chief Kepuha and the other ancient Chamorro chiefs have children?"--"What do you mean?"--"Well, did men have babies back then?"--"Are you serious?"--"Considering, you know, that there were no women."--"What makes you think that?"--"Have you ever read about a single Chamorro woman in the history books? I haven't."

Stunned into silence, the profound message of this short dialogue hit me like a shower of coconuts detached by an unexpected gust of wind. I was not quite prepared for the immense task of responding to such an innocent inquiry. The young Chamorro girl who raised the questions waited patiently for an answer. I managed to blurt out a rather badly articulated one: "There were always Chamorro women who had the babies even if they were rarely written about in the books."

For students in the Guam History class I was addressing during "Chamorro Week" activities at the Guam Vocational and Technical High School in March 1977, the issue was laid to rest. For me, that moment marked a beginning. I resolved to resurrect Chamorro women of the past from their graves of silence and to serve as a mouth piece for Chamorro women of today so that their stories would not suffer the same fate.

This book addresses status, roles, and contributions of Chamorro women in three ways.[1] Firstly, I have examined the historical record and have attempted to weave together the bits and pieces of information on women, sprinkled throughout the literature about Guam, so as to write a history of the roles and significance of Chamorro women in their culture. Scholarship on Chamorro women is virtually nonexistent. Only a handful of studies have given partial attention to Chamorro women. Aside from these efforts and the occasional newspaper or magazine article featuring particular individuals, the experiences and contributions of Chamorro women remain unrecorded. It is unlikely that contemporary Chamorro women will write of their experiences themselves.

Nevertheless, their role as active participants in Guam's history is a vital one, indeed half of the Chamorro story. I hope that some of the gaps in the historical record will have been filled by answering such questions as: What was the female experience? How did women live? What did they do? What would history be like if it were seen through the eyes of Chamorro women and ordered by values they define?

These concerns lead directly to the second aim of this work, actually to document the life experiences of at least a few Chamorro women. The selection of a focal group was based on the rationale that the tasks Chamorro women have performed demonstrate their ability as formal and informal organizers. Some are recognized as skillful managers and powerful activists by the Chamorro community. These women have been instrumental in organizing political campaigns, social and cultural movements, single-issue causes, community or family activities, and women-centered programs which call for leadership capability above and beyond the organizational and managerial skills expected of most Chamorro women in the home or domestic sphere. Given the assumption that organizing has been utilized by Chamorro women as a viable means of participating in the creation of history and effecting change, I considered Chamorro women organizers as an appropriate choice of subjects. The intensity and visibility of their involvement as makers and shapers of Guam's history make them important resources. Furthermore, social historians and feminists--in their attempts to correct the bias in written history and expand it to include the lives of the poor, Blacks and other minorities, and most recently women--did begin with leaders or activists in the public sphere. In this context Chamorro women organizers as a group are a logical starting point in the process of "bringing women out of hiding." Material comprising the case study portion of this work is the result of this documentation process.

My task is guided by several inquiries: What factors motivated women to organize? What did they organize? What resources or organizational strategies did they utilize? How did they view their work as organizers? Did their organizational experience give rise to any development of personal consciousness? And lastly, how does this study of Chamorro women organizers contribute to our knowledge of the experiences of Chamorro women and the roles they play in contemporary Guam?

The third and final objective is to achieve a better understanding of how Chamorro women are perceived and how they perceive themselves--their contributions, their position, and their status as women. Although generalizations are necessarily limited to the women portrayed in this study, I make tentative observations regarding principles of feminism in the Chamorro context.

The cross-cultural literature on women suggests a characteristic pattern of female exclusion from participation and influence in community policy, official positions of power, and politics. The experience of Chamorro women is somewhat different when compared with that of American women or the prevailing reality of most contemporary societies of the Third World in that they are increasingly assuming top level official positions of authority in proportionately greater numbers than women elsewhere. Frequently observers ask: What cultural factors can account for the tendency of women who assume official positions of leadership on Guam to become more powerful than their male counterparts? What can explain the fact that women on Guam dominate the upper levels of the power structure in the field of education?

Speculations abound. Among the most popular is the explanation that this emergence of women in positions of power parallels the women's liberation movement in the United States and elsewhere in the world. Another explanation is that

3

although women comprise the bulk of Guam's educational leadership, when compared with positions of power that men hold, education is traditionally a women's domain anyway. Consequently this attainment is not so unusual or significant.

Others, myself included, contend that, in comparison to many of their sisters abroad, Chamorro women on Guam do have considerable power in both the public and private spheres. Are there historical antecedents which account for this uncharacteristic pattern? Have historical circumstances worked to the advantage of the Chamorro female? Is there a difference between the prescribed behavior imposed by societal institutions and the actual behavior of Chamorro women? Does modernization pose a threat of diminishing status for Guam's women? What factors could contribute to the possible breakdown of female power in Chamorro society? How do contemporary Chamorro women perceive their status and gender? How do they view feminism? This book seeks to answer these questions.

My commitment to the preservation and development of the Chamorro culture provides the underlying motivation for this work. As a Chamorro woman activist, I have observed and participated in the activities of contemporary Chamorro women in the everyday life of the Guam community. I derive a tremendous sense of fulfillment in documenting a small part of our collective experience.

Chamorro women today, particularly the younger generation, are caught in the swirl of an unprecedented period of change in the values, customs, and traditions which once provided stability and a source of cultural identity and pride. We are fast becoming victims of cultural marginality. Young women are faced with dilemmas regarding, on the one hand, their sense of personal fulfillment as career women and, on the other, the values and traditions which they believe in and want to hold on to including their roles as wife and mother. This record of the lives of nine Chamorro women, their coping strategies and resolution of personal conflicts, can serve as both inspiration and role model for Chamorro women attempting to

4

make personal decisions which deal with the contradictions that so often become a source of frustration and lack of fulfillment.

Haga' means blood. Pronounced slightly differently, *haga* means daughter. I am a blood-daughter of my Chamorro ancestors who migrated to *Guahan* over three thousand years ago. Our people created a new life on an inconspicuous volcanic peak in the vast waters of the Western Pacific and called our homeland, "the place which has." This work is an attempt of one *hagan-haga'* to discover and share a part of the continuing story of our Chamorro cultural heritage.

As a Chamorro student, I hope to contribute to the development of scholarship from an indigenous and female perspective. Revisionists in all fields are striving to correct the hidden biases of conventional Historiography. Most of Guam history has been written from the myopic perspective of Western males. The work of native writers has been greatly influenced by Western methodology and perspective. While I do not discount the usefulness of this methodology, nevertheless I attempt to question the general applicability of Western scientific research methods by sharing the conflicts and research problems I have experienced.

I am hopeful my endeavor will make several broader contributions. Research by, for, and about women has proliferated in the last decade, receiving the greatest impetus from feminist scholars who offer alternative theories and methods for studying women. The material contained in this study will add to our knowledge of women. It also enables further testing of the new theories and methodologies that feminists are in the process of developing. Another area of major concern to feminists relates to the issue of the universality of the female experience. Third World feminists, for example, are questioning the applicability of Western feminist resolutions to their unique problems.[2] While there is growing recognition that cultural differences and varying experiences divide Western feminists from their sisters in the Third World, prevailing theories have not bridged the gap. There is a need to explore cross-cultural perspectives on feminism more openly before an understanding

5

can be reached. Studies of the particular experiences and perceptions of different cultural groups, such as this, can provide the necessary basis for comparison. Alternative views form the basis for revising existing feminist theories. Furthermore, this study will provide information on an indigenous culture caught in the throes of modernization while highlighting the manner in which women in transition are coping with change. Thus it should find its place in the fast-developing genre of literature identified as Women's Studies.

On another level, this effort can contribute to the steadily growing body of literature on American minorities. The indigenous cultures of Pacific Americans have been ignored by U.S. Government agencies and officials as they have implemented programs, which have reflected American mainstream values and practices. In order to achieve a more sensitive and balanced relationship between Pacific Islanders and the official organs of the U.S. Government in the Pacific Territories, greater understanding is essential. In-depth studies from an indigenous perspective can provide a means to that end. Moreover, a basic assumption of this study is that the Chamorro story is not merely an interesting saga of a Pacific people of the distant past. It is a contemporary illustration of the struggle for meaning and identity which complicates the lives of many Americans in pursuit of that ever-illusive "American Dream." If an informed and culturally sensitive perspective on Chamorro women is gained from this research endeavor, the study will have established its relevance to American Studies.

Central to the existence of all Chamorro women are two essential ingredients of identity--being Chamorro and being female. A brief overview of Guam history is provided in Chapter II as a means of generating understanding about the historical-cultural circumstances which have influenced and altered Chamorro ways. In addition Chamorro perspectives on history and developments in women's history are briefly reviewed in this chapter. Together, Chapter II and the following sections illuminate the factors which account for the absence of

Chamorro women from the official historical record since contact with the West.

A Sense of History and Herstory

My attempt to reconstruct the historical experience of Chamorro women takes into account what I call the "Chamorro sense of history." Chamorros conceive of time as either *antes* (before) or *pa'go* (now). This conceptualization views the past (*i manmaloffan na tiempo*) as "lived experience." While such a definition may appear straightforward, a caveat is necessary. Chamorros generally interpret "lived experience" in the literal sense to mean the immediate past (relative to one's own experience), rather than the collective and long-range experience of Chamorros over time.

The subjects in this study hold this view, which is narrow in scope. In order to understand how Chamorro women organizers perceive their changing status and roles, the reader should be aware of the *antes* and *pa'go* dichotomy. However, to appreciate fully the position of Chamorro women in the past, an expanded vision is needed.

Unfortunately, despite its expansiveness, the conventional historical record about Guam fails to convey a sense of the actual experience of Chamorros themselves, let alone Chamorro women. Historians writing about Guam have generally devised timelines based on events or periods which have had significance in a formal, political, and Western context, that is in terms of Guam's relationship with world powers. This inclination has led to a division of Guam history into five basic periods: Precontact or Ancient Chamorro (1500 B.C. to A.D. 1521), Spanish (1521 to 1898), Naval Administration or First American (1898 to 1941 and 1944 to 1950), Japanese Occupation or World War II (1941 to 1944), and Post World War II or Second American (1950 to present).

In contrast, a women-centered approach calls for reordering history on the basis of the female experience. In proposing a revision of conventional periodization, I do not discard the importance of the aforementioned political events, which obviously affected the culture and people of Guam. Rather, I contend that when Guam history is examined with a "double vision" representing the indigenous and female perspectives, a more accurate reflection of "herstory" emerges. Although what we know of the female experience has been recorded by male observers until recently, when perceived through this doubled vision, different "turning points" begin to take shape.

The available information suggests that the first known turning point in the position of Chamorro women occurred with the introduction of Catholicism in the 1670s and the ensuing conquest of the aboriginal Chamorros by Spanish colonizers. For the next two hundred or more years ancient Chamorro culture absorbed new values, Christian traditions, and Spanish customs. This process of adaptation and assimilation eventually produced a stable hybrid traditional culture which persisted with only slight modification up through the early twentieth century, at which time a second turning point occurred.

With the advent of American rule, naval administrators enacted laws which imposed new restrictions on the rights and activities of Chamorro women. The U.S. military's concerted effort to transform the subsistence-level farming and fishing economy of Guam into a cash-based market economy created new arrangements in the Chamorro division of labor, which resulted in the separation of the home from the work place. Men became wage-earners. The domestic sphere became increasingly identified as the woman's place. Puritanical views led to the re-institution of restrictions on the moral conduct of women, which had been laxly enforced by the Spanish clergy. Gradually, Chamorro-Spanish ways amalgamated with American ways to form a pool of syncretic cultural traits which present-day Chamorros call traditional Chamorro culture or *kostumbren Chamorro*.

The sixties heralded another major turning point for Chamorro women. Rapid modernization, compounded by a growing heterogeneous population, characterizes this contemporary period. The experiences of the Chamorro women organizers in this study illustrate the distinction between the traditional and modern periods well. Subjects were either adolescents or adult women at the onset of the modern period. Hence their understanding and experience of it differ from that of the post-sixties generation. In addition their lived experience encompasses both the traditional and modern periods. In this sense, they are clearly transitional figures in contemporary Chamorro history.

Recording and Interpreting Women's Experiences

The basic historical approach for this work derives its conceptualization from the new social history and women's history. Until the early twentieth century academic American history was noted for its so-called objective and elitist portrayal of American political and legal institutions to the exclusion of all else.[3] Revisionist historians writing at the turn of the century challenged conventional historical analysis through an application of social science methods. This new school of progressive historians criticized American political and economic institutions and

> called for a dynamic "new history" that would encompass social and economic developments as well as legal and political institutions, that would deal with conflict among classes and interest groups rather than stress national unity, and that would be relevant to contemporary social concerns.[4]

Despite their revolutionary departure from traditional interpretations, these "new historians" continued to write from the perspective of the dominant culture. Social and cultural historians of the post World War II era have attempted to correct this bias in their Historiography.[5]

While it is true that these revisionists of American history caused a significant shift in the focus of subjects for historical analysis, the inclusion of women as a legitimate topic of history was by and large ignored.[6] Many modern social

9

historians have tended to focus on women in their work. Several progressive historians also addressed the subject of women. Mary Ritter Beard's **Women as Force in History** is a classic example. Beard was one of the pioneers who made a case for studying women.

Overall, such concerns had little effect on the writing of history until the recent emergence of a new genre of literature which coincides with and is succored by the American Women's Movement of the Seventies and Eighties. Many of the works categorized as Women's Studies have applied social science and humanities methods in an effort to create a holistic and inter-disciplinary approach for the purpose of documenting and analyzing women's experiences.

The works of feminist historian Gerda Lerner are germane to the development of a branch of Women's Studies referred to as Women's History.[7] When Lerner first began writing about the need to record the story of the "majority of humankind," among her recognized and well-respected male colleagues in American academe, she was a "lone voice crying in the wilderness."[8] She wrote an article in 1969 entitled, "New Approaches to the Study of Women in American History," which outlined the state of the art at that time. Lerner, incensed by blatant distortions in the historical record, urged that "a fresh approach to known material and to available sources" be developed.[9] She argued that the subject, "Women" was too vast and diffuse to serve as a valid point of departure and that the subject should be subsumed under several categories which recognized status differences based on race, class, economic status, family status, and political-legal status.[10] While the oppressed group model which feminists and social historians were inclined to use did offer significant insights, she stressed the need to go beyond looking at official positions of power and investigate the different forms of power women did in fact wield.[11] Lerner proposed that cross-cultural comparisons among groups of women across time be undertaken. She further pointed out the need to "distinguish the ideas society held at any given moment in regard to women's proper 'place' from what was actually women's status at that time," a point she elucidated in subsequent writings.[12] Finally, she addressed a fundamental question which has challenged scholars writing about women to this day: How are the contributions of women to be judged?

Are women noteworthy when their achievement falls exactly in a category of achievement set up for men? Obviously not, for this is how they have been kept out of the history books up to now. Are women noteworthy then, as the early feminists tended to think, if they do anything at all? Not likely. The fact remains that women are different from men and that their role in society and history is different from that of men. Different, but equal in importance. Obviously their achievements must also be measured on a different scale. To define and devise such a scale is difficult until the gaps in our historical knowledge about the actual contributions of women have been filled. This work remains to be done.[13]

Many historians have since joined Lerner in challenging conventional Historiography by questioning basic assumptions, posing new questions to bring women into view, revising the accepted historical periodization based on political and economic events, challenging patriarchy, and ultimately creating new categories of analysis. Historiographers of women's history are seeking new theoretical and conceptual methods to understand women's experience from a women-centered perspective. No definitive frameworks have as yet been established although many are being developed and used in research.

If women's history claims no clear-cut methodology, what is it? Is it a field, a subfield of social history or an aspect of family history? Gerda Lerner provides a succinct definition:

In the face of this time-honored neglect, the effort to reconstruct the female past has been called "women's history." The term must be understood not as being descriptive of a past reality but as a conceptual model, a strategy by which to focus and isolate that which traditional history has obscured.[14]

The writing of Guam history with few exceptions to date has been conventional in its assumptions and approaches. On a general level I hope this study will challenge the profile of progress or unilinear method of recording history which does not account for the dialectical nature of cultural change nor does it seek to uncover the hidden cultural realities in its portrayal. More specifically, I want to begin filling in the gaps about Chamorro women. The basic concepts of social history and women's history form the underpinnings of the historical perspective developed for this study.

Three approaches characterize the recent writings of women historians: the "women worthies" or compensatory approach; contribution history; and the female perspective, which draws its source and framework of analysis from the actual experience of women, i.e., oral histories, diaries, letters, autobiographies, and literature by women.[15] This work uses a combination of all three.

Research Methodology

The methodology used for this study is interdisciplinary, drawing its research framework from Women's Studies, the Humanities, and Social Sciences. These disciplines inform the issues studied and have shaped the types of questions raised. Furthermore, they provide a structure and the scholarly literature from which working concepts have been formulated. History, Anthropology, and Sociology have been the most useful.

Scholars studying women have increasingly turned to oral interviews or the life history method used by anthropologists as a way of getting at the heart of the contemporary female experience. A major portion of the material central to this study has been obtained through oral history interviews.

A thorough description of the use of this data gathering tool is found in **Lives: An Anthropological Approach to Biography**.[16] The authors, Langness and Frank, state that their book "comes out of a movement at this time toward what might be called 'person-centered' ethnography" ... and that, anthropologists who use the life history method convey directly the reality that people other than themselves experience.[17]

Of the six reasons they listed for utilizing this method, three are relevant to the objectives of this work:

> To portray culture; ... to illustrate some aspect of culture not usually portrayed by other means [such as women's view of their culture]; and to communicate something otherwise not communicated [for example, the humanist side of anthropology or, more typically, the insider's view of culture].[18]

Oral interviews also serve as an invaluable research tool for studying peoples with an oral tradition or the functionally illiterate populations of the world among whom the largest segment across cultures is female.[19]

Women historians and anthropologists have based numerous studies on oral history sources.[20] This documentary technique has assumed new levels of meaning for women researchers. In the words of feminist historian, Sherna Gluck:

> Women's oral history, then, is a feminist encounter, even if the interviewee is not herself a feminist. It is the creation of a new type of material on women; it is the validation of women's experiences; it is the communication among women of different generations; it is the discovery of our own roots and the development of a continuity which has been denied us in traditional historical accounts.[21]

Lynn Z. Bloom, Professor of English, has written extensively on biography and autobiography. In discussing the importance of the oral history interview for women, she states:

> ... every oral history interview with a women is a means of enhancing not only the woman's individual place on this earth, but the significance of women generally. The oral historian can raise the self-esteem

13

of the women interviewed, for in talking about themselves, women can recognize the worth of their roles, their efforts, their contributions, their lives.[22]

These considerations account for the suitability of the oral history method for my endeavor.

This data gathering tool provides a rich record of individual lives. So despite the claims that it is unscientific or subjective, what it offers cannot be duplicated by quantitative methods.

A literary and evocative presentation style is deliberately employed in this book to convey a personal sense of the living subjects. The objectification of the subjects in the case studies to follow or an implied distancing through the use of scientific language between interviewer and interviewees is alien to the interpersonal interaction between the writer and the subjects. Furthermore, it is imperative for the reader to bear in mind that the oral history documentation process itself is characterized by a similar dialectical relationship. Thus, my roles as interviewer, participant observer, and cultural insider have interacted with the subjects' roles as Chamorro women organizers, inteviewees, and friends to create a joint articulation of their experiences.

The climate of the interviews and the nature of the relationship between each subject and myself has been footnoted at the beginning of every case study. These disclosures are an essential prerequisite to understanding the tone and manner in which the nine case studies are written; for example, how I refer to each of the subjects in the context of the case studies reflects the relationship I have with her.

Another challenging responsibility as researcher became evident during discussions with subjects about how they would like to see themselves portrayed in the case studies. While all the subjects vested me with the task of sculpting the data into an acceptable form, they did express views about what they did not want: "Don't put words in my mouth"; "I'm simple, so make my story simple"; "I've never thought about my gender, so don't call me a feminist"; and "I hope you don't analyze me the way some óf those academics do." During a lengthy session with Cecilia Bamba, we discussed the kind of publicity she had gotten over the years--often superficial and unsatisfactory. I reiterated to her then, as to other subjects, that I wanted to do justice to them and their activities. I explained that I perceived my role as perhaps an artist or sculptor would: in attempting to characterize a person, create a profile, I hoped to capture the mind and spirit of each subject while recounting selective experiences in her life. These considerations guided the process of shaping case study materials.

A Profile of Chamorro Women Organizers

Chamorro women organizers represent a select group in the cast acting out the drama of contemporary Chamorro life. It is a basic contention of this study that they play a leading role. This section summarizes the responses of 82 subjects who comprised the sample population of the original study, to a preliminary survey questionnaire. The 20-page survey was designed to collect information for a tabular portrayal of the organizers as a distinct segment of Guam's female population. Demographic descriptors such as age, religion, place of birth, residence, education, occupation, and marital status were obtained. Data regarding family background, marital status, motherhood, Chamorro cultural practices, support systems both public and private, opinions on social issues, and details on the respondents' voluntary and organizational work were solicited to provide the necessary descriptive background for becoming acquainted with and understanding organizers as a group.

The data obtained through this field instrument were computer tabulated using the Statistical Package for the Social Sciences. Content analysis of open-ended responses supplemented this approach. The following is a profile of Chamorro women organizers drawn from information collected in the survey.

Chamorro women organizers unquestionably come from all walks of life. Their natal family backgrounds, present family life, demographic characteristics, and occupational, voluntary, and organizational experiences span a wide range with marked variations in life-style, attitudes, interests, and social circles.

Notwithstanding these differences, a composite portrait of Chamorro women organizers has emerged. She is likely to be a middle-age married woman with more than the average number of children. Her husband is probably Chamorro. She views him as a significant source of support, understanding, and encouragement. Her ties with both her natal and extended families are very strong. She is closer to maternal relatives and turns to them, most especially to her mother and sisters, for assistance with both domestic and public responsibilities. She visits her in-laws fairly regularly but is not as close to them as to her own family. A fluent speaker of both English and Chamorro, she nevertheless prefers Chamorro as it is the language of her childhood and the one most used by family members and friends. While she practices Chamorro traditions actively, she is quite concerned that her children's generation is losing touch with cultural values embodied in the extended family and Chamorro language.

The prototypical Chamorro woman organizer is a well-educated professional who has remained active in the labor force throughout her adult life. She is an active community volunteer who spent her nascent years as an organizer working with church related groups. Undeniably, her organizing has been facilitated by the support networks she has formed through contacts at school, her volunteer work, and organizational activities. These public sources of support augment the support and assistance she receives from her parents, husband, children, and relatives. Her sense of responsibility toward improving the quality of life and future community for her children serves as a major motivation for her involvement. She typically organizes formal activities on an islandwide scale. Community and women-centered organizations provide a locus for her organizing efforts.

Case study subjects Cecilia Bamba, Clotilde Gould, Pilar Lujan, Carmen Pearson, Annie Roberto, Elizabeth Arriola, Ernestina Blas, Geraldine Gutierrez, and Delgadina Hiton personify this archtypal organizer in various ways. The lives and experiences of these nine women organizers may not mirror those of all Chamorro women. Nevertheless, they are women in transition. They were born and reared at a time when Guam's population was culturally homogenous, yet they have lived a substantial portion of their adult lives in the last two decades. They have witnessed unprecedented change in values, customs, and family life. Having experienced firsthand the lifestyles and traditions characteristic of Guam prior to modernization, their cultural perspectives differ considerably from those of their children. These women have their feet planted in two worlds, so to speak. They have attempted to bridge the gap between the domestic and public spheres in their efforts to serve their community. In so doing they have become present-day notable actors in the Chamorro story. Moreover, each embodies in her own unique way the contradictory images that characterize Chamorro women. The particulars of how they fit in and how they differ will be discussed in later chapters.

Sources

Published Guam materials which figure prominently in this study span a range of disciplines and types of sources. Journals, ship logs, Spanish colonial and American military documents, census records, and the official reports of explorers, missionaries, administrators, and traders comprise the bulk of primary sources available on Guam's historical relationship with the West. Secondary sources portraying the history of Guam since contact draw heavily from these accounts. The reports of several archaeologists and anthropologists which provide clues about Chamorros prior to contact augment the primary historical data. These descriptions and speculations have been authored almost exclusively by Western males. Despite their inherent biases, they comprise the only known pool of written documentation on the Chamorro historical experience.

The post-World War II period has seen a significant increase in written documents pertaining to Guam. Government reports, including demographic data, economic information, and narrative description of the island's problems and public programs, are the most prevalent. The **Guam Recorder**, periodic magazines and newspapers, a few research reports, and academic papers constitute the bulk of published information today. Several academic theses and dissertations have focused on Guam-related topics in recent years. These efforts are most heavily concentrated in the field of education.

Written information on Chamorro women is limited to a few dissertations, a compilation of articles entitled **Women of Guam**, the work of anthropologist, Laura Thompson, and sporadic references in historical accounts and contemporary published material about Guam.

Cognizant that traditional sources were clearly insufficient as a data base for this study, I explored new techniques of American social historians, particularly feminist scholars. Tamara Hareven in her preface to **Anonymous Americans** discusses a major pitfall in adhering strictly to traditional historical sources:

> The common excuse for omissions in traditional social history has been the unavailability of sources. True, there has been a dearth of sources for the history of the inarticulate and the non-heroes of America. The experience of silent participants seeps through fragmentary documents only and is often presented through the biases and perceptions of the recorders or compilers. Even the U.S. Census, a relatively neutral source, is slanted by the peculiar biases and omissions of the census taker. Historians presently engaged in the effort to recapture the experience of the anonymous are not oblivious to these limitations of sources. They are determined, however, to ask new questions of traditional materials, as well as to develop methods that would enable them to explore often untapped sources, such as census manuscript schedules, school

records, marriage and birth certificates, wills and tax records.[23]

Since Chamorros have written only a minute percentage of available material, and further, because so little has been written about Chamorro women, I pursued the task of looking at untapped sources. This included a review of sources that had until recently been discounted by so-called serious scholars as being too popular to be academic. In his article entitled "Slave Songs and Slave Consciousness: An Exploration in Neglected Sources," Lawrence W. Levine points out that:

> Negroes in the United States, both during and after slavery, were anything but inarticulate. They sang songs, told stories, played verbal games, listened and responded to sermons, and expressed their aspirations, fears and values through the medium of an oral tradition that had characterized the West African cultures from which their ancestors had come. By largely ignoring this tradition, much of which has been preserved, historians have rendered an articulate people historically inarticulate, and have allowed the record of their consciousness to go unexplored.[24]

The same contention can be made about Chamorros. Although we have no written literary tradition, our legends, proverbs, and songs evidence a rich oral folklore. Content analysis of a selection of these songs and stories has offered exciting insights heretofore overlooked.

There are problems inherent in the use of the type of data collected for this study. The information contained in the transcriptions and survey responses is not generalizable to all Chamorro women. Further, it was delimited by the questions which guided the interview sessions with subjects. However, during the course of each interview, subjects were given free reign to discuss those aspects of their lives which they defined as important. Because all subjects were free to determine which questions to answer and how to answer questions, there is a risk that their responses were skewed to represent what they would like others to believe rather than reflecting reality. In all cases

19

the subjects chose not to discuss the intimate details of their private lives and their personal relationships with their husbands, children, friends, and natal families.

This problem of selective reporting is compounded by the concern for reliability. There is a greater inclination to accept as truth what subjects recounted as personal experience rather than their descriptions of activities and events which involved the larger community. While the subjects' views of the activities they have organized were in all likelihood influenced by personal bias, the perspective of individual organizers is crucial to a study which seeks to balance the propensity of historians to focus on institutions rather than on the people these purport to serve. My main concern was to obtain the subjects' own accounts of their lives and activities. Consequently, what the subjects related is considered accurate for the purposes of this endeavor. Reports, brochures, newspaper articles, private records, and personal interviews with other informants have been used to supplement the oral history data and as a means of balancing any distortions caused by personal idiosyncrasies.

Organizational Scheme

This book consists of seven chapters which reflect the foci of the study. Chapter II, "Island Metamorphosis: Guam's History of Conflict and Adaptation," provides an overview of historical events which have shaped and influenced the history of Guam since Western contact occurred in 1521.

Conflicting stereotypes used to depict Chamorro women in the historical record and the ways in which these images reflect the ideal and real position of Chamorro women throughout history provide the central theme of Chapter III, "Chamorro Women: Myths and Realities." The behavioral, ideological, and legendary antecedents of these images are examined as a means of understanding the changing status and roles of Chamorro women in the context of various spheres of their experience.

Chapters IV, V, and VI comprise the oral history portion of the book. The nine case studies are divided into three clusters. Chapter IV focuses exclusively on one subject, Cecilia Bamba. The rationale for setting this case study apart from the others is twofold. Firstly, Mrs. Bamba is well recognized as having been a long-standing and outstanding organizer in the Guam community. Her scope of activities spans the range of the whole survey sample. Secondly, this subject has provided the most comprehensive oral history material for this study. Her untimely death has brought added reason to share as much of her story as she wished to tell. Furthermore, her extensive contributions warrant the in-depth treatment accorded to Mrs. Bamba as "Lady Extraordinaire."

Four of the nine case studies are presented in Chapter V, "Women Organizing in Their Professions." These women specifically identified work-related or profession-associated activities to be the most meaningful in their organizing experience. Each case study write-up includes a biographical sketch and brief descriptions of the activities, motivations, and strategies related to the subject's organizational work with particular emphasis on the activity that each chose as a focus for the case study.

Chapter VI, "Women Organizing Through Formal and Informal Networks," provides a more in-depth examination of the support systems Chamorro women have and how the four subjects featured in this chapter have utilized socially structured, formal and informal networks as an effective organizational strategy. A similar presentation format is used for Chapters V and VI.

"New Perspectives on the Chamorro Female Experience," Chapter VII, attempts to integrate historical perspectives on Chamorro women with contemporary realities as reflected in the lives of Chamorro women organizers. This chapter analyzes the implications of the material presented in view of the questions raised at the beginning of the book. Subjects' opinions on the position of Chamorro women and gender-related issues are incorporated into a concluding discussion which explores perspectives on feminism in the Chamorro context. Recommendations for future research complete this effort.

Ile Guam: Usages des anciens habitans by J. A. Pellion, 1824.
    The nude woman depicted in this engraving shows how she carries her infant. The basket is woven with diamond designs and is finely woven. The man on the right is holding a woven basket with similar designs probably used to hold his betelnut, *afog* (lime) and *pupulu* (pepper leaf). (Photo courtesy of Nieves Flores Memorial Library and the Guam Museum.)

Ile Guam: Usages des anciens habitans by J. A. Pellion, 1824.
    The woman featured in this close-up is holding a *fa'lu* (wooden double ended pestle) with a stone mortar (*lutsung*) to her left. (Photo courtesy of Nieves Flores Memorial Library and the Guam Museum.)

Agaña, Ile Guam: Occupations domestiques by Js. Arago, 1824.
     A close-up of an engraving showing a woman feeding a
young child, *tortillas*. The woman is wearing a long sleeved
blouse (rolled up to the elbows) with a fine checkered skirt.
She wears a long *lisayo* (necklace) with her hair tied in a bun.
She is smoking a *cigarillo*. (Photo courtesy of Nieves Flores
Memorial Library and the Guam Museum.)

Femme de l' ile Guam: Josephine Cortes by Js. Arago, 1824.
  The young woman is the daughter of the *alcalde* of
Umatac. Her name is Josephine Cortes. She wears a long
sleeved blouse with the waist located below the bosom and a
long checkered skirt. Her beaded pendant reaches to her waist.
Her hair is allowed loose behind her back. (Photo courtesy of
Nieves Flores Memorial Library and the Guam Museum.)

CHAPTER II

ISLAND METAMORPHOSIS:

GUAM'S HISTORY OF CONFLICT AND ADAPTATION

Contemporary traditional cultures are threatened, as never before, by the homogenizing effects of modernization. The indigenous culture of the American Pacific Territory of Guam is a case in point. The Chamorro story is also a contemporary illustration of the struggle for meaning and identity which complicates the lives of many Pacific islanders as they move beyond centuries of colonialism. Because of its long and colorful history of colonization, many are skeptical that an indigenous culture even exists on Guam. This chapter provides an overview of external forces which have influenced the evolution of Guam and its people.[1] The set of beliefs and behavior patterns which comprise the cultural complex known as Chamorro derives from a dialectical relationship between the ancient Chamorro order and the everchanging realities wrought by historical circumstances.

The Birth of an Island and the Origin of Its People

... in the beginning, in the limitless space of the Universe, before the creation of the earth and the sky, there lived an omnipotent being named *Putan*. As eons of time went by *Putan* felt himself about to die, so he called his sister, *Fuuna*, who, like himself, had been born without the help of father or mother, and gave her explicit directions as to the disposal of his body, and conferred upon her all his miraculous powers. He decreed that upon his death his eyes

27

should become the sun and moon; his breast, the sky; his back, the earth; his eyebrows, the rainbow; and the rest of his anatomical parts, the lesser things of the world and the nether regions.

In due time *Putan* died and *Fuuna* carried out her brother's wishes to the letter, and so the world was created. When *Fuuna* contemplated the beautiful earth that had been brought into being by her brother's command, she decided that it should be peopled with men and women created in the likeness of her brother and herself. So, to this end, in order to best accomplish her purpose, she established herself as a sea-girt rock in the Southern part of *Guahan* and after she had done this she decreed, on her own account, that a certain kind of earth on this rock should first become a stone which would in time give birth to all people. So she gathered a great quantity of this earth, mixed it with the waters of the sea and caused it to solidify into a great stone. Then she commanded that this stone divide itself into many stones, a great number of which she imbued with life, and thus they became the human stock from which the races of men were disseminated throughout the world.[2]

Geologists have established that the birth of the island of Guam occurred within the last fifty to sixty million years of geologic time, in the Cenozoic era. As a result of a succession of massive convulsions at the bottom of the Pacific Ocean, the Marianas wrinkle developed. Through time, explosion followed explosion. These eruptions repeatedly deposited lava and limestone forming a peak of volcanic debris 14,000 feet high. As this initial phase of volcanic activity subsided, other natural forces went to work to form the island's topography and its surrounding reefs. Subsequent volcanic eruptions created the now familiar rolling hills and peaks in the landscape. The ocean's activities made further alterations. A stable ecosystem evolved long before the first brave voyagers ventured into the Pacific in search of a new homeland.

Anthropologists, archaeologists, botanists, and linguists have provided several theories of migration. Material remains give us our only clues regarding the first human settlements on Guam. While the exact details of Oceanic prehistory remain unknown, it is generally accepted that mass migrations from Asia into the areas known as Polynesia and Micronesia began over 4,000 years ago. Seafaring people from the Asian Continent migrated eastward to settle in the Marianas at least as early as 1500 B.C. Recently excavated archeaological evidence suggests even earlier settlement dates by several thousand years. These settlers brought breadfruit, bananas, taro, and coconuts with them on their long voyages across the uncharted seas. Their swift, seaworthy canoes allowed them to travel great distances. Those who inhabited Guam were descended from the rice-growing and betelnut-chewing peoples of Southeast Asia. Much of the evidence being uncovered by modern science links the ancestors of present-day Chamorros with Malaysia, Cambodia, and the Philippines. Stone, shell and bone implements, pottery sherds, the remains of latte structures, petrographs, and human skeletons unearthed by excavations shed some light on where the first inhabitants lived, the tools they made and used, their living arrangements, and burial practices. Missing pieces of this archaeological puzzle far outnumber what is available. Nevertheless, these speculations have irrevocably altered prevailing views of the early Chamorros.

The First Encounter with the West

Douglas Oliver in his book, **The Pacific Islands,** gives a succinct description of the initial period of contact between the indigenous population of Guam and the Spanish explorers who first sailed the Pacific:

> The rape of Oceania began with Guam. Two and a half centuries before the unsuspecting savages of Polynesia welcomed white masters to their shores,

Guam's fate was already sealed. Magellan led the procession in 1521 and left the usual calling cards.[3]

Magellan's chronicler, Pigafetta, recorded the first known account of contact in this way:

> After sailing sixty leagues on the aforesaid course, and being in twelve degrees of latitude and one hundred and forty-six of longitude, on Wednesday the sixth of March we discovered a small island to the northwest, and two others toward the southwest. One of these islands was larger and higher than the other two. And the captain-general wished to approach the largest of these three islands to replenish his provisions. But it was not possible, for the people of those islands entered the ships and robbed us so that we could not protect ourselves from them. And when we wished to strike and take in the sails so as to land, they stole very quickly the small boat called a skiff which was fastened to the poop of the captain's ship. At which he, being angry, went ashore with forty armed men. And burned some forty or fifty houses with several boats and killing seven men of the said island, they recovered their skiff. Soon after, we left, taking the same course. And before we landed several of our sick men had begged us, if we killed man or woman, to bring them their entrails. For immediately they would be healed.[4]

Pain and misunderstanding abounded at that moment of fatal impact. Magellan's visit set the tone for many subsequent encounters. It is not surprising that historical accounts since have reported conflict albeit with an overwhelming Western bias. Descriptions, like the following, abound in the literature depicting Chamorros:

> The character of the natives, which at first seemed to be very simple and free from all deceit; for which they were highly praised by the first Jesuit Fathers and Spaniards who dealt with them, and who allowed themselves to be persuaded by the kind reception and

hospitality shown to them, proved afterwards deceitful and treacherous, as they would hide their wounded feelings for a year or more until opportunity for revenge arose; and as to the truth, they had so little regard for it that they would never let a promise stand in the way of what they really wanted to do.[5]

Unfortunately, secondary sources of the history of Guam have reinforced such views and have consequently had a denigrating effect on the modern Chamorros' perception of the past.

Spanish Missionaries and the Establishment of a Colony

Despite the unsavory beginning marked by Magellan's brief stopover, the next century and a half was a period of relative quiet punctuated intermittently by the activities of a handful of adventurous explorers in search of land, riches, knowledge, and souls. In 1565 Legaspi claimed the chain of 15 islands situated between the 13th and 20th parallels of north latitude and along the 145th meridian east of Greenwich, which were later named the Marianas by Sanvitores in honor of the Spanish Queen Mariana of Austria. Guam lies at the southernmost end of the chain and covers approximately 212 square miles. This barely visible dot on the map called *Guahan* was a sacred place to the Ancient Chamorros who believed that all life sprang from its soil. It was treated as everything but sacred by the long line of visitors who have since alighted on its shores.

The establishment of the first Spanish settlement and mission in 1668 signaled a succession of violent clashes between the Chamorros and their conquerors. With the *padres* and later the Spanish soldiers to protect them came a code of ethics, ideology, and social system completely alien to the ancients. Spanish-Chamorro Wars spanning the 30-year period 1670 to 1700, resulted in the decimation of the Chamorro male population.[6] Disease and natural disasters further reduced the number of indigenes from between 150,000 and 100,000 at contact to less than 5,000 by the end of the seventeenth century.[7]

In the lifespan of one generation the Chamorro social and political order, which had evolved through several millennia, was profoundly threatened. Carano and Sanchez, writers of the first comprehensive history of Guam, summarize the effects of this era thusly:

> At the end of the period of conquest, Christianity, which was to play a major role in the history of Guam, was firmly established as the religion of the people. As a result of the various commanders and Governors who administered the affairs of the island during the wars, Spanish law and the Spanish pattern of government became an integral part of the life on Guam. Such influences were to prevail until 1898 and even after.[8]

To the ancient Chamorros of precontact times, who believed that they were the original race and that their island of *Guahan* was the center of the Universe, the biblical account of creation and its concomitant explanation of the physical world which was introduced as part of the mental baggage of the early explorers must have been totally incomprehensible. Through several centuries of contact with Western Thought, the ancient Chamorro world view, unable to compete with foreign conquerers and their ways, gradually gave in to the prevailing explanations of whence and how *Guahan* and its people came to be. Thus, the legendary creators, *Putan* and *Fuuna*, have been replaced by the Judeo-Christian God.

The Galleon traders between Mexico and the Philippines made regular stopovers on Guam. Expeditions from Russia, France, England, and America visited the island throughout the centuries under Spanish rule. American whalers called at Guam's port. These Filipino, Mexican, and assorted Western influences contributed to the cultural hybrid which became characteristic of the Chamorro way of life. Intermarriages between Chamorro women and men of other races resulted in miscegenation. Spanish colonial influences are still quite evident in Chamorro beliefs and practices today. Many Chamorros have Spanish surnames and the Chamorro language has incorporated numerous Spanish words. Over two centuries of Spanish colonization had made its indelible imprint on the cultural identity of Chamorros by the late 1800s. Ironically, Spanish officials and native inhabitants of this island possession knew nothing of the turn of the century political movements which would alter the course of Guam's future. The isolation of island administrators and residents was clearly illustrated in the chain of events surrounding the transfer of control over Guam from Spain to the United States.

American Takeover and the Americanization of Guam

As is typical of world powers negotiating settlements, Spain and the United States arbitrarily attached Guam to the purchase agreement for the Philippine Islands. Thus, on June 20, 1898 the North American cruiser, **Charleston**, and her convoy arrived on Guam. Captain Glass was ordered to take possession. In a civil exchange of letters between Captain Glass and the Spanish Governor, Juan Marina, the situation at hand was communicated. Spain gave up her colony in a most peaceful and dignified manner.[9]

American military authority was established. President McKinley placed the control of Guam under the Department of the Navy. For the next fifty years, interrupted only by the Japanese occupation during World War II, Naval Governors administered island affairs through a series of executive orders which dictated appropriate standards and acceptable behavior for the people of this newly acquired territory. These edicts proclaimed who could marry whom; when church bells could ring; what language would be used; and prohibited whistling and spitting, particularly of betelnut spittle as the unsightly splotches of red offended the delicate wives of naval officers during their afternoon strolls. Many of these orders had profound effects on how Chamorros in the early twentieth century began to readjust their perceptions of themselves. The first four decades of American rule could be characterized as a period of do's and don'ts. Through the institution of a new form of government, health programs, and an American education system, implemented primarily by U.S. military personnel, the people of Guam were introduced to the American way of life.

From the perspective of American Historiography, World War II and the postwar years proved to be a more active and challenging period in the Americanization process.[10] Guam was captured and occupied by Japanese armed forces from December 8, 1941 to July 21, 1944 when American troops liberated the island. The Japanese occupation caused severe hardship to Chamorros, who were coerced into serving the Imperial forces and complying with their demands. The people suffered atrocities such as rape, physical injuries and even death, enforced manual labor, and inhuman treatment in concentration camps. They put their hope for freedom in the hands of God and the American G.I.'s. The refrain of an underground song composed during the war expressed the prevailing sentiment well: "Oh, Mr. Sam, Sam, my dear Uncle Sam, Won't you please come back to Guam?" Loyalty to the Stars and Stripes reached fanatic proportions during those years.[11] It is no wonder that Chamorros were described as being more patriotic than the patriots.

Gratitude to the United States for liberating them from the Japanese fueled a sense of patriotism in the period following World War II. Chamorro leaders were more determined than ever to achieve United States citizenship for their people. There was a move to establish civilian government. It is doubtful that Washington was responding wholly to the clamor over "inalienable rights" across the continent and the Pacific Ocean. Nonetheless, Congress passed the Organic Act of Guam and President Truman signed it into law in August, 1950. This new "law of the land" transferred jurisdiction over the Territory to the Department of the Interior. A presidentially-appointed Civilian Governor replaced the Naval Administrator as the highest ranking American official on Guam. The establishment of civilian government and the newly conferred citizenship status were interpreted then as a measure of self-rule. Island residents elected a non-voting Delegate to Congress in 1965. The first gubernatorial election was held in 1970.

In addition to postwar political developments, other factors served as major catalysts for change and cultural adaptation. The early Sixties is considered the threshold of the modern era on Guam for several reasons. In 1963 the heretofore required Naval Security Clearance for entry into Guam was lifted. The island's relatively homogenous population was now exposed to large groups of alien laborers, foreign investors, and statesiders in growing numbers who, for economic and other reasons, decided to make Guam their home. The lifting of the security closure provided the impetus for unprecedented non-military and non-governmental economic growth. Tourism developed as a major industry. Today over a quarter of a million tourists visit Guam annually, most of them from Japan.[12] The animosity towards Japanese during the war has trickled down through several generations and occasionally surfaces as crimes against these visitors.

The composition of the local population has changed drastically. In 1940 Chamorros constituted 90 percent of Guam's inhabitants. This percentage was reduced dramatically in the next few decades so that by 1970 Chamorros comprised roughly 56 percent of the island's residents.[13] The 1980 U. S. Census puts Chamorros at 47 percent of Guam's population. Once the dominant cultural group on Guam, Chamorros are fast becoming a minority in their homeland. The United States continues to control immigration to Guam. Without local control, Chamorros are likely to either leave the island in search of better living conditions or remain as an underclass. The lack of control over who is allowed to reside on Guam is a critical problem for several reasons. Guam's finite resources cannot sustain a population which is inflated unnaturally through in-migration. The growing number of non-Chamorros on Guam also poses a real threat to indigenous control of the local government. While Chamorros no longer control the economic institutions on island, the Government of Guam is still Chamorro controlled. This is changing, however. The issue of numbers is central to the quest for Chamorro self-determination as well. The political aspirations of newcomers and statesiders who relocate to Guam are distinctly different from the aspirations of Chamorros. Outnumbered, Chamorros can be prevented from ever excercising their inalienable right of self-determination. This threat grows as the number of Chamorros diminishes in proportion to the rest of the population. Although most island politicians like to describe the population as a heterogeneous melting pot, the reality of ethnic conflict cannot be ignored. Tension between Chamorros and Filipinos or statesiders is a product of competition for employment, services, and other benefits available in the name of progress. Limited opportunities have worked to the disadvantage of Chamorros, who often do not possess the training or skills in demand. The struggle for political control also presents problem.

Two other events have been associated with the cultural upheaval which thrust Guam into the modern age. Typhoon Karen hit on 11 November 1962, flattening the island and killing seven people. The catastrophe was declared a national disaster. Millions of federal dollars poured into Guam to assist in reconstruction. New homes, schools, churches, health facilities, and businesses were built. Public projects proliferated. The military expanded its installations. Post-typhoon rehabilitation funds created an economic euphoria. Chamorros abandoned their farms to join the ranks of civil service and private sector employees. Old neighborhood patterns were disrupted by subdivisions designed after the grid system of America's cities and housing developments. Another boom occurred with rehabilitation funding after the onslaught of Typhoon Pamela in 1976. The development which followed these so-called "blessings in disguise" paved the way for tourism, which is an industry second only to the military on Guam today. With the emergence of Japan as a world economic power, Guam is experiencing a "third" Japanese invasion *vis* Japanese corporate investors who are buying land at inflationary prices and through their investments control the tourist industry.

Economic prosperity has taken its toll. Crime, the cost of living, and competition for limited resources have increased tremendously. The number of recipients of food stamps and other government handouts is steadily growing. Guam has shifted from being a self-sufficient community to a consumer society which imports most of its food requirements and nearly all other commodities. This, coupled with the sale of land to outside investors, has created a totally lopsided economy which is externally controlled. Programs in agriculture, fisheries, and local industrial enterprises have reduced Guam's dependence on outside resources somewhat. But, until development is internally initiated and the sale of land is stopped, the dream of regaining some vestige of economic control will be out of reach for Chamorros.

Air travel has given mobility to island residents. For those who remain on Guam, television brings the world into their living rooms. Chamorro historian, Robert A. Underwood, has recently described the impact of mass media as the most effective vehicle of Americanization today. The following are selected excerpts outlining his position:

> As the institution to which all groups come into contact with, the media is in the rather influential position of being able to project images of the island to the people who live in it.

> ... it tells us what is going on at home and does so in every aspect of the way information is given to us.

> ... This function of the media is acculturative in a very unique way. Not only does it make us feel homesick for places we have never been, but it gives us the uneasy feeling that what we experience daily is abnormal. The real world, the normal world, the model world is what we read about, hear about and visualize on television.

> ... This normal world is in reality the world of the American, suburban middle-class family.

The underlying message is that the lifestyles and expectations of the people of Guam and of Los Angeles share a common denominator. Thus, artificial bonds and false ideals are engendered by this type of daily exposure. Underwood argues further that:

> Mainstream America, the America that we all want to become a part of simply does not exist on Guam. Despite the increasing numbers of "statesiders" on Guam, there is no white middle class. Despite attempts to construct similar communities to those found in the States, islanders regularly confound the planners by raising chickens and building outside kitchens. Yet, the mainstream American cultural image is what we seek to emulate without having personal experience with it. Since it doesn't really exist on Guam and the School does an imperfect job of producing the mainstream, it is left to the media to interpret and purvey the image of mainstream to a society 5,500 miles away from it.

> Television programming is the clearest purveyor of this image of what constitutes the mainstream. In fact, the media becomes the mainstream.[14]

Definitions about what constitutes normality based on mainstream values exacerbates the identity crisis brought on by modernization. Addressing the cultural implications of the mass media on Guam, Underwood states:

> Culturally, mass media on Guam behaves in two distinct ways. The first is that they actively engage in cultural genocide. ...

> By cultural genocide I mean that the media messages promote a disengaging from Chamorro Culture, the indigenous culture of Guam. The Chamorro Culture becomes, when it is mentioned, a relic of the past, an entity seemingly alien to both the sender and the receiver of a mass media message. This process of

objectifying the Chamorro reality quickly leads to its
dehumanization. It is no longer a human activity
subject to human change and innovation. It is a static
object which is beyond our input as humans in the
present. All questions about it have been previously
resolved and all that is left to us is a decision to make
reference to it or not.[15]

I do not subscribe to the media's image of Chamorro Culture as
a relic of the past. Unfortunately, many Chamorros and most
of the non-Chamorro ethnic groups on the island unquestioning-
ly accept the white middle-class reality in America as the cultural norm which must be aspired to at all costs. For Chamorros whose only homeland is the Mariana Islands, such influences have challenged their cultural identity.

Chamorros have paid a heavy price in the course of
pursuing the "American Dream." According to the **Guam
Comprehensive Development Plan of 1978**:

The colonial history of the island has benefited
Guam's development in many ways. It has introduced
many new political ideas, scientific advances, and
economic progress. However, the island's people have
had little input into the development of Guam's political and social institutions. Outside forces in control
of the island have viewed Guam's culture as a stum-
bling block to what they have defined as progress.
This has resulted in an unnatural and unbalanced
development of the island's culture. A serious conse-
quence has been the development of a negative self-
image regarding island values. The comparison of
local lifestyles to "stateside" lifestyles in order to
measure progress and success often results in negative
self-images of Guam and its culture.[16]

The extent and desirability of Americanization on
Guam is a debate that promises to rage on for years. The point
to be recognized is that the Chamorro way of life exists as a
fully established cultural system known, valued, and practiced
by the descendants of the indigenous inhabitants.

Thoughts on Chamorro Culture and Identity

The cultural challenges facing Chamorros in the 1980s are necessarily different from those encountered through 460 plus years of contact with other cultures. The identity problem is introduced here as a way of characterizing the cultural climate that pervades on Guam today. The issues surrounding Chamorro identity are extremely complicated and can be dealt with only briefly in this overview. Awareness that the situation exists, however, is essential to understanding the lives of Chamorro women. It is also an important consideration as we begin to address the question, how American is Guam?

Residents of Guam, excluding non-immigrant aliens, are American citizens, who have not yet 'earned' the right to vote for the President. Almost everyone on Guam can speak English. We have American political, economic, and educational institutions. Guam boasts the regular fast-food and entertainment attractions of most American communities its size. But, as military personnel who still consider assignment to Guam as hardship duty often attest, once one starts peeling away the veneer, things become increasingly unfamiliar. Department of Commerce statistics reveal that in 1978 Guam's population breakdown including military personnel and their dependents was 47.8 percent Chamorro; 23.5 percent white; 20 percent Filipino; 1 percent Chinese; 2.9 percent Korean; 1.4 percent Japanese; 2.7 percent Micronesian; and 1.2 percent other races.

Besides looking different, the local people act differently. For example, having strong extended families and a collective sense of reciprocal obligation are characteristic of at least half of the islanders. Other behavioral anomalies defy the conventions of the mainstream American culture.

Nonetheless, many Chamorros are convinced that Guam has become an overseas suburb of Los Angeles County. They operate under the misguided impression that they are faced with an either/or dilemma. The Chamorro identity crisis is often defined in terms of how American one is. In other words, the problem is perceived in terms of whether one is 'allowed' by societal norms to be Chamorro in an American context. The identity question has been mysteriously linked to such concerns as to whether one can in fact be Chamorro and American at the same time. Being of Chamorro ethnicity is somehow rationalized as being acceptable; after all, America is a nation of subcultures. In this manner the fundamental issue of cultural sovereignty, i.e., the inalienable right of Chamorros to continue to be Chamorro, speak Chamorro, and live a Chamorro way of life in the face of rapid modernization and change, is avoided.

Those Chamorros unconvinced by the above argument manifest their resistance in various ways--by continuing to raise chickens in a suburban neighborhood, by promoting language and culture programs in the schools, by organizing nationalistic groups such as the Organization of People for Indigenous Rights (OPI-R) and by raising issues related to political status and economic development.[17]

This brief discussion of Chamorro identity may lead the reader to expect a succinct definition of what is Chamorro? I am personally opposed to the view that a concise definition can be given. Yet, the necessity of clarifying what is meant by Chamorro in the context of this study prevails. The subject of Chamorro identity is rife with controversy, especially when considered in relation to who should vote on political status and other similar concerns. This chapter attempted to familiarize readers with the background needed to understand the various components of the identity question. It is fair to say that there are as many definitions of Chamorro as there are individuals who choose to discuss the term.

I proceed with the assumption that contemporary Chamorros are the descendants of the indigenous inhabitants of the Marianas. Thus all residents of Guam are Guamanian, but not all Guamanians are Chamorro. One may argue that being Chamorro is equivalent to practicing the Chamorro way of life, speaking the Chamorro language, marrying into a Chamorro family and so forth. While these factors are integral to a discussion of the behavioral manifestations of cultural identity, they do not, in and of themselves, constitute Chamorro identity.

Being Chamorro is first and foremost being of Chamorro blood. For some this is a birthright. Many skeptics proclaim that the historical record invalidates such a contention. Chamorros do not deny that our racial mixture precludes a purist argument. Therefore, we do not speak in terms of actual per centage of bloodline as, for example, Hawaiians do. Nevertheless, the historical record does document that a persistent racial strain has survived to the present day. The practice of Chamorro traditions and the transmission of Chamorro values have been maintained in conjunction with this adaptive form of racial continuity despite the implementation of genocidal policies since contact. The dialectic between the colonizers and the colonized and between tradition and modernity are clearly manifest in the values and behavior of Chamorro women.

CHAPTER III

THE POSITION OF CHAMORRO WOMEN:
MYTHS AND REALITIES

Conflicting stereotypes of the Chamorro woman and their influence in shaping her identity have affected her status and roles in
contemporary society. The Chamorro woman is at once culture-bearer, cultural preservationist, and agent of change. She
is the embodiment of many contradictions. She is admired for
her assertiveness, yet praised for being submissive. She is
expected to obey her husband, but hailed for succeeding in
controlling him and their children. She defers to her husband
as an authority figure; however, it is common knowledge that
she actually "rules the roost." She is extolled for her virtue and
at the same time applauded for her lack of inhibition. She is
both the madonna-like lady on the pedestal and the *dama de
noche* or woman of the night. This inheritance of contradictory
images forms the backdrop against which the contemporary
Chamorro woman is perceived and perceives herself.

The position of the Chamorro woman today can only be
understood by examining her changing status and roles
throughout Guam's history. While this task is difficult because
the Chamorro woman is virtually invisible in formal historical
accounts, I have nonetheless attempted to provide a conspectus
by assembling references found in records about the culture and
people of the Marianas.

Social Organization

Ancient Chamorro society was characterized by a rigid
caste system comprised of three distinct levels. A woman's

position in that society was determined first by the caste into which she was born. Her caste defined her "life choices" and prescribed the relationships and obligations that would dominate her life.

Guam was divided into well-organized districts, each composed of several clan hamlets. Next to caste, membership in the clan was the most significant determinant of status. A clan consisted of several extended families tied together by mutual obligations which involved the exchange of labor, food, and other resources, the use of land, and the ritual and ceremonial activities of its members. Descent within the clan was reckoned through the female line. This matrilineal principle conferred power and prestige on Chamorro women.

Among kin, age determined rank. The oldest woman (*maga'haga*) and her oldest brother (*maga'lahi*) were the highest ranking individuals. Together they wielded considerable control over clan affairs and property. According to the French explorer Freycinet, who visited Guam for several months in 1819, rank within the clan was determined by seniority along the direct first-born uterine lineage from the highest to the lowest as follows: great-grandmother, grandmother, mother, grand-aunt, aunt, sister, female first cousin, and daughter. Married women took precedence over the unmarried.[1]

Caste distinctions were perpetuated by patterns of intermarriage which prevailed during the period of Christianization and Spanish control. Women of the *matao*, the highest caste, married top Spanish officials, thus enhancing their positions within a colonial context. While Chamorro women could reinforce their status through marriage, Chamorro men did not have a similar option. These circumstances worked to the advantage of Chamorro women. After World War II intermarriage between Chamorros and statesiders (and other incoming ethnic groups) were more frequent. Initially, this involved marriages between Chamorro women and American military personnel. As more Chamorro men left Guam for U.S. military service, a balanced pattern developed.

The rigidly defined caste system no longer exists. Former determinants of status, i.e., birthright, ownership of land, and craft/trade have been lost or devalued by the introduction of new forms of social organization and wealth. Although respect for the aged has dwindled somewhat, in most Chamorro families elders still command esteem and authority.

Ancient patterns of settlement (i.e., over 200 clan hamlets located both inland and in coastal areas) began to change with the establishment of village communities by the Spanish. These *pueblos* (later called villages) centered around the parish church. Nevertheless, kin continued to live within close proximity and share resources. This communal lifestyle has been profoundly altered in visible ways. Chamorro families are now scattered all over the island, across the United States, and in other parts of the world. Ancestral lands have been either confiscated by the U.S. Government or broken up into smaller parcels as a result of changes in inheritance patterns. Individual family residential units in subdivisions have all but replaced the less-structured village clusters (extended family compounds). Despite these changes in living and subsistence arrangements, extended families continue to function as vital support systems irrespective of the distances which often separate family members.

Another major change in Chamorro social organization occurred with the changeover from Spanish to American administration of island affairs. Matrilineage was outlawed. The Spanish custom of allowing children to take their mother's name had predisposed Spanish officials to accept this preference among early Chamorros. American naval officers, on the other hand, took exception to this practice. Hence, Chamorros were forced to abide by patriarchal notions of descent. Executive Order No. 308 promulgated by the Naval Government on April 3, 1919 declared that a married woman should bear the surname and follow the nationality of her husband; and further that children should bear the surname of the father. In addition, the people of Guam were exhorted to Americanize their children's names.

Outwardly, Chamorros have conformed. But their ancient emphasis on the maternal family has not diminished. Anita Johnston in her study of Chamorro women in the 1970s observes that:

> Even today, the kinship ties and obligations are perpetuated and socially transmitted by the female members of the family, and in the typical Chamorro home it is the woman who rules. Relatives on the mother's side of the family are considered more important in terms of kindred obligations than those of the father's side.[2]

Different interpretations and definitions of the family have challenged the heart of the traditional Chamorro social system. Clans have virtually disappeared. Yet the family--both the "household unit" (typically composed of a married couple, their children, and other relatives) and the "extended family" or *parientes* (maternal and paternal parents, siblings, grandparents, aunts, uncles, cousins, nieces and nephews, regardless of residence)--continues to be the foundation of Chamorro social organization. A system of reciprocal exchange and obligation exists as strongly today as it existed in ancient times. Rites of passage, many linked with a centuries-old Catholic tradition, provide the occasions during which mutual obligations among kin are reciprocated. The extended family is also a valuable source of support during the life crises of its members.

Chamorro women play a pivotal role, indeed an essential one, in sustaining the family and perpetuating traditions which form the core of Chamorro identity. So, despite the imposition of patriarchal values by colonial powers, which led Chamorro women to accommodate themselves to the beliefs and practices of their "foreign" or "acculturated" husbands and fathers, Chamorro women do hold significant and powerful positions in Chamorro social structure today.

Sex and Marriage

Nowhere are the changing patterns which have affected female status in Chamorro society more evident than in the values, laws, and traditions associated with sex and marriage. Prior to the introduction of Catholicism in the Marianas, "premarital consorting of the sexes was institutionalized."[3] In fact, "a virginal bride would have been an embarrassment to her family.[4] The *Urritao*, associations of unmarried young men, bought or rented young girls from their parents for two or three iron hoops and a few turtle shells, according to *Padre* Diego Luis de San Vitores.[5] Guam's first missionary was determined to destroy this institution as he considered it the root of evil and moral decay in Chamorro society.

Although Spanish *padres* preached virginity as the ideal state of purity for unmarried girls, it is not clear how extensively it was practiced during Spanish times. While prescribed behavior did create a drastically different sex code for Chamorros, commentary on the sexual mores of Chamorro women in the literature provide ample evidence that old ways persisted. Consider the following accounts.

Writing in 1839, Des Graz stated:

> Several times we braved vermine to enter into the houses and to assist in these evening prayers. Unfortunately our presence bothered them. It also happens that following these acts of piety to see the young women give themselves up to disrobe to demands of our sailors who confront at the same time, leprosy, ugliness, and vermin.[6]

Des Graz goes on to note that:

> One of the women that we have seen at the padres in Agat came with him here; only to preserve a little of the propriety, she did not appear in the public eye. The Governor told us, "Monsieur, the priests do not edify their flocks; on the contrary, they give them the worst examples."[7]

Surprisingly, Frenchmen expressed the greatest scorn for this so-called "promiscuous" behavior. In another account Antoine-Alfred Marche declared:

The easiness with which indigenous women gave themselves to the first comer permits one to affirm that the crews of all the ships which came to the Marianas left behind quite a few descendants.[8]

Modesty was also a virtue the missionaries stressed. Chamorro women did don garments as fabric became available. It is likely that the cult of virginity and modesty was more rigidly enforced for upper-class women than for those who labored in the fields or fished. Regarding this subject, Des Graz remarked, "As with men, the women take off their shirts while doing housework and put it back on only when they appear in public, more often, this precaution is neglected."[9]

Having children out of wedlock was considered sinful by the Catholic Church. Nevertheless, while never condoning the practice publicly, Spanish priests apparently tolerated the high incidence of illegitimacy. It is known that they frequently contributed to the numbers of "fatherless" children.

The only fair conclusion we can make is that Christianity introduced new ideals which were accepted by Chamorros. Their actual practice probably varied considerably and may have been applied with varying levels of intensity to women of different classes.

The first American Naval Governor and his staff found the sexual mores of Chamorros as despicable as did the first Spanish missionaries. Consequently, Executive Order No. 5 was issued on September 15, 1899 to remedy the situation.

The existing custom of concubinage, rearing families of illegitimate children, is repulsive to ideas of decency, antagonistic to moral advancement, incompatible with the generally recognized customs of civilized society, a violation of the accepted principles of Christianity, and a most degrading injustice to the innocent offspring, who is not responsible for the condition of his unfortunate existence.

The aforesaid custom is henceforth prohibited, and is declared to be an offense punishable after November 3rd, 1899, by fine and imprisonment; and all persons in this island so living together out of the bonds of wedlock are commanded to procure from the Government the necessary marriage license and to be married by either the civil or church authorities, or both, in order that their children may become legitimized.[10]

The prescribed sexual behavior for unmarried Chamorro girls has been radically reformulated during the several centuries of Western colonization. So much so, that what is now considered "traditional" represents a complete reversal of ancient Chamorro prescriptions.

Laura Thompson in **Guam and Its People** has provided an evocative description of the "traditional" upbringing of young girls on Guam in the 1930s.

After the first menstruation, which usually occurs between the ages of twelve and fourteen and is not marked by any ceremony, a girl is called *soltera* (from the Spanish equivalent) until she married or becomes pregnant. A *soltera* in prewar Guam was not allowed outside the house alone at night. Shutters of rooms in which adolescent girls slept were frequently closed to guard them from prowlers. In fact even during the day most young girls rarely went out unaccompanied by a sister or other relative, especially in the villages.

Formerly, many parents were opposed to sending their girls to school, according to informants, because they did not want them to learn to write love letters. Although parents were eager that their girls should receive an education, many took them out of school at puberty because they did not want them to associate with boys. [11]

The last few decades have been marked by a "liberalization" of attitudes about sex, which is usually attributed to exposure to the "American sexual revolution," co-education, and a gradual decline of control by parents over their children's behavior. This may be true. However, to my knowledge Chamorros both young and old have always viewed sexuality as an integral, desirable, and natural part of human existence. It seems to me that while virginity and modesty have been ideal virtues that young girls have been expected to uphold, in practice it has been understood that imperfect behavior is a fact of human nature. This may account for the tremendous tolerance shown by parents when ideal expectations have not been fulfilled by their daughters.

Marriage among ancient Chamorros was regarded as a contract between two intermarrying clans.[12] These unions were always between members of the same caste and were marked by premarital service to the bride's family by the groom.

> Marriage amounted almost to purchase. A young suitor would be forced to offer his service to the parents and a fee for his bride. The fee might be collected either from him or his relatives. In frequent cases the groom himself might have enough property of his own to make a present to the father of the bride.[13]

This custom, which constituted a form of "male dowry", served as one indication of the favorable position of the female in Chamorro society.

Fray Juan Pobre, who observed husband-wife relations during his visit to the Marianas in 1602, wrote:

> When a man or a woman marry and live together in a house, although they may have been married twenty or thirty years, if the husband is unfaithful to his wife, or takes a mistress, and if it should anger his wife, she will leave the house, taking the children and all of the household furniture and effects, and will go to the house of her parents or of other relatives, where she

will remain. During all this time the children will not acknowledge their father, even though he might pass very close to them. Before the wife will return to the husband, his relatives will have to go to great lengths and beg her to do so. If the wife is unfaithful to the husband, her relatives do not have to go to such lengths because it is easier to obtain the husband's pardon since this sin is considered less serious for the women than for the men.[14]

Padre San Vitores expounded further on the marriage practices of ancient Chamorros thusly:

They do not have many wives nor do they marry relatives, if one can call marriage that which might be better called concubinage for its lack of perpetuity, for they may separate and take another husband or wife at any trifling quarrel. However, if a man abandons his wife it costs him a great deal, for he loses both his property and his children. Women can leave their men without inconvenience, and do so frequently through jealousy, and suspecting their husbands of disloyalty, punish them in many ways. Sometimes the women, who has evidence against her husband, calls a meeting of all the women of the village, who, wearing hats and armed with spears and lances, advance on the house of the adulterer, and if he has growing crops, they destroy them. They make him come out of the house and threaten to run him through with their lances, at last driving him away. At other times the offended wife punished her husband by leaving him. Then her parents go to the husband's house and carry away everything of value, not even leaving him a spear, or a mat on which to sleep. They leave nothing more than the mere shell of the house and sometimes they destroy even that. If a woman is untrue to her husband the latter may kill her lover, but the woman receives no punishment.[15]

These customs led Le Gobien writing in 1700 to remark:

> To the wives are given all the rights attributed to husbands elsewhere. The woman has absolute command in the home. She is the mistress, she has all the authority, and the husband cannot dispose of anything without her consent.[16]

Along the same vein the French artist Arago, who accompanied the Freycinet expedition in 1819, concluded that, "the relationship between the sexes at that time indicated that the women had exercised great influence and that the men were in a species of subjugation to them."[17]

The advantaged position of married women encountered its first major challenge with the institutionalization of the Sacrament of Matrimony on Guam in 1668. In addition, divorce was prohibited. Conventional historians would have us believe that Chamorro women complied with these radical changes consentingly and without regret. Le Gobien provides evidence to the contrary.

> Marriage presented greater difficulties. It was the custom of the people to have only one wife, but they were free to change them. Indissolubility of marriage seemed to them to be an unbearable yoke. Above all, the women accustomed to dominate and change husbands whenever they pleased, could not subject themselves to a maxim which was contrary to their natural levity, and they considered the law which obliged them to live with their first spouses until death a real tyranny. It was necessary for them to subject themselves and renounce their mistaken rights of freedom and independence. The rules concerning marriage prescribed by the Council of Trent were published throughout the island and all were obliged to observe them.[18]

On the other hand, Chamorro men were apparently more willing. They seized the opportunity to gain control. Padre San Vitores reported that upon seeing how obedient, diligent, and "circumspect" the wives of the first converts were in relation to their husbands, "the Indios wished that their wives might be like them; and when they were told that this was a grace conferred only by matrimony, they acquired a fondness for the Sacrament."[19]

In time Chamorro women embraced the Catholic faith and observed the Sacraments with zeal. In fact they became the pillars of the Church. Religious marriage practices and the concomitant changes in husband-wife relations were deeply ingrained by the eighteenth century. The rites and customs that evolved are still practiced today.

The ancient tradition of a bride-price has been altered, but the groom is still under obligation to pay tribute to the bride. Responsibility for the wedding lies with the groom's family.[20] Up to the modern period, parents often chose the spouses for their children. This customs has changed. Love marriages are currently the dominant trend.

Civil marriage was instituted in 1899. Divorce was also legalized under American rule. Naval regulations prevailed until 1950 when civilian government was established with the passage of the Organic Act of Guam by the U. S. Congress. Since then, the Civil Code of the Territory has determined the rights of wives and husbands in relation to each other.

Part III, Title I (marriage) of the Guam Code was enacted in 1953. Among its provisions were three which portrayed the general tenor of legislation regarding marriage at that time.

1. The marriage of a female has the legal effect of changing her last or family name to that of her husband.[21]

2. The husband may choose any reasonable place or mode of living, and if the wife does not conform thereto, it is desertion.[22]

3. The husband is the head of the family.[23]

The first of these provisions was amended by the Fourteenth Guam Legislature. Women can now take whatever names they choose at marriage. The second and third were changed by P.L. 15-133 enacted on March 20, 1980. The three female members of the Fifteenth Guam Legislature introduced a series of amendments making Guam's marriage laws more equitable for both spouses.[24]

Motherhood

Chamorro mothers have been figures of power and authority throughout history. We can assume with reasonable certainty that the Chamorro culture has been mother-centered, a pattern which was established before Western contact. While the position of Chamorro women in relation to their husbands has changed as a result of transformations in the institution of marriage, the centrality of motherhood in Chamorro culture has not.

This matrifocality is manifested in various ways. "Mother-praise" songs are a popular means of celebrating the esteemed status of mothers. The lyrics of "*Si Na Gi Familia*" (A Mother in the Family) provide a classic example of this genre of musical poetry which Chamorros enjoy.

A Mother in the Family

A mother in the family
Whether ugly or pretty
Is always like an angel to us.
My mother was not pretty.
She would not have been chosen a
    beauty queen
But my mother is more beautiful
Than an American blond.

My mother never tried
The latest styles at the store.

But we were always clothed
Even though our clothes were mostly
   hand-me-downs.

The importance of mothers is also the subject of many proverbs. For example:

Y salape un sosoda, unjujute, lao unu ha nanamu.

You may have all the wealth in the world, all the comfort of luxuries and friends, but you'll only have one mother.

Maolegna un putan nana ki ni tai nana.

A mother is everything, even a whore for a mother is better than no mother at all.

Atan este y patgon bastado namas suesuete ki ni un patgon ni gai tata.

A bastard child is oftentimes more successful than a child with a father. (Implying that a mother's care is the essence of success.)[25]

One of the most well-known and frequently told Chamorro legends is the story of "*Sirena*". This legend of *Sirena* and her mother captures the power and decision-making authority of women in the family. It also illustrates the significance of the role of godmother. *Sirena*, an avid swimmer, disobeyed her mother once too often by stopping at the Minundo River in Agana for a swim at the expense of ignoring an errand she was asked to run. Her mother called her repeatedly but to no avail. Incensed by her daughter's disobedience, *Sirena*'s mother uttered a curse just as Sirena's godmother entered their home for a visit. Upon hearing the curse, *Sirena*'s godmother shouted, "If you desire that she turn into a fish, let the part that belongs to me remain human." Instantly, *Sirena* felt a tingling sensation from her waist down. The legendary mermaid begged her mother's forgiveness but the curse was irreversible. Through such legends, the young girls of Guam were taught to obey and respect their mothers' wishes.

In addition to folklore, there are other sources which lend credibility to my contention that motherhood has provided a context through which Chamorro women have exercised power and control, both within the family and in all other spheres of society, if not directly then through their children. The importance of children cannot be overstated in this regard. As childbearers, Chamorro women have long achieved prestige and honor, and enhanced their status in society. Early accounts illustrate this.

In 1597 Fray Antonio de los Angeles, the first clergyman to remain in the Marianas for nearly a year, observed:

> The first time the woman is pregnant, she goes to the home of her father or to that of the principal. There everyone takes her presents of whatever they have. And when she feels that the time for delivery is near; she goes to the home of the relatives where she can be the most favored with gifts.[26]

Fray Juan Pobre, who jumped ship and lived among the Chamorros for seven months in 1602, wrote:

> So great is their love for their children that it would take a long time to describe it and to sing its praises. They never spank them, and they even scold them with loving words.[27]

Padre San Vitores described the ancient Chamorro family thusly:

> In each family the head is the father or older relative, but with limited influence. A son, as he grows up, neither fears or respects his father. In the home it is the woman who rules, and her husband does not dare give an order contrary to her wishes, nor punish the children, for she will turn upon him and beat him. If the wife leaves his house the children go with her, knowing no other father than the next husband their mother may select.[28]

More recent works by Thompson, Beardsley, Munoz, and del Valle have illustrated the continuity of the mother's role at least until the modern period.[29] Sister Joanne Poehlman in her study entitled, "Culture Change and Identity Among

Chamorro Women of Guam", has summarized the traditional role of mothers succinctly.

"Traditionally," then, the role of mother in Chamorro culture has been one primarily characterized by a sense of responsibility, the woman exercised a near-absolute control over the behavior of her children, regulating their activities, determining their whereabouts, censoring their wishes.[30]

The premium Chamorro women place on having many children, irrespective of the tremendous responsibility and burden involved, baffles many modern observers especially feminists, who maintain that motherhood is at the root of female subordination. Although Chamorro women no longer top the record of having the highest birthrate in the world as they did in 1954, they still have unusually large families.[31] It is not at all uncommon for them to have ten or more children. The large-sized families of some Chamorro women organizers in this study attest to that fact.

Sister Joanne Poehlman has offered a likely explanation about why Chamorro women have attached so much importance to motherhood.

As every Chamorro woman also knew ... a life devoted to her children would be repaid by her children's devotion to her ...

If it was important for a man to have a child to prove his manhood, it was crucial for a woman to produce a family for her own security.[32]

Poehlman notes that the benefits of motherhood may be threatened by modern trends.

For many, the expected has never materialized. Ironically, by exerting control, by directing her children into new paths of success, the Chamorro mother in some ways has lessened her control and has supplied her children with new tools for independence.[33]

If motherhood becomes more of a liability than an asset for Chamorro women, will their attitudes toward it change? Already younger women are having fewer children. Perhaps contemporary realities will force an unprecedented turning point.

Socialization and Education

Mothers have been the primary agents of socialization in diverse cultures throughout history. Chamorro women are no exception. Early accounts of child-rearing illustrate the tremendous responsibility ascribed to Chamorro women in the family. We can safely assume that their role as mothers was a source of stability and continuity amidst the changes brought about by colonization. Mothers transmitted cultural values and practices to their children. As new codes of behavior were instituted, they took it upon themselves to teach the new ways along with the old.

Within the Chamorro matrifocal kinship system, girls were socialized to become strong and active women and mothers. They emulated their mothers and other female relatives and learned how central their various roles were to the survival of the Chamorro culture. On the other hand, boys were trained to imitate their fathers, many of whom were non-Chamorros. While values and attitudes were probably taught to both male and female children alike, gender-specific roles or trades were not. This may help to explain why the ancient Chamorro skills and arts practiced by women (like the *suruhana's* services and weaving) have been maintained, while most of those performed by men (such as canoe building) have been lost.

Perhaps the most significant aspect of the Chamorro woman's role as educator involved the preservation and transmission of the Chamorro language to her children. William Haswell, who visited Guam in 1801, remarked:

The present inhabitants are the descendants of Spanish, French and Englishmen who settled on the island and intermarried with the Chamorros, and the children learning the language from their mothers, have preserved it to the present day, somewhat modified by the introduction of Spanish words and idioms.[34]

Numerous other observers have recorded this fact, and Chamorros themselves agree that their language is spoken today because women have continued to speak it in the home along with the other "officially imposed" languages since contact with the Western World.

Besides acquiring the language, children, especially daughters, learned the fundamentals of Chamorro life by observing their mothers and often assisted them as they participated in religious rituals. They led prayers (*techa*), met mutual obligations through exchange of services (*chinchule*), and performed a variety of tasks in the household. They were taught the importance of the family and kinship ties. As apprentices from an early age, young girls learned to care for siblings and take greater responsibilities for managing family affairs as they grew older.

The tradition of *manginge* (kissing the hand of an elder to show respect), which is still observed today, is one example of how effectively ancient cultural practices have been preserved by Chamorro women through the centuries. Identifying kin and teaching children about their lineage has also been the mother's responsibility. Chamorro genealogist, Anthony Ramirez, revealed in an interview that, "most resources on genealogical information in Chamorro society are recorded and related by women." He based this remark on the extensive research he has conducted with Chamorro families. He also said that, "although the newly formed Society of Chamorro Genealogists is composed chiefly of men, the resources always being quoted are the *tan*, female elderly."[35]

Inherent in the Chamorro mother's responsibility for her children's future and for developing their ability to cope with new realities, was the need to assume an active role in promoting change. Although this often conflicted with her role as cultural preservationist, her foremost concern was for her children's survival and success.

Describing the role of contemporary Chamorro women as agents of change, Sister Joanne Poehlman writes, "The Chamorro woman, then, as wife and mother, was no mere spectator on the periphery of change. Rather, she was a significant contributor to the post-war transformation of her island."[36] Poehlman concludes that,

> For Chamorro women the situation sets up a particular dilemma. Because of their central role within the family, they have been a strong influence on the direction of change. Because of these same roles, they are held responsible for the maintenance of a sense of cultural continuity.[37]

This dilemma is clearly evident in the lives of the Chamorro women organizers in this study.

This paradox also extends to the Chamorro woman's role as educator in the occupational or formal sense. Reports show that formal training for children was an urgent priority of the Spanish missionaries. During Governor Saravia's term in office (1681-1683) for example:

> The new Governor also undertook the construction of another building in which newly Christianized girls might be educated under the care of a female teacher from among the leaders of this island, who is conspicuous in Catholic practices and the liberal arts proper to her sex.[38]

Reporting on the institution of education on Guam in the 1860s, Governor Felipe de la Corte wrote that there were 26 teachers in seven *pueblos*; six were women. And,

> In addition to the *colegio* for boys in the city, four boy's schools, five girls's schools, and nine for both sexes were maintained. In like manner, a scholarship position should be created at the *Escuela normal* for women teachers from the Marianas. The objective would be to supply women teachers for Agana and,

sequentially, for the *pueblos* in the manner described
to supply *maestros* (school masters).[39]

These accounts illustrate that the teaching profession was one
of the first salaried occupations opened to Chamorro women as
early as 1681. Since then, women have steadily embarked on
careers in the field of education, initially as teachers and in the
modern period as administrators as well. Women have also
been involved in religious instruction as catechists at *escuelan
pale* (literally, the priest's school), an institution dating back to
Spanish times. As religious and secular educators, they continue to impart new values and rules of conduct which frequently
challenge the validity of or actually contradict the traditional
ideology and customs which, as mothers, they teach to their
children at home.

While the culture has undergone major transformations, the Chamorro woman's responsibility for the socialization
and education of children has remained constant throughout
history. Modernization has introduced other influential forces
of socialization, such as the media, which have lessened the
control of mothers and teachers. Still, Chamorro women are a
powerful force in the home and in Guam's educational system.
Their resolution of the tension between being agents of change
on the one hand and cultural preservationists on the other
influences their future impact and status as socializers and
educators.

Social Life

Chamorro society has always been sexually integrated;
no strict division of the sexes into separate spheres or physical
spaces has ever been socially enforced. As sex relations and
gender roles are often reinforced by such spatial arrangements,
it is likely that the unrestricted mobility and interaction between
Chamorro men and women also reflected the esteemed position
of Chamorro women in ancient times. Several references in the
literature, coupled with visiting artists' renditions of Chamorro
social life from the time of contact through the Spanish period,

suggest that at least until the American Naval Administration of Guam, most Chamorro women enjoyed an active social life. They were by no means "cloistered ladies of the domicile."

Women had their own festivals. In addition they participated in leisure activities with men, presumably their husbands or relatives. In paintings and sketches they were also portrayed fishing, planting, and cooking alongside men. When the parish church became the center of social life for villagers, both sexes gathered for religious or community celebrations.

Visitors to Guam have depicted Chamorro women in other interesting ways. Des Graz noted that both men and women attended cockfights, a popular sport in the Spanish colonial world. Chamorro women were apparently fond of smoking cigars. Des Graz remarked that they "appear to make a greater usage of it [cigars] than the men. One continually sees in their mouth a cigar from three to four inches long and very fat. They were made of tobacco grown in the Marianas."[40]

F. H. Von Kittlitz who stopped at Guam with a Russian expedition in 1829 recorded,

> that the women were not inclined to be segregated or secluded from visitors as they were on some islands. He reported that the women of Guam were courteous to strangers and talked easily and pleasantly with them. In fact, he found that women here were apt to monopolize any conversation.[41]

The log of the **Emily Morgan** of New Bedford, a whaling ship commanded by Captain Ewer which stopped at Guam on April 6, 1852, included under the entry "Females":

> The females of Guam are remarkably fair-looking; keen black eyes, flowing black hair, smooth complexion, and possessed of a robust and well-rounded form; their step light and elastic, and very graceful in their movements. ... After vespers we passed a very pleasant evening with these lively, chatting beauties from whom we learned much of interest in regards to the island.[42]

It seems women have always played an important role in the flow of communication about island affairs as they do today. Beardsley wrote, "everyone welcomed a visitor who might bring interesting news from another sector. Women visitors were especially esteemed."[43] They not only exchanged information; some women served as "guides." Lt. Governor Safford recorded such an instance in his journal in 1899.[44] While these excerpts from various accounts do not give a detailed or comprehensive picture of social life, they do evoke a scenario of social interaction.

Using linguistic evidence to make her point about interaction between Chamorro men and women, Lolita L.G. Huxel, in a paper presented at the Guam Women's Conference in 1977 entitled "Explaining Culture Through Linguistic Structure," stated:

> The Chamorro language shows absence of gender distinctions and suggests how it is probable in reconstructed Chamorro culture that men and women work together as a team, set or whole in their communal everyday activities.[45]

Perhaps the social attribute which Chamorros have been noted for is their hospitality. Whether at a fiesta or in the home, Chamorro women personify the essence of this tradition.

The early twentieth century on Guam was characterized by many changes in the lifestyle of the Chamorro people. Women rarely ventured outside the home except to perform household tasks, garden, or fulfill obligations. Only church activities were sanctioned. Unmarried girls were chaperoned wherever they went. Their retreat into the home was a departure from the long-standing social freedom they enjoyed. The "Victorian" views of U. S. Naval Administrators coupled with legal restrictions they imposed on the populace effected a redefinition of "women's proper place." Ironically, Chamorro women lost their freedom of movement and status in the public sphere at approximately the same time that "flappers" in the

United States were discarding all symbols of the "Victorian lady" and more importantly as American women gained the suffrage. Contemporary Chamorro women have overcome many of these artificial barriers as they seek full participation at all levels of society once again.

Myths, Rituals, and Religion

Creation myths provide an original source for identifying attitudes about sex roles and relations that different people develop as their cultures evolve. Though the Catholic population of Guam today believes in the account of creation found in the **Book of Genesis**, ancient Chamorros believed that a female spirit was the life-giving force. The Chamorro legend of creation was first documented by Fray Antonio de los Angeles in 1596. He wrote: "They say that a woman gave birth to the land, and to the sea, and to all that is visible."[46] The story of *Fuuna* and her brother *Putan* is a more popular version.

It is important to recognize that ancient Chamorros believed in the ultimate power of women as the source of life and controller of their environment. Several other legends illustrate this well. "The Coconut Girl" tells of a young Chamorro maiden who despaired because she had no contributions to make to her village. She grew melancholy and refused to eat. Family, friends, and suitors all sought as a cure the fruit from an unknown tree that she had seen in a vision. No one could find the fruit of which she spoke. She died. After her death, heavy rains prevented anyone from visiting her grave. When the rains finally stopped, her parents and friends were amazed to find a tiny unknown plant growing where she was buried. In time the plant grew into a tree which bore a strange fruit with the aspects of a human face. The white meat of the fruit gave sustenance; the fluid provided liquid refreshment; and the fronds gave shelter and were woven into many things. Her people learned to use many of its other parts. Though she lived among them no more, her loved ones knew that the maiden had finally contributed a most valuable gift to her people. This theme and that of the creation myth are rooted in the actual role of women as mothers, i.e., they give birth and nurture.

The "protectress" image also has a legendary origin. The "Maidens Who Saved Guam" tells of a monster from the sea, who long ago began to chew his way through Guam, for it was determined to destroy the island. Night after night the men went out in search of the monster but could not find it. The young women would talk about the monster whenever they gathered to wash their hair with soap oranges. Their favorite spot was Agana Spring. When they finished, the pool would be covered with soap orange peels. One day a girl noticed these peels floating in Pago Bay. She was puzzled by their appearance. After some thought, she surmised that the monster must have eaten a hole all the way under the island from Pago Bay to Agana Spring and that was where it was hiding. The next day, when the girls gathered at Agana Spring, they wove a net with their long, black hair, then sat around the pool and began to sing. The monster, enchanted with the music, swam up from the bottom of the pool to listen to the girls sing. Suddenly the girls spread their net over the spring and they all dived in. The monster was caught and the island of Guam was saved.

Legends, as they are told today, reflect the influences of Catholicism. Many are associated with the Blessed Mother (*Santa Maria*). For example, a later version of the legend just narrated features *Santa Maria* as the "Maiden Who Saved Guam". Chamorros believe that *Santa Marian Kamalin* floated onto the shores of Guam, escorted by two crabs with lit candles on their backs, to reside among them and protect them from harm. She is the island's Patroness. Her feast is celebrated with an islandwide procession. Many Chamorros, especially women, have a devotion to her.

An interesting extension of the "caretaker" image is found in the role of the *suruhana* in Chamorro culture. The spiritual world of the ancient Chamorros revolved around an ancestor cult. *Aniti* (souls of ancestors) and *taotaomona* (people of before) were believed to be sacred and powerful and could cause great harm when crossed. A class of sorcerers called *makana* or *kakana* invoked these supernatural beings to bring success in warfare, to insure a good catch, to obtain rain, or to cure illness. Whereas the *makana* used supernatural means to cure illness, *suruhana* healed with herbs and ointments. Catholicism led to the demise of the sorcerer class. Some people on Guam still believe in the *taotaomona*. *Suruhana* attend to ailments believed to be inflicted by these ancestral beings. Besides administering to the spiritual and mental well-being of Chamorros today, *suruhana* continue to treat physical maladies. Some have incorporated prayers into their method of treatment. God, the Blessed Mother, and a whole litany of Saints are often called upon to restore an individual.

Today priests are more frequently turned to for guidance regarding spiritual or emotional matters, and modern medical practitioners are visited for treatment of health problems. These changes have caused many to believe that the traditional healing practice of the *suruhana* is disappearing. A recent study by Ann Marie Pobutsky has shown otherwise. The results of a survey to determine the current use of traditional healers revealed that, "Chamorro women, women of childbearing age and young people (less than 35 years old) show a greater frequency of use of the services of traditional healers than their respective counterparts."[47] Pobutsky also states that "interviews with *suruhana* supported an earlier study that most of the clients of the *suruhana* are women and children," and that "*suruhana* specialize in the treatment of women's problems." This study has provided convincing evidence that female healers still play a vital role in the community.

The esteemed status of Chamorro women is also evident in Chamorro rituals. Women played a key role at ancient burials. According to Fray Juan Pobre (1602):

> After the body of the deceased, especially a high ranking leader is wrapped in a mat [shroud], two of the deceased's female relatives arrive, who are among the oldest women of the village, and lay pieces of tree bark or of painted paper on top of the body. Then they begin mourning.[48]

Freycinet reported that, "every year fishermen were expected to give their first catch of each kind of fish to their female relatives."[49]

The distribution of the traditional Chamorro wedding cake--a pyramid of cooked rice--provides another example of the high rank accorded to women in ceremonial events.

> This cake was first offered by the mothers of the nuptual pair to their husbands' eldest sisters. The wedding cake, which was constructed upon a special litter, passed via appointed bearers from person to person until it finally was received by the eldest woman in the family. She alone had authority to divide it among those to whom it had been presented.[50]

Though priests perform the religious ceremonies for baptisms, marriages, and funerals, Chamorro women have traditionally played a significant role in cultural rituals which are still practiced--although slightly modified--at family or extended kin celebrations and during more solemn occasions like the death of a family member.

No study of the position of Chamorro women would be complete without addressing the centrality, influence, and effects of Catholicism in their lives. Catholicism revolutionized ancient Chamorro conceptions about women. It discredited mythical beliefs about creation, which reflected female power and subsequently replaced them with Western/biblical views. A totally new ideal personified by the Blessed Virgin Mary became the measuring stick for appropriate female behavior. Novel Images prompted Chamorros to rethink and adjust their views on gender and power. A rigid code of chastity and submission was instituted. Though it was neither strictly enforced by men including the clergy nor always observed by women, as evidence presented earlier demonstrates, its effects were profound.

Ultimately, then, Catholicism imposed an alien moral code which restricted the Chamorro woman's freedom and redefined her "proper place" in society, with the family, and in relation to her husband. The religious conversion of Chamorros undeniably threatened and altered the high status women enjoyed in ancient Chamorro society. While the introduction of Catholicism marked a turning point in the Chamorro female experience, it nevertheless established a "framework" which allowed women to continue their powerful roles as mothers and teachers within the limited confines of their homes and the church. So despite the devaluation and loss of power women experienced in the political sphere and in terms of patriarchal notions, the Catholic Church reinforced the Chamorro woman's position in the family. Because she had direct and continuous access to the colonial power structure through her active participation in the religious life of the community--this being the most important institution in Spanish colonial times--she was able to regain some of her former status. In many ways Chamorro women were better off than Chamorro men throughout colonial history. As was pointed out earlier, Chamorro women could enhance their status through marriage. Men could not. Though the "woman's world" had narrowed in scope, they retained their high status among kin. Chamorro women continued to control all affairs related to the family. Chamorro men, in contrast, could neither compete with colonial officials for status and control in the "man's world" nor could they compete with priests, who held considerable power. Hence Chamorro women maintained their high rank in relation to Chamorro men during the Spanish period.

Once Chamorro women embraced the Catholic faith, they were noted for their religious fervor. Governor Felipe de la Corte commented on their zealousness.

> In general, the Marianos are generous to the point of extravagance, hospitable, and religious--at least they go through the motions, especially the women with their fanatical and superstitious passementerie (beads, cords, etc.)[51]

Attendance at mass, bible readings, novenas, and rosaries were an integral part of their daily activities. The village church became the center for social gatherings. Young girls joined the Sodality of Mary. Married women became members of the Christian Mothers Association. Participation in church activities was, for most women, the only sanctioned involvement outside the home.

The *techa* have served as lay ministers of the Catholic Church on Guam for centuries. Today they are also assuming other roles. In these various capacities, they have worked hand in hand with their parish priests to fulfill diverse community needs. In addition, Chamorro mothers are considered guardians of religion in the home; this has added to their prestige. Sister Joanne Poehlman describes this role in terms of actual responsibilities. While she refers to women in prewar Guam, her description is also applicable to many women today.

The Chamorro mother was ultimately responsible to God who had entrusted to her her souls to be readied for heaven. The priests and selected laywomen provided formal instruction in church doctrine and taught prayers at *eskuelan pale*. It was the mother's responsibility to see to it that her children attended classes, said their prayers on a regular basis, and attended Sunday Mass .... Every family had its patron saint after whom children were named and in whose honor parties were given. Each year, for nine consecutive evenings before the saint's day, neighbors were invited and a *techa* was called to lead the *Nobena* prayers and hymns .... *Nobena* obligations (which are handed down within families from mother to daughter or mother to son and daughter-in-law) were sacred; something had been promised and one found joy infulfilling that promise. *Nobena* were family feasts turned into neighborhood celebrations .... Passed on from one generation to the next, they reinforced ties between mother and daughter. And if, by some chance, a child went wrong, a mother could find hope in prayer. Here her ultimate responsibilities could be fulfilled.[52]

Chamorro men have certainly been active in the church and have also taken responsibility for the religious well-being of their children. Nevertheless, Chamorro women remain the "moral keepers" of the family and society. Many of the activities organized by women in this study attest to their own understanding and fulfillment of this responsibility. The centrality and influence of Catholic beliefs and practices in the lives of Chamorro women and the concomitant significance of the roles they play as active members of their parishes reflect an important aspect of their status and identity. This will become increasingly evident as we examine the views and experiences of Chamorro women organizers.

Economy

Guam's economic history can be divided into two major phases. The first phase is characterized by a cooperative system of shared labor and exchange based on subsistence needs and trade. In contrast, the second phase is characterized by a competitive cash-based system, which reflects a separation between economic activities in the household from those in the marketplace.

The shift from one phase to the other began at the turn of the twentieth century and is a direct result of the concerted efforts of the first Naval Administrators to promote capitalism with its emphasis on wage-employment and production.

Women were an integral part of the subsistence and barter economy of the early Chamorros. Class, more than gender, determined the division of labor. Though women performed tasks in or near their homes, caring for children, weaving, making pottery, and cooking; they also worked alongside men in the fields, at the ranch, or fishing. Men and women often shared roles. The contributions of both sexes were essential to the livelihood of the family.

In addition to the subsistence activities they performed, women controlled property through their lineage, managed the exchange of goods and services among kin, and controlled commerce. We know that married women could confiscate their husbands' property. Children also belonged to her. This was clearly illustrated in descriptions of the ancient divorce settlement.

Other accounts of this period also reported the economic power of Chamorro women. Freycinet, for example, described how the wealth of a family was in the hands of its women.

> If a woman needed a piece of land, a part of the harvest, a canoe, or any other thing belonging to a man of her family, she presented a piece of shell "money" to him with a request for the property, and her request was immediately granted without further payment.[53]

They also monopolized trade. Antoine-Alfred Marche wrote:

> One can still see dominating the harbor the ruins of an ancient Spanish fort and the village of Sumay whose inhabitants and especially the women, trade with the whalers coming there every year to replenish their food supply.[54]

Women exchanged sexual favors for goods brought by the Galleon trade and explorers that made their way to Guam. Several were "employed" as servants, cooks, and laundry women. By and large though, wage employment did not adversely affect the advantaged economic position of women until capitalism was introduced along with extra-domestic wage employment for men.

In his description of the first few years of American rule on Guam, Captain Frederick J. Nelson of the U. S. Navy presented the "philosophy," which forced a reversal of the old economic order.

> Thus the difficulties faced by the government in making and collecting the first taxes were due largely to the transition from a barter to a money economy. This transition was especially slow due to the most

oriental reluctance of the Chamorros to adopt new ways and customs, even though their leaders, at least, appreciated the need for such changes. In order to encourage further the practice of wage earning and the development of a money economy, and also to get vitally necessary public works done, Safford found it necessary to eliminate the almost continuous general celebration of religious feast and saint's days, and ac cordingly an Executive Order was issued prohibiting all holidays except those prescribed by the laws of the United States. Thereafter the obstacle to regular and continuous economic activity was removed.[55]

A new division of labor relegated women to the home. If women worked for wages, they were maids, housekeepers, cooks, store clerks, bar girls, Nurses, and school teachers.[56] Men, on the other hand, were lured from their farms or ranches to fill semi-skilled, skilled and white collar jobs, which were created by economic development.

Before World War II, a modified subsistence economy prevailed despite the changes which were instituted by the Naval Government. Intense economic development in the postwar era has resulted in a complete changeover from sub-sistence/sufficiency to production/consumption. Women have entered the job market in full force. The principal motivation for their participation has been to increase family income in order to meet the growing needs of their household and to afford education for their children. While many women are engaged in traditionally female occupations, they are quickly rising to the top in these and other professions.

Many Chamorro women have developed home-based businesses--baking, sewing, providing childcare, and catering services--as a source of income. Small-scale family businesses are also operated by husband-wife teams or extended family members.

In prewar Guam women's confinement to the domestic sphere did not lessen her economic power in the family. Though she was often not the wage-earner, she controlled the purse-strings as her husband's and children's salaries would be given to her. She apportioned family finances as she saw fit and distributed *chinchule* and other resources to meet kinship obligations. Modernization created new needs. It was often the Chamorro mother who devised ways and means to make home improvements, purchase labor-saving appliances, and provide her family with other luxuries. The desire for a college education for her children has further taxed the fiscal management skills of many Chamorro mothers.

Chamorro women continued to own property after the American takeover. Safford's journal is replete with references regarding property disputes concerning female owners. He purchased land and houses from several women.[57]

While these observations seem to indicate that women were not adversely affected by the economic shift which began at the turn of the century, the valuation of "women's work" has steadily declined since "men's work" became identified with the public sphere. Although almost as many women are now active in the labor force as men, their work status has not improved. Working women now endure the double burden of performing their household tasks--at least being responsible that these tasks get done--in addition to their responsibilities as employees outside the home. The fact that they earn less than men for comparable work heightens the frustration of many working women. Chamorro women are fortunate in that they have a large support network on whom they can rely for assistance with household responsibilities. This lightens the load. However, it does not lessen the growing dissatisfaction expressed by some regarding these inequitable arrangements. The good news is that changes in sex roles are already beginning to occur. Women are demanding equal pay for comparable work.

Modern values have also taken a toll on the Chamorro woman's traditional role as keeper of the purse-strings. Mothers can no longer "expect" their children to hand over their paychecks. The philosophies of self-reliance and independence have altered this practice in recent years. The current economic position of Chamorro women reflects these disparate realities.

Government and the Law

Governing councils directed public affairs in ancient Chamorro society. These district councils were composed of the high ranking men and women of the *matao* caste. According to Freycinet, every question of family honor and anything vital to the interests of the district were submitted to the council.[58] Members of both castes were subject to the decisions of this governing body. It is not known whether all the members of a family or clan were affected by an individual's transgression of the rigidly enforced Chamorro code of behavior. But the record indicates that women were subject to the law in their own right; they were not treated as wards of either their fathers or their husbands. In fact they received preferential treatment.

Even in feuds women were accorded special treatment. If a woman was engaged in a quarrel, the whole clan took her side; no one interfered in arguments between men. A person who could mobilize the limited energy resources available in such a society commanded political and economic power. If a plea for assistance was directed to a male, he alone came. But if it were directed to the women of highest rank in a Chamorro family, all the relatives, including the in-laws, had to turn out.[59]

Pere Charles Le Gobien, French Jesuit and historian of the Mariana Islands, wrote in 1700 that the women controlled everything except navigation and war.[60] These descriptions provide convincing evidence of female power and even dominance in the political sphere of ancient Chamorro society. However, the status and roles of Chamorro women in the realm of government began to change with the imposition of Spanish laws and governance.

As late as the 1670s, women still assumed official positions of power. This was documented by Padre San Vitores.

During this year [circa 1672] the astuteness and courage of the Islanders themselves served quite as well as the Spanish arms to rid the island of malefactors. This was started by a woman who governed, insofar as the Marianos will suffer government, the district called Sydia, in the southern part of Guam. This noble matron who was devoted to Christianity, counseled her people, who were already tired of constant unrest, to buy peace and friendship from the Spaniards by means of the punishment of delinquents. Thus it was done.[61]

It is interesting to note the opposing roles women were said to have taken in reaction to Spanish conquest. The above Chamorro woman urged capitulation.

Compare this stance with that taken by women who practiced abortion as an act of defiance against Spanish domination. The Spanish-Chamorro wars, which lasted for thirty years, decimated the aboriginal male Chamorro population. Notwithstanding the drastic reduction in their numbers, some women apparently chose to terminate pregnancies rather than give birth to children whose "freedom" would be denied.[62]

Nearly a half a century after the wars, the Spanish Crown responded to these female acts of rebellion.

Spanish King Philip V issued a royal decree on May 28, 1741 that women of the Marianas were to be exempted from tasks and occupations not suited to their sex, "and the men shall cultivate the land." It was a dozen years before Governor Enrique de Olivide y Michelena issued orders to the *Alcaldes* of Guam's villages to see that the women did not do any hard labor. The Governor specifically authorized women to weave sails, mats and roof coverings. The intent of the decree, of course, was to free women sufficiently so that they could focus their attention on building up the labor force. Women who voluntarily had abortions were whipped and sentence to forced labor.[63]

"Tasks and occupations not suited to their sex" were defined by non-Chamorro men. For Western males, government was one such area ill suited to women. Although an innovative form of Spanish colonial government was established in the Marianas empowering native leaders to govern over local affairs, to occupy principal positions in each village, and to be appointed to high positions in the King's army on the island, none of these official posts was occupied by women.[64] In time Chamorro men held all but the very top local government positions. Chamorros were given Spanish citizenship and legal equality with other Spanish subjects. The Law of the Indies became the legal code. Presumably it applied to Chamorro men and women alike. Women did possess some legal rights. They could enter into contractual agreements, own property, and seek reprisal for criminal acts against their persons or property.[65]

With the establishment of American Naval Government, Chamorros lost all vestige of political control over their lives. Naval Governors ruled with an iron fist. Executive Orders imposed one restriction after another.

Descendants of the Chamorro ruling class were among the first to be allowed limited participation in government through the Guam Congress. Chamorro men filled the political and administrative positions opened to indigenes. Still, Chamorro women made some inroads in the formal arena of elected politics. Six women served in the Guam Congress between 1946 and 1950. This promising start proved deceptive as only five women held office between 1953 and 1978.[66] Since then, many more women have been vying for seats and getting elected to the Guam Legislature. In addition, as shall be discussed in greater detail in a later chapter, more women are assuming top-level positions in the Executive Branch of government.

Chamorro women have also been active in international politics. Two of them head Guam's involvement in the Nuclear Free and Independent Pacific Movement.[67]

In summary, the Chamorro woman was vested with formal power in ancient Chamorro society. In many ways she was more powerful than her male counterpart. Her official status changed somewhat during the Spanish colonial period.

While she did not occupy official positions of power, she wielded a great deal of informal power within and through her family and maintained important legal rights. American Government curtailed many of her former privileges. In the modern period she has begun to regain power.

Prescriptive ideals and actual behavior, oftentimes at odds, have been interwoven throughout history to shape perceptions about the position of Chamorro women in their culture. Myths have influenced reality, and in turn, reality has given rise to new myths. Chamorro women have played a dynamic role in this dialectic process of change. The record illustrates unequivocally that Chamorro women have not been mere bystanders or passive recipients of the changes in their status and roles, which were brought about by external forces. Chamorro women of the past--legendary and real--collectively created a unique legacy to which the contemporary Chamorro women featured in the following three chapters are adding their own perceptions, experiences, and contributions.

Cecilia C. Bamba

CHAPTER IV

"LADY EXTRAORDINAIRE"

Introduction

As a researcher, I have had the challenging task of structuring and presenting a portion of the life experiences and selected contributions of nine Chamorro women organizers in a format that provides coherence for the reader while attempting to preserve the subjects' "voice." To achieve this goal in this chapter, I utilized lengthy passages of Cecilia Cruz Bamba's own description of her experiences and activities. These have been interspersed with less personal summaries of information she provided in the interviews or through written documents. While this format may prove disruptive to some readers, it intentionally reflects the interview dialogue.

Cecilia Bamba's story is told in a distinctively positive tone. The style of telling captures the personality of the subject and how she saw her life and work. Although the other personal testimonies have necessarily been written in a more compact form, a similar attempt is made to preserve the vitality and perspective of each organizer.

As we begin Cecilia Bamba's story and those of the eight subjects, it is important to ask what information is gained from the lives of these women regarding their status, roles, and contributions? Of concern to this chapter are such questions as: What motivated a woman like Cecilia Bamba to devote much of her life to community service while she fulfilled her roles as wife and mother to a large family? How did she balance her" career" in volunteerism with responsibilities at home? What strategies did she utilize for her lengthy lists of accomplishments? Did she consider herself an activist? What were her views on the position of women and feminism? And, ultimately, what value did her various involvements as an organizer have both for her personally and for the community which she served? Cecilia Cruz Bamba answers some of these questions as she recounts "her story."[1]

Cecilia C. Bamba[2]

Early Tuesday morning on September 30, 1986 at Sequoia Hospital in Redwood City, California, Cecilia Bamba passed away quietly in her sleep after a long and painful bout with cancer. She was only 51 years old. She spent the last few years of her life in great pain. She never complained. To the contrary, she grew in faith, was always hopeful, and exuded love in all she said and did. Her strength and character have left an indelible mark in the hearts of her children, grandchildren, relatives, friends, and all whose lives she touched.

Her beloved island of Guam honored her with a state funeral. The people she loved and served so generously in the five decades of her life paid tribute to their mother, grandmother, relative, and friend at the Agana Cathedral Basilica where she laid before Santa Marian Kamalin in whom she put total trust. Hers is a legacy of service which is evidenced in the pages that follow.

Some Guam residents are familiar with Cecilia by name only. During the hot and sticky tropical summer of 1982, islanders were barraged by political campaign slogans which lined the major streets of Guam. One could have been introduced to Cecilia Bamba through bold-fuchsia-colored letters which caught the eyes of passers-by at the junction of Chalan Santo Papa and O'Hara Street in Agana, where an election poster urging voters to re-elect Cecilia Cruz Bamba to the Sixteenth Guam Legislature billed her as "Lady Extraordinaire."

Others who have personally met her would probably describe her as a well-dressed, attractive, middle-aged, active community volunteer. These are simply superficial descriptors. Only she can reveal the inner layers of reality as she has lived it.

Childhood Memories

I was very close to my father, more so than my mother. I don't know if it's because I was always with my
mother. We had a big ranch up at the Naval Communications Station. My father was very industrious and
a very ambitious man. He had a job with the Navy as
Supervisor of Naval Supply, but he maintained the
ranch. He took over land he bought from his father
when his father could not pay the real estate tax .... .
He hired some other Chamorro men to be ranch
hands. He was exporting copra and making oil for the
Ada's factory. They started planting fruits and different kinds of produce. His routine was every Friday
afternoon after work he comes home and he would
get all the supplies ready to bring up to the ranch. He
would usually come back before dinner or in time for
a late dinner. You could tell we were very close. His
absence affected me. Whenever he came home late,
or if he didn't come home by ten o'clock, I would start
getting a fever. I would have a high temperature. But
immediately after he comes my temperature would go
down .... . I'm the apple of his eye. So there's nothing
in this world I couldn't have within his reach. That
was the relationship that we had. I was very close to
my father. It just devastated me when he was beheaded by the Japanese, when I lost him. After losing my
mother, he was still around. When I lost my mother, I
was really lost, but I guess because my grandmother
was around, she kind of just stepped into that role.
But when my father was taken away from me it was
something. I thought that I was going to die, that I
would never survive (pp. 7-8).

Victimized by the cruel, destructive onslaught of World
War II, at age nine Cecilia Cruz was thrust into a world of adult
responsibility. She survived the personal losses of her mother,
Rosario, and her father, Jose Leon Guerrero Cruz. The
strength and inspiration of her maternal great-grandmother and

grandmother, her love and concern for her baby brother John and positive childhood memories armed her with the courage to do something with her life. Remembering was both painful and heartwarming:

> My mother was a very strict lady. She was a perfectionist. I guess her personality and my father's were just opposite .... She died at 27. She was so strict with my upbring. I tell you, I don't think there's anybody that was reared the way I was reared. When I was a little girl, it even made me feel resentful sometimes. She deprived me of being an ordinary girl. Others would go out and make mud pies and run around with the neighborhood kids and play with them. With me no, she had a room in our house fixed up with furniture, small china. She selects who plays with me; she controls everything. The only time I would have a little freedom is everyday after lunch. The nurse, a young girl in her 20s or 30s, would bring me to the beach so that I can play in the sand, with the thought that I would get tired and take my nap .... In the morning I would be brought to school. I could never walk to school with the kids. After school somebody would pick me up. When I had to walk, someone would stand beside me with an umbrella. I was just like a prisoner in my own home .... I admired her--she was a beautiful person--but I think in that area it made me tend to be a little more liberal with my own children (pp. 25- 27).

Young Cecilia's rigid training had a mixed impact on her. She never lost sight of the discipline that her mother tried hard to instill in her at the tender ages of six and seven. This is evident in her relationship with her own children and grandchildren and in her approach to her various undertakings.

Looking back, she revealed that childish resentments often turned into humorous episodes:

> When I was a little girl, I couldn't understand [my mother]. Because when you are little you want to do

what you want and when somebody stops you, you
turn around and say she's mean, but that's the way. I
loved to eat raw eggs when I was little. My mother
would be just furious because she thinks it would hurt
me if I eat them. I could eat six or seven eggs. She
would leave explicit instructions that eggs should be
put in a place where I couldn't find them. Everyday
fresh eggs would come from our farm; so I would
bribe our housegirl to give me some .... I would
find little things. They had boyfriends, and my mother
was so strict she didn't allow the boyfriends to visit.
Sometimes I would see one of the housegirls talking
to her boyfriend. She would be afraid that I might
squeal to my mother about her; she knew that I knew
the policy. So I would use that on her. "You better
get me some eggs or I'm going to tell my mother." I
was only about 5 or 6 years old at the time (p. 28).

After her mother's death, Cecilia's father remarried.
His second marriage was short-lived. He was executed by
Japanese military forces toward the end of the war. In the brief
interim between their father's remarriage and his death, she
and her baby brother moved in with him and their stepmother.
A stepbrother was born of that union. The orphaned Cecilia
and John were taken by their maternal grandmother to her
postwar home in Agana Heights, the village where Mrs. Bamba
resided till her death. Contact with their stepfamily ceased until
Mrs. Bamba's own marriage prompted her to seek them out
and re-establish ties.

In spite of these hardships at such a young age, Cecilia
had many wonderful memories of her youth. She was forever
grateful to both her grandmother and great-grandmother, who
served as a sustaining force in the difficult years of maturation.

My grandmother became the key [figure] in my
growing up and [in] the formation of character (p. 20).

After I lost both parents, my grandmother and
great-grandmother reared me. I took care of
them after I married until they passed away. My

great-grandmother died in 1957 at the age of 92. Ever so often I say, I don't know why I didn't tape all those stories that she would tell me. A lot of things she told me really guided my life. I quote her even now to my children and grandchildren .... They helped me to appreciate and understand how it is to be old. It made me sensitive to the elderly (p. 6).

My great-grandmother always reminded me that to every grain of rice wasted you have to spend one year in purgatory, because those are God's graces and when you waste God's graces, God will punish you. This lesson has stayed with me (p. 30).

Mrs. Bamba repeatedly expressed regret at not having recorded the numerous anecdotes and teachings that her great-grandmother taught her. She vividly recalled how the last decades of the Spanish colonial era on Guam came alive for her during such storytelling sessions:

She [great-grandmother] was born in 1865 so she remembered all those days in Agana when they had to draw water from a well. And how as a young girl she would be the one to fill a big earthenware container with water. When the container was about to be filled someone would start washing and the water would go down again and she would have to keep going back .... She was a governess for one of the Spanish Governors, she and her sister. She went off island; in fact they were taken to Shanghai. And she would tell me about all the children she had to take care of. I think it was just beautiful to have experienced something like that (pp. 6- 7).

It was with her mother's mother, whom she called *Nana*, that she found refuge as a child. *Nana* was an advocate, friend, inspiration, guide, "mother," and a constant source of support until she died in her seventies.

She was a very gentle woman, very devoted and religious. She's the only one who really guided my life into being close to the Church and being attentive to my studies. She often said that education is the only gift that I can give you that no one can take away from you. Even though you may not have any worldly possessions or wealth, if you have a good education, you can go out in this world and make a very comfortable life for yourself. She instilled in me the value of education and was forever prodding me to continue (p. 29).

She had a lot to do with my attitude about helping people because she was forever very conscious of helping people; so people would come to her ... . She's a very good seamstress. She would sew children's clothes and give it to people that she think needed it (p. 29).

Mrs. Bamba, herself widowed in 1978 at the age 44, described her grandmother as being a truly independent woman, a role model in countless ways:

Being a 21 year old widow, she [grandmother] had only my mother. She was a very attractive woman. [I] often asked her why she never remarried at that age and only being married for two and a half years. "How can you survive not having a man in the house?" She said, "it's not that I wasn't asked and I have thought about it." But she had seen so many lives where the mother remarried and having a young daughter she said she doesn't want to bring to her home someone that would be resentful to her daughter. Sometimes they [men] marry you because of your daughter, and then you would be hurt because sometimes the stepfather would do something to the daughter. I guess she's seen a lot of this. And she would not subject her child to that so she reared my mother alone ... . My mother wasn't even born when her father died. My grandmother was seven months pregnant with my mother. She was remarkable woman in that circumstances; rearing her child. She

became very independent. She knew how to handle
the manly duties and the maternal duties of the family. She taught me a lot how to conserve and not to
waste. In her own life she could not afford to be
wasteful about things. She had to earn her own living,
and she furnished her house, which was passed down
to my mother, where I lived and grew up before the
war (pp. 29-30).

Cecilia greatly admired her grandmother's tact and
diplomacy in her dealings with family members and others.
Even in the most hurtful situations, she was always kind:

She would go into pains of giving me an analogy
instead of being directly critical. She taught me a lot
of things about being diplomatic (p. 34).

Friends and colleagues of Cecilia Bamba will vouch
that such a description aptly characterized her as well. She said
of her opponents and detractors, "I have no ill feelings towards
them." Also: "I really don't like to be the harbinger of any ill
feelings or bad tidings." (pp. 34-35)

Marriage, Motherhood, and the Family Business

Marriage was the opening of a new chapter in my
life .... When I got married, I took over the rearing of
my brother. I was like a mother to him. I was only
sixteen years old when I got married. I graduated
from high school in June and married in September.
Actually the reason I thought of marrying young was
not because of getting married. Not having a mother
and father, and my grandmother also a widow, there
were no men. So I guess I was looking for the security
of a man in the family .... I had two scholarships to go
off island to go to school. But I chose not to take it
[scholarships] because I felt that it was more important to be here. I couldn't see myself going off and
leaving my grandmother and my little brother. I took
that as my own responsibility at that time. I felt that

they were looking to me since I'm going into womanhood. I felt that I should take the role of being breadwinner in the family. This is the reason why I sacri-
ficed instead of going off island to go to college when
I had the opportunity. This is the reason why I also
encourage my kids too. To me formal education is
very important, because I knew how important and
what sacrifices I had to make and why. I thought that
maybe I could get my education later, and here on the
island. Not to be away from my family, that's the
reason why I got married young (pp. 8-9).

After graduating from George Washington High School
in 1949, Cecilia Cruz became Mrs. George Mariano Bamba.
She took a short respite from school in the first few years of
their married life. Later she enrolled in classes at the Territorial College of Guam from 1952 to 1955. Throughout the course
of her active career she has attended professional training
seminars and conferences, including the Business Management
Institute, University of Guam; the Hospital Planning and
Design Institute in Hartford, Connecticut; and the Governing
Boards Management Institute in Grossinger, New York. In
1970 she received an Honorary Degree in Humanities from the
University of Guam.[3]

As a 16 year-old bride, there were other immediate
adjustments that Cecilia had to make. George Bamba, a 20
year-old Chamorro from Agana Heights, was "very active in
both village and islandwide levels of service."[4] He was a
member of the prewar church choir and served as a long-
standing member and President of the Holy Name Society in
Agana Heights. Cecilia approximated that he belonged to over
30 clubs or organizations in his lifetime, often as an office
holder.[5] Being married to such a man presented a series of
challenges to his young spouse.

When I got married I had the notion that my responsibility is to take care of my family. Well, I didn't
know how; so I had to learn. Being reared by my
grandmother, she really spoiled me. I didn't even

know how to boil water; so I was determined by my own volition that even though I wasn't prepared for being a homemaker and mother, I would learn. I'm going to shine and make my husband proud of me. This was my aim. I didn't tell my husband this, but I wanted him to be proud of me. Two weeks after we got married, he invited friends to dinner; they became my guinea pigs, testing my cooking (pp. 9-10).

My husband, Mr. Bamba, never showed me that he wanted just the two of us. He took over the rearing of my younger brother. We sent him to Catholic schools from the time he was young; we sent him to private college in the States. He wasn't selfish at all. Other men can say well I have my family already coming up and I can't afford to detour my finances to other people. He took over and we took care of my grandmother and great-grandmother also (p. 9).

The Bambas have five sons and five daughters, who ranged in age from 14 to 31 at the time of our interviews. Her expectations for them all were:

... to be resourceful and constructive in their pursuits in life, to be a credit to themselves, their family, their island and their Creator.[6]

She wanted the same for her 15 grandchildren.

With a "ready-made" family at the onset of her marriage, the pivotal role her husband played in his own natal family, and ten children arriving on the scene in rapid succession, how did Cecilia Bamba manage her family and home and still have the energy and motivation to do anything else? Mrs. "B" answered that question with no hesitation. Her husband and grandmother gave her the support she needed. Although the Bambas did have hired help, Chilang did not feel comfortable relying on them to run her household. Neither did her grandmother.

She was devoted. She didn't want anyone [else] to take care of my children; so she's the one I relied on as the person who supports me and provides at least the attention to make sure that the hired help does what they're supposed to do. I didn't trust anyone with my children other than my grandmother .... What made me feel relaxed and at ease while leaving was that she was there. She's the person or anchor that I could count on (pp. 11-12).

From her husband, she received encouragement and the freedom to explore the world beyond the confines of home and to get involved. "My husband gave me a lot of encouragement to develop as a person and to broaden my experiences in life."[7]

Four years after we were married we started our own insurance business and again I put myself in the role that I wanted to support him. I wanted to help him because I know I have my own talents and I know I can use these talents in order to develop our future financial capabilities. So George and I started our business together. He didn't just go open the business. I was the administrator; I stayed in the office and took care of the operations while he goes out and solicits the business. We were a team from those very early years, in our case, I was active, he was active. We just happened to complement each other. You know, not too many couples can work together. I hear this from couples who would say to me, "Gee, don't you fight when you are working on something?" and I say, "No!" Being in business together, normally the husband does one thing and the wife wants something else too; so they clash ever so often. But because of our respect for each other's judgment, he does have a lot of respect for my feelings and what I believe in and I did the same for him. When he sees something that is really not the same as I see it, I give him the benefit of the doubt, and he does with me. Normally husbands can make it very hard for a woman to go out. That's one of the very major setbacks to women, because sometimes even though they want to go out into the community, the husbands are possessive. They're jealous and feel insecure of their own status. They're afraid that when their wives go out that they might outshine them. Really, I see a lot of that. In the case of George, he gave me a free hand. In fact, sometimes it's too much because people would come to him and talk about some problems and he would say, "Why don't you talk to my wife because she can help you on that." And I would say, "Gee, thanks a lot." But he does this because he has a lot of confidence in my ability and so he gives me a free hand in developing my own human potential. If anyone is to be given credit for what I am now, I will give him credit, If it was not for his total tolerance .... (pp. 10-11).

At the time of her death, Mrs. Bamba was owner and president of the Bamba Corporation, Cecilia Bamba Insurance, Chamorrita Enterprises, and Oceania Associates, Inc.[8] The deaths of her husband George in 1976, her grandmother in 1973, and her brother John, who passed away shortly before these interviews were conducted, were deeply felt by Mrs. "B." She said, however, that with the Blessed Mother as her spiritual guide and her older children to confer with in decision-making, she and some of her children were able to operate the family business much the same way she and George did when they started out in 1952.

The Road from Politician's Wife to Elected Office

The Organic Act of 1950 heralded a new political era on Guam. Civilian government and U.S. citizenship were topmost in the list of "benefits" that poured in from Uncle Sam. However, the Organic Act did not provide sovereignty nor did it end colonialism. It provided citizenship as a means of securing the continued utilization of Guam and its resources by the U.S. government. Because Chamorros had been in political limbo regarding their status as "colonials of the United States" any change was welcomed. Local participation in the political process, albeit limited, was called for. George Bamba took up the challenge. He vied for a seat in the Guam Legislature in

1952, won, and subsequently served nine consecutive two-year terms.

That year marked another turning point in Cecilia's life. At the "ripe old age" of 18, mother of a young brother, two toddler infants and another baby on the way, Chilang, taking her partnership with Mr. Bamba quite seriously, joined him in his political pursuits.

> I am one person who is interested in whatever my husband does and I share those interests. I make it a point, unlike some wives who do their own thing and their husbands do their own thing. With me, when my husband first came into the legislature, I really wanted to learn about law-making, the process of law- making, the things he does. I wanted to so I could understand what he's going through and I can be a supporter of his at home. Because I believe that when a man goes to work he needs an understanding wife at home; so when he comes home and he's kind of a grouch, well, you'd understand why .... Because of that I began to start reaching out, outside the perimeters of my home. Even though I have kids already, I feel that my place is beside my husband in his work. So I would go to the legislature and when he goes on conferences for the legislature or for his other activities, he wants me to come along. He always invites me and I always go along unless there's something at home or my previous commitments deprive me of doing so (pp. 53-54).

Adopting the role of an apprentice, Cecilia eased her way into politics through several channels. From 1954 to 1960, she was a member of the Popular Party of Guam, the predecessor of the present Democratic Party. With the formation of a rival group, the Territorial Party, some of whose members became the future Republican Party of Guam, competition for seats in the Guam Legislature triggered the development of a campaign style currently taken for granted as an integral element of the Guam political scene. In the early days of civilian government, however, hitting the campaign trail was a novel experience. It soon became apparent that Chamorro women would take the lead and experiment with innovative strategies for winning elections. Initially, women's activities were limited to the preparation of food for political gatherings. Mrs. Bamba remembered that although a formal women's political organization had not yet been established in the early sixties, both male and female members of the Popular Party/Democratic Party were deeply concerned over losses to the Territorial Party. In the 1964 election Democrats lost control of the Legislature. "The complacency that prevailed before was because we were always winners. We never experienced defeat until then; it was a bitter defeat" (p. 78). The first election of Guam's non-voting Delegate to Congress in March 1965 became a catalyst for action.

> We had to do something and you know that it was really the women that got everybody back on track. In 1965 the Women's Democratic Party was not [yet] organized. It was the women's activities for that March election. We went around the island, that was the first time we ever canvassed. We pounded the pavement and knocked on doors. We women had rallies and conferences. Not the men. The men just sit there. We are the ones that are running the show. The [male] candidates will come and talk. This is proof that it's the women that made that election.... 1964 to 1966 were a hard two years. But I said I'm not going to sit back and take this for another two years. So that's when we organized the Democratic Party; we changed the name. In every village we had women's rallies. Because it's all women's activities. We raised the funds and we started the Democratic Party .... Even when we sent [representatives] to the political convention afterwards it was the women that funded the bill to send the delegates. Everything comes from the women. We never stopped raising funds and programs throughout the year to get our women to gether, to increase our membership and be active. So

this is an example of what women can do in changing things. In 1966 while the men are going out to meetings at night, we in the daytime took shifts in the morning or afternoon. Because this is new to the women to go out and canvass, so we had to have orientations to teach them what to say and how to react because it would be very cruel; it was the women that delivered (pp. 77-79).

In 1965 Mrs. "B" was elected Secretary of the Democratic Party Women's Activities. She served in the same position for the Women's Association of the Democratic Party of Guam from 1966 to 1968. She admitted that she hated being secretary to anything, but someone had to do the work. It was not any easier when she became the association's president for the following four years.

She chaired the Democratic Party Finance Committee from 1968-1970 and in 1972 chaired the Jefferson-Jackson Dinner Celebration. For personal reasons her husband changed his party affiliation in the next election. Following her long-standing practice of supporting her husband, Cecilia became an active member of the Republican Party of Guam and its Central Committee. True to form, she continued to chair committees including the Calvo-Palomo Write-In Campaign, Co-chairperson 1974; Lincoln Day Dinner Celebration, 1975-1976; Finance Committee, 1975-1976; and the By-Laws and Constitution Committee, GOP Women's Club, 1976. She also belonged to the National Republican Legislators Association, 1979-1982; and the American Academy of Political and Governmental Studies, 1980-1982.

Her first involvement with politics at the national level took place when she accompanied her husband to the National Conference of Legislators in Phoenix, Arizona to 1962, and again in 1964. The same year she was voted delegate to the Democratic National Convention held in Atlantic City, New Jersey. She was later elected to attend the Chicago Convention in 1968.[9] Her political participation did not end there:

In the arena of law-making, the higher echelon of politics, they're very cruel. The men are very cruel to the women. To them that's the only realm that they still have in control and once that is given up, there's nothing for them. I think that is what made me accept the challenge to run for office. I don't like to be in that position. But in a way I always like to prove [things] to myself. I don't like to read about it or be told by somebody. If I can live through it and get the firsthand knowledge, that to me is the best way to get my experience. I knew of the cruelty of politics, the dog eat dog type of life. I also knew what it takes to make a good lawmaker, like teamwork and helping each other .... I also know because it is a man's world; you cannot expect to be treated like a woman. You've got to expect to be treated like a man, whatever it is. One thing that I proved when I was there, what I didn't know before, was the envy and jealousy that prevailed among the members; I can't fight that. I don't like to work under those situations .... You're in there to serve the people; you're not in there to serve yourself. And you're not in there to build your empire. Your empire will be built by the people who put you in there. The ultimate is based on what you have done. But when you go in there and you have to always be looking behind your back to find out how many knives are stabbing you, it's a very unethical situation. I knew what I was getting into. It was like jumping from the frying pan into the fire, for me, being the wife of a legislator for 20 years and knowing the mechanics of what goes on (pp. 74-75).

Cecilia Bamba won a seat to the Fifteenth Guam Legislature in the 1978 November election as a Republican candidate from the central district. Her first and only term as a Senator was an active one.[10] She sat on 16 different legislative committees. Of these she chaired five. She identified two in particular to which she felt she had contributed most--General

Governmental Operations, Military, and Veterans Affairs; and Cultural and Municipal Affairs.

In her roles as Chairperson of the Committee on General Governmental Operations, Military, and Veterans Affairs, she established two advisory councils, one on women's concerns and the other on community concerns. This committee's extensive scope involved the Senator in government reorganization, public services, municipal development, and a variety of other issues.

The controversy over political status of Guam generated much interest during this period. Senator Bamba aired her views publicly on several occasions. In a report she presented to the United Nations Decolonization Committee Mission entitled, "Guam and Its Relationship with the United States," she stated,

> Although placed under 'temporary' naval rule by President McKinley in 1898, pending action by the U.S. Congress, the Congress did not act. Consequently, the Guamanians for a period of 50 years--half a century--were at the disposition of each of 41 governors, all appointed by U.S. Presidents and all military officers.
>
> ... The entire island was designated and ruled as a naval station. In a comparative sense, the Guamanians were not mistreated and the quality of life improved under military rule.
>
> ... The major drawback for the Guamanians was the overriding concern of both the federal and military government to preserve Guam as a strategic defense base; the citizens were secondary in importance. So although governed with America's basic humanitarianism, they were denied self-rule and U.S. citizenship. From that standpoint, they themselves were U.S. possessions. This engendered deep disappointment in the Guamanians.

... In spite of this, Guamanians, have remained intensely loyal. But the disappointment will endure until such time as we were afforded the dignity of making decisions that directly impact upon our lives and restrictions that limit economic growth are lifted.

... Guamanians want to be regarded fully as Americans, not as an incompetent child in some remote backwater. America has been unquestionably generous with financial aid; what Guamanians yearn for is America's generosity of spirit. After three quarters of a century of what in essence amounts to colonial rule, it is untenable to be denied the freedom of choice of all American citizens any longer.[11]

Additionally she addressed the University of Guam Conference on Public Administration on the topic "Commonwealth and the Role of the Community."[12] Her most widely recognized presentation occurred at the First International Sovereignty Conference held in San Juan, Puerto Rico, from April 26 to May 2, 1980. The following are excerpts from Senator Bamba's remarks given at that conference:

First of all, and speaking only for myself, although this perhaps may also represent the views of most Guamanians, I do not have the slightest interest in considering any program for Guam which would lead to independence from the great nation, the United States of America. On the contrary we in Guam are proud of our American citizenship, and have demonstrated, upon many occasions in the past, that we are willing to fight for it, and for the United States, when it is necessary to do so. However the fact that the people of Guam are proud to be Americans, does not mean that we agree with everything that the huge bureaus and agencies of the United States do... .

... I have found that is very easy to become angry and upset because of these frustrations with federal officials, but then, I begin to analyze some of the

things that our own local government does, which
likewise causes frustrations and distress in our population. The conclusion I have reached, therefore, is that
dealing with government is always going to be a
somewhat frustrating, but necessary experience.

... Nevertheless, it is our government, and I believe
that it is our responsibility to present well reasoned,
well documented, plans and petitions for change, as
we believe it is necessary, and then persist in gaining
recognition for these plans.

... Further, if independence is under consideration, we
must carefully consider how lonesome we are going to
be without the protection and the benefits of one of
the few major powers in the world that really cares
about our welfare. Further, I believe that it is also
imperative that we consider, at every step of our
studies, the economic impact of whatever it is we may
wish to do.... . We, who are elected to lead them,
should not take the slightest chance of depriving them
of any of these necessities by some adventure, or
experiment, in the government process.[13]

Senator Bamba's patriotism towards America did not eclipse
her commitment to a more acceptable political status for her
people. In January 1981 she was selected Executive Director by
the Commission on Self Determination, a position she held
throughout the Commission's existence under the Republican
Administration of Paul Calvo (p. 124).

As Vice Chairperson of the Legislative Committee on
Cultural and Municipal Affairs, she demonstrated her interest
in the arts and culture. She co-sponsored legislation which
would provide government land for the construction of a center
for the performing arts. Inspired by visits with the Curator of
the El Prado Museum, King Juan Carlos of Spain, and Marianas
history researchers in Madrid during her stopover enroute
home after attending the First International Conference on
Cultural Planning and Economics at the University of Edin-
burgh, in 1979, Senator Bamba introduced a bill appropriating

funds to restore the old Governor's Palace in the Plaza de España and to designate the Palace as the Museum of Guam History.[14] This act became P.L. 15-141. Preliminary restoration planning is now underway. In 1982 Senator Bamba addressed the International Congress on Arts and Communications held at Queens College, Cambridge University in England.[15] She supported other measures relating to Chamorro language and cultural preservation.

Throughout her brief term in the Guam Legislature, Cecilia Bamba capitalized on national opportunities to promote Guam's interests. Such forums were: the 1980 National Conference of State Legislators in New York; the National Assembly of Legislative Leaders; the Council on State Government's Governing Board Meeting in Nevada; the American Academy of Political and Governmental Studies Seminar in Washington, D.C. and even President Reagan's 1981 Inauguration.[16]

The Senator did not win her bid for re-election to the Sixteenth Guam Legislature. When I asked her to comment about it during the interview she replied:

> As a woman Legislator and serving with two other women and 18 men who are strong individuals, too, it was really a challenge. The only thing is the petty jealousies, the petty enviousness. It's just terrible. You've got to really want to be a Senator bad in order to want to go back--and I'm not there. But I encourage young women to go into that field. Because I think that if more women are dedicated and sensible and have good background to back up their work, their endeavor, I think Guam will be better than when you have mostly men in there... .

> Then the rules might change. Now the rules are the rules of men. If there were enough women to change the rules, then the rules will be much better (p. 75).

This statement clarified Mrs. Bamba's position regarding women's involvement in politics and as decision-makers. In her view, women have a unique perspective to offer, and furthermore, they should be active agents of change for the betterment of the community.

Women-Centered Organizations, Issues, and Activities

Organizing for women ranked high on Cecilia's list of priorities. She strongly believes that women are assets to their community:

> I believe in the capability in women, the value of women in any endeavor. I tend to lean on women more to bring them into joining with me in whatever work I'm doing. So a lot of my work is woman-centered (p. 61).

This genre of organizing in her life began in 1962 with the Agana Heights Woman's Group, Cecilia's inaugural effort as a grassroots organizer. During a decade of being actively involved in community organizing, she had ample opportunity to observe the role of Chamorro women in the myriad activities to which she had dedicated much time and energy. Disappointment and frustration, born out of a developing consciousness, gave way to a powerful motivation to do something about the wasted talents of women who remained in the confines of their homes.

> In our culture the women stay in the house and take care of everything in the home ... when a girl becomes a young lady, that's the time to quit school and learn how to be a homemaker. I think that's the most unfair thing to do to a young woman, because I'm not looking at a woman as just a homemaker. I think the quaalities of a woman are just the same as a man's (p. 2).

> ... The woman stays at home and the man is the spokesperson of the house. But, actually the man never makes a decision without consulting with his woman. In other words all the policies emanate from the woman in the house.... In reality we are strong, the motivating factor of everything that happens in the home and through our husbands (p. 63).

It bothered Cecilia that cultural mores limited Chamorro women from exploring their full potential as "makers of society" (p. 63).

> They're seen but not heard. They do work but no one ever hears from them. Nobody ever bothers to ask them what they feel about certain things. And nobody ever recognizes what they have done to make success of anything that happens in the community. We have to bring ourselves together and with one voice we can be active in civic action. We can change a lot of things that we don't like (p. 1).

So, she started the Agana Heights Women's Group:

> My purpose for that was, I saw the talents of women and what we women can do. What we women have been doing all along. And I said that this energy, talent has to be harnessed and channeled into an organized group so that our work can be not only recognized, but can be effective. When women speak out as an organization, we have a tendency to be heard more readily than [if] we speak individually.

> They're very good campaigners. They are the ones that are sensitive to the needs of the community. The men aren't. Normally the men just see what's in front of their nose. But women, because of their children, because of their church, because of their school, they're the ones that can see these needs ... in that group there was nothing we couldn't do (p. 69).

Mrs. Bamba had difficulty convincing the women of Agana Heights to step beyond the boundaries of their homes to become active in village affairs. She patiently prodded capable women into leadership roles. She saw their involvement as "in-service training" (p. 70). Chilang proudly recalled their accomplishments:

> We were active politically. We took over during meetings, pocket meetings or just membership meetings. We got in there; we planned meetings as well as

providing refreshments. All the men have to do is come in and sit down.... Then we went into raising funds for the means of our community. We sponsored an Independence Day Carnival and we raised money to buy playground equipment for Agana Heights, plus to operate the ball field. That was in the sixties. At that time the Vietnam War was accelerating, we extended our hospitality to the Vietnam wounded. We have a Thanksgiving dinner event in the ball field and we invited the Vietnam wounded and the B-52 crews too. That's our way of showing them that we appreciated their going through this hell to keep our country free (p. 70).

The significance of these efforts must be understood in the context of Guam's role as a strategic American military "outpost." Military presence is evident everywhere on the island, many island activities revolve around this role.

Throughout her first few years as an organizer, Mrs. "B" represented the women of Guam as a delegate to several Federation of Asian Women's Association's Conferences in Manila, Taipei, and Guam. She was a Charter Member and sat on the Board of Trustees of that organization. Her memberships in other women's organizations included: the Guam Women's Club; Guam Business and Professional Women's Club; Guam Girl Scout Council; Guam Beauty Association; General Federation of Business and Professional Women's Clubs; and the League of Women Voters of Guam.[17]

Of all her past involvements, Cecilia says she would choose to assist the Guam Girl Scouts again, if her business schedule and other commitments permitted. Her attachment stemmed from being a mother, her main incentive for getting involved. When Mrs. "B's" daughters were younger, they belonged to Girl Scouts troops located in the military installations. She would transport them and their friends to meetings. It was a very good learning experience for her girls. At the time that a representative from the National Scouting Headquarters came to Guam to explore the possibility of expanding Girl Scouting beyond the military bases, Cecilia was president of at least five organizations simultaneously. Nevertheless, the Girl Scout representative had been told Cecilia Bamba was the person to get the expansion project off the ground. Her desire to see such a program benefit youth everywhere on the island and not just those who were fortunate to go on base prompted her to accept the challenge. She tackled the task zealously. As was true with many of her other organizing activities, reaching out to the community became her strategy. She visited schools, spoke out at PTA meetings around the island and got the Commissioners and VISTA Volunteers to assist in persuading parents of the merits of the program. Parent support was essential because scouts needed uniforms, supplies, and most especially troop leaders. At the onset of this pilot effort there were 200 Girl Scouts located at Anderson Air Force Base and the Navy installations. By 1966, 60 troops were distributed throughout the villages and membership had climbed to over 2,000. Despite her efforts to bow out once the islandwide Scouting program was firmly grounded, Council Members insisted she stay on. Chilang acquiesced and remained President of the Guam Girl Scout Council from 1966 to 1972. Guam Girl Scouts became visible helpers in the community. The organization developed solvency. Her attendance at several president's seminars and Girl Scout conventions in the U.S. contributed to the enrichment of what she perceived as her new mission at home. She had many fond memories of her years spent building up Girl Scouting on Guam (pp. 54-55; 100-106).

Guam women were not excluded from the excitement being generated by the First International Women's Year Conference (IWY) in Mexico City in 1975. The IWY meeting provided the impetus for an American conference in Houston, Texas, which would bring together representatives from the 56 States and Territories. As national planning progressed, Mrs. "B" remembered receiving a letter from a Hawaii Senator, "asking me to host a conference on Guam and I thought that was very irregular" (p. 118). She recalled that her late husband was the author of the bill which created the Commission on the Status of Women and that, "if anything that group should be the forerunner of this" (p. 118). So when she received a call from Guam Congressman Won Pat's office inquiring whether she was interested in organizing Guam's pre-Houston activities, she suggested that the leadership should go to the Commission on the Status of Women. Nevertheless, she became actively involved.

> I thought I would just be a supporting member. I ended up taking care of the Role of Women Workshop which had nine sessions. It was very exciting though because it was the first time Guam had a woman's conference strictly for women (p. 118).

Cecilia was elected as one of the 12 Guam delegates to the National Women's Conference at Houston in November, 1977.

> ... we really went all out to show that even though the others are burning their bras, the Guam contingent came in their colorful outfits, their orchids and the media took shots at us because we were the group that exemplified femininity, but yet with a purpose. We're there to make our voices heard too that the women of Guam are also not timid and passive women who bear children, but they are of course someone to contend with (p. 119).

Exposure for Guam was not the only benefit of the Houston conference. Delegates and those who had attended the Guam meetings became more acutely aware of discriminatory practices and issues affecting women. Mrs. Bamba expressed disappointment that the momentum for organizing around women's needs has not been maintained locally. As Senator, she worked to remedy this situation. An item in **Tolai Mensahi,** a quarterly newsletter to Senator Bamba's constituents, announced her creation of an Advisory Council on Women's Concerns thusly:

> Composed of representatives from women's organizations on the island the Council has been formed by Bamba in a desire to gather information on the problems encountered by women on Guam.

"This is not just to be a discussion group," the Senator said. "It is an advisory group, and I am excited about the valuable input they can provide which can be translated into legislative output."

The visibly dynamic group expressed a multitude of common concerns ranging from battered children and spouses, redefining sexual offenses, properties of married persons, female representation, and recapturing the strength of the family unit.

Bamba said one of her long term goals is to establish within GovGuam, a Women's Bureau. "The concerns of women are not limited to the problems of women," she noted, "but rather cover the total spectrum of social ills. We are not content with the status quo," she emphasized. "Perhaps that is some nurturing instinct in females, but from whatever it stems, the essential desire is for improvement in the quality of life for all Guam's citizens."[18]

The economic role of women was another area of major importance to Mrs. Bamba.

More and more, our women have to prepare ourselves for the world. Not just to be a homemaker but to face the world as a breadwinner and ultimately to take care of their own families. Even if she happens to marry into a family where she is very secure and comfortable and she doesn't have to go out and work. In life you can never guarantee that can always be. So I believe that a woman should prepare herself so if something happens she won't feel lost. Right now there are a lot of widows on Guam, young widows. Being a widow myself, they come to me and they talk about life and how they are faring. They tell me about their anxieties, that they never learned about supporting the family. They're afraid to go out and they feel that they don't know anything but how to tend to children and how to clean the house. And I say it's never too late to develop your potential ... .

I encourage any woman because a lot of them now have found themselves without their breadwinner. They have to go out into the world to seek their own livelihood. Coupled with the fact that most of their children have grown up, they're at an age when they're on their own also. So the woman finds herself alone. She's lost. She can't even turn to her own children because they have their own families already (pp. 2-3).

Chilang earned a reputation for being a good listener, steadfast friend, and women's advocate. Her advocacy was further manifested in much of her public speaking. The following titles of selected keynote speeches she delivered represent her range of interests on the subject of women.

"The Role of Women, and a Vital Member of an Action Team" -- Conference of Women's Organizations on Women's Concerns

"Women--A Partner in Politics" -- Federation of Asian Women's Association Convention, Republic of China, 1963

"Women, an Equal Partner" -- Rotary Club of Guam

"The Role of Women in Politics" -- Kiwanis Club of Guam

"Women, Our Culture Bearers" -- American Association of University Women

"Women in Politics and Legislative Process" -- Guam Business and Professional Women's Club

"Women in the Military" -- U.S. Armed Forces Day Celebration

"Women in Education" -- Guam Women's Club and Guam Nurses Association

"The Pacific Island Woman" -- Asian-Pacific Women's Conference, USC, Los Angeles, California, March 1980[19]

The April 1980 issue of the **Asian American Journal** printed Mrs. Bamba's address at the closing session of the

Asia-Pacific Women's Conference in California. The following excerpts from that speech emphasize her commitment to identifying and breaking down the barriers that prevent Pacific-American women from fully participating in American life.

From the Pacific women's viewpoint, there are many problems which flow from a propensity to group all persons from the Pacific region into one category. The most obvious ones are invisibility and overgeneralizing. Pacific Islanders do not constitute a numerous group. Consequently, they are rarely recognized in forums, government-sponsored assistance programs and media reports on minority groups. For those Pacific Island women who do live on the U.S. mainland (approx. 75,000 Pacific Islanders, including 30,000 from Guam and 35,000 from Samoa), this means a sense of invisibility. In addition to the problems of coping with general American society faced by all minorities, Pacific women have the additional difficulty of not even being recognized as having particular problems. This lack of identification as a unique group with unique difficulties results in a sense of rootlessness and insignificance. Unlike Latinas and Asians, they do not come from large or powerful nations. Unlike the Black woman, Pacific Island women are not numerous enough to be politically significant. It is a major problem not to be valued for what you are. It becomes more problematic not to even be recognized.

... For those Pacific Islanders who remain on their home islands which are under the United States flag, being strong in heritage yet small in numbers also poses certain difficulties. There is always the sense of being an adopted people, of being Uncle Sam's distant nephew. **In much the same way the Native Americans were asked in the past to be loyal to a Great White Father, Pacific Islanders are frequently expected to generate similar loyalties. Let us take care to see to it**

**that the American women's movement does not take
up this role in relation to Pacific women under a
similar guise** [emphasis mine]. Another major inherent problem in the gathering together of diverse
women in the Asian-Pacific category is overgeneralizing and stereotyping. When Pacific women are recognized and are no longer invisible, they often run into
the more serious problem of stereotyping.

**... The view of Pacific Islanders as being carefree and
indolent comes from total ignorance and cultural
bias. There is nothing about living in the tropics
which makes one irresponsible, unwilling to work or
incapable of serious planning. These are the make-
believe notions of conquering peoples from temperate
zones** [emphasis mine].

These problems can be remedied by taking certain
steps in the political, economic, and educational institutions of the U.S. The American woman should lend
support to her Pacific-American sisters in their struggle by endorsing the following measures:

1. Full Political Equality for Pacific Islanders.

2. An End to Media Stereotyping of Pacific Islanders.

3. Support of Educational Studies of the Pacific in
   the Form of Research Grants.

4. Support of Educational Opportunities for
   Pacific Women.

5. Recognition of Pacific Islanders in Government
   Forms and Government-sponsored Programs.

6. Support for Pacific Studies Programs at American
   Universities and Inclusion of Some Pacific
   Studies in the Public School Curriculum.[20]

She concluded with the statement, "We do not demand special
treatment, we only ask for recognition as Pacific Island
Women." She again represented Chamorro women when she

attended the National Women's Bureau 60th Anniversary Conference in September, 1980, in Washington, D.C.

During her legislative term, Cecilia Bamba discovered she had breast cancer. A mastectomy and treatment did not deter her from active involvement in her political work. Nor did it slacken her enthusiasm.

Community Activism

A veteran volunteer for over 30 years, Mrs. Bamba described her lifework in this way:

> I belong to a vast and diversified group of people and organizations from health, youth, elders, economics, professional, political and cultural. I spent over half of my life time pioneering causes, organizing. And served in leadership capacities in all of the organizations I belonged and helped to foster and perpetuate.[21]

A cursory review of Cecilia's wide assortment of volunteer activities reveals a clustering into several main areas.

Her initial activities centered around school and church. At George Washington High she was editor of the school paper, **Banana Leaf.** At church she was president of the Junior Sodality of Mary and an Agana Heights choir member. Although she was just 16 when she had her first child, she joined the Confraternity of Christian Mothers, making her the youngest member. At first this was her only involvement outside her home because she felt her place was with her husband and family. She quickly broke out of her self-imposed confinement. She admits that her level of activity with Christian Mothers, as with all other associations, has been irregular, peaking when there was a need and tapering off when others took over responsibility. Through the years she headed retreats and special projects for the Agana Heights Christian Mothers. She has also assisted other parishes with dedication ceremonies and clergy dinners. She was Program Committee Chairperson in 1981, and in 1983 she chaired the Sub-Committee on Entertainment for

the Visit of the Apostolic Delegate to the United States.[22]
One of her most rewarding experiences, beside nurturing her
spiritual life, has been working for over 20 years with a small
group of women who take care of decorating the Agana Cathedral. In addition, Chilang has organized fundraisers.

> After Typhoon Pamela, the church of Agana Heights
> found its roof leaking, a lot of damages. It needed
> repairs. The pastor came to me and asked me if I
> would help in doing something to raise money so that
> we could have the church repaired. I said, of course,
> then he turned around and asked me if I would chair a
> raffle. I said, I hate raffles (pp. 113-114).

The Agana Heights priest insisted. So Mrs. Bamba recommended several capable people in the village. They formed the
Agana Heights Thanksgiving Association (circa 1976) and she
became the vice-president. They ran a very successful carnival
and were able to raise $50,000. Cecilia and her husband alone
sold 1,000 raffle books. Later, "Father wanted to do the Fatima
Hall" (p. 114). The social hall was deteriorating. Chilang did
her share by selling another thousand raffle books. After the
Agana Heights Thanksgiving Association disbanded, a Fatima
Hall Committee was established to raise funds for construction.
To avoid another raffle, Mrs. "B" initiated a "guild system of
fundraising of pledges. Each family of Agana Heights pledged
$100 which they paid throughout the year" (p. 115). This was
the beginning necessary to secure a bank loan. The new social
hall now graces the church grounds.

With so many children who have all gone to Catholic
schools, Mrs. Bamba has also been active in numerous PTAs
since 1955. At all of the following schools she served as an
officer at one time and chaired various committees: Father
Duenas Memorial High School, Academy of Our Lady of
Guam, Bishop Baumgartner Junior High School, Cathedral
Grade School, and Saint Anthony's.[23]

Another area to which Mrs. Bamba has contributed
with characteristic gusto is civic affairs. She was appointed by
several governors to government boards and commissions,

among them: the Governor's Committee on Education, 1963-1965; Federal Employment Council, 1963-1966, Economic Opportunity Commission Council, 1963-1969; Guam Memorial Hospital Board of Trustees, 1963-1975; Guam Health Planning Council, 1974-1975; and the Agana Heights Planning Council, 1978-1980.

While a Trustee of the Guam Memorial Hospital, she became the first women to hold the presidency of any Government of Guam governing board, a position she maintained from 1967 to 1973. In this capacity Mrs. Bamba attended several American and Western Hospital Association conferences, which increased her sensitivity to the problems of administering health services.[24]

Undoubtedly the most significant outgrowth of her hospital work is the Guam Memorial Hospital Volunteers Association, which she founded. Her awareness of patients' needs led her to establish a link between the community and the hospital. The Association sponsors fundraisers such as the Annual Charity Ball and the Holiday Homes Tours, both of which Mrs. Bamba has organized. They operate a gift shop. The proceeds of their efforts are used to purchase expensive hospital equipment and for refurbishing rooms and lounges. She remained active in this group to her death as it was dear to her heart.

Charity organizations have frequently turned to Cecilia for help with projects. The Guam Chapter of the American Red Cross was having great difficulty raising funds and establishing a solid foothold in the decade following World War II. Mrs. Bamba recalls that they simply were not popular. The seemingly discriminatory distribution of goods to the people of Guam after the war created a bad image. Chilang joined the organization in 1962. She served as Secretary of the Board of Directors for nine years. Her main aim was to improve the image of the American Red Cross on the island. Typhoon Karen devastated Guam in November of 1962. The Red Cross contributed substantial assistance to the territory. Through continuous promotional efforts and upright practices, the people were eventually won over and began to contribute. The current Red Cross facility was built during Chilang's term of office. Many of her efforts were channeled towards assisting military families, especially the victims of the war in Vietnam (pp. 92-94).

As a member of the Guam USO Council, she engendered good relations between military personnel and the local community through hospitality programs. She recruited civic organizations and families to open their homes, provide dinners and entertainment to "those lonely boys" (pp. 117-118).

Cognizant that the people of Guam were continuously supporting fundraising activities. Chilang explored new and innovative ways to make donating money more palatable. For the American Lung Association, now the Guam Respiratory and Health Association, she instituted the "Mother of the Year Award" and the first "Miss Charity Contest Benefit Drive". There was the Jerry Lewis Telethon for the Muscular Dystrophy Association, which she chaired for two consecutive years. This fundraiser was especially meaningful due to the high incidence of *litigo* and *bodig*, muscular diseases affecting the people of Guam and the Northern Marianas (pp. 115-116).

The American Cancer Society opened a unit on Guam in 1970. Mrs. Bamba extended support during its infancy. As President of the Guam Women's Club, she was "instrumental in the first Cancer Prevention Program here on the island" (p. 117). She wrote to the American Cancer Society asking for films on breast and uterine cancer and on preventive measures.

That program started the first pap-smear test program on Guam. It really made women aware of this. I had the films shown all over the island. Christian Mothers meetings islandwide, the women's clubs, and even the men's clubs. Anyway because of that, when the unit was started here in 1970, I was asked to help; so I did (p. 117).

Mrs. "B's" latest involvement with a charitable cause before her death was as Chairperson of the Board of the Guam

Rehabilitation and Workshop Center, Inc., a center of training and sheltered employment for the physically and mentally handicapped. Because proceeds from the workshop often fall short of covering operational expenses, Mrs. Bamba organized the Foundation for the Disabled to receive endowments, gifts, and other contributions for the handicapped and to assist the Center in upgrading its training and workshop activities (pp. 119-120).

Among the numerous community improvement projects that Mrs. Bamba spearheaded, one in particular stood out in her mind as being memorable. She laughed as she recounted how a solution to the dog problem sprang from the beautification campaign that was tied to her membership in the Guam Women's Club.

Celebrating its thirty-first year, the Guam Women's Club, a service organization, "had a very influential and a very strong organization of women who really dedicate their time and sincerity to help Guam grow and to provide a secure and comfortable environment for those who live on this island" (p. 84). Although she was invited to the first meeting in 1952, she had to refuse because she and George had just began their family and business. She had her hands full. When she did join, she plunged into clubwork with her customary fervor.

> I think I must have served practically 90 percent of the offices. I served as Standing Committee Chairperson in special projects and special events. This was before I became the Corresponding Secretary, then I became its Treasurer, and then President. It was such a challenge when I became President because I was not only very young, but that year was the tenth year of the founding of the club (p. 85).

Many community projects were pioneered by the club, e.g., the multipurpose civic auditorium and the Guam Youth Building. Mrs. "B" envisioned and implemented many firsts as President despite Typhoon Karen, which hit shortly after she assumed office (pp. 85-87).

Several years prior to the typhoon, Chilang as Chairperson of the Civic Improvement Committee, launched the first islandwide clean-up and beautification campaign. Private homeowners, neighborhood stores, and villages were given incentives to landscape their surroundings and plant colorful flora. Mrs. Bamba reached out beyond the club to involve the Governor, Commissioners, and businessmen who donated prizes and plants. The project snowballed and soon became a separate entity, the Guam Beautification Association. The Guam Women's Club continued to organize it until 1975 when the Guam Visitors Bureau took over.

Around 1961, when Cecilia was leading the clean-up campaign, she was determined to do something about Agana. She recalled being embarrassed to admit that Agana was Guam's capital city as it was real eyesore. There was *tangantangan* (a bothersome weed) everywhere! Multiple ownership of lots made it impossible to force the responsibility on private landowners. She sought assistance from the Legislature and the Governor. A compromise was reached to everyone's satisfaction. Consequently the government was spurred into action. "And so we got Agana cleaned up" (p. 14).

Every three months a committee of judges would travel around the island to select the most beautiful village, home, and neighborhood store. During the course of these journeys, she was astounded by the number of stray dogs, which were a nuisance to both villagers and visitors. When she inquired about what could be done, Commissioners replied there was no place to put them. Occasionally the dogs would be taken to the Department of Public Safety and killed by carbon monoxide poisoning. Driven by the feeling that such a method was horrible, she proposed that the Women's Club purchase a tranquilizer gun. But, that was like patching a leak in the dam with a band-aid. A more permanent remedy was sought. Members lobbied the Legislature for appropriations to build a government kennel. Their efforts paid off. She wondered how she ever got involved in canine control, of all things. When the Guam Women's Club entered the international civic improvement contest co-sponsored by the General Federation of Women's Clubs in Washington, D.C. and the Sears Roebuck Company, Guam won first prize. The club was awarded $500 for the efforts just recounted (pp. 14-15; 84-91).

Being an adventurous organizer, Mrs. "B" often found herself in unfamiliar places doing unusual things. The Bambas co-founded the Guam Beauty Association, which sponsors the annual Guam Beauty Pageant. Each year girls are selected to represent Guam in the Miss Universe, Miss International, Miss Teenage Intercontinental, Miss Young International, and Miss Asia Quest Competitions. A major goal of the Association is to promote peace and friendship through Guam's beauties. Chilang presided over GBA activities from 1968 to 1982. When the Miss Guam's were invited to attend the 1971 South Pacific Games in Tahiti. Mrs. Bamba accompanied them as chaperon and member of the hospitality contingent. While they were in Tahiti, the Speaker of the Guam Legislature asked Chilang to organize in two days' time a fiesta-style dinner for 2,000 people. Banking on the assistance of other members of the delegation, she agreed and proceeded to arrange for use of the hotel kitchen, after hours of course, and to shop for the ingredients. The menu consisted of stuffed roast suckling pig, *eskabeche*, barbequed *ta'taga*, taro and breadfruit in coconut milk, red rice and chicken, fish and shrimp *keleguen*. They had *ahu* for dessert. She got the shock of her life, when everyone convened at the appointed hour of 10:00 p.m., to discover that no one, not even the oldest woman in the group, knew how to cook rice in a huge pot. She estimated that five G.I. pots would be sufficient. She had no one else to turn to. She had never cooked rice in that quantity either; besides there were 200 pounds of fish to be fried. She plunged in and prayed many "Our Fathers" as she and her makeshift crew labored all night. She recalled:

> It was really quite an undertaking and quite an accomplishment. If it were on Guam, I wouldn't even blink an eye, but gee over there ... we had a Guam talent show, we outshined all the other countries that hosted, even Tahiti (p. 113).

When the Fifth South Pacific Games were held on Guam, Mrs. Bamba took charge of hospitality once again.

In addition to promoting Guam through international hospitality activities and through the participation of Miss Guams in various functions and pageants worldwide, Chilang did her share on the homefront through successive Liberation Day festivities celebrated annually on Guam (pp. 108-113).

Taking on the Federal Government

Painful experiences leave scars. The hurt can keep recurring long after the wounds seem to have healed. It was that way with Cecilia Bamba's memory of what happened in the two and a half years following that eventful morning of December 8, 1941.

I was seven years old when the war broke out. It was the day of my First Holy Communion. So it was a very significant day in my life. I remembered how fortunate I was as a young girl, having a family that is full of love and security for my future... .

About one month after the war broke out, my mother died. She died of hemorrhaging after giving birth; it was because of the cruelty of the occupying enemy forces which caused that. That was the first blow in my life. I still had my father. He took care of me. The feeling of insecurity wasn't so great because he was still around... . But then before the war ended my father was beheaded by the Japanese enemy forces for saving an American pilot... .

My father was devoted to his family; he was patriotic, very loyal to the United States... .

At the end of the war I had lost both my parents. It was ironic though that the United States who liberated me from the enemy forces took over our land after Liberation--my resources for my livelihood. This really changed my life (pp. 129-131).

Was it the pang of a childhood nightmare that compelled Cecilia to seek justice for herself and for all her people who had suffered similar atrocities and losses in the Second World War?

A combination of factors made 1976 a year of awakening for her. The recollection of her personal experience hurt deeply. The people of Guam had endured tremendous hardships because of their patriotism as "would be Americans". Other groups in the United States and the American Pacific were agitating for just compensation of losses to property, life, and land as a result of the war. Two such precedents for seeking retribution were being spearheaded by Japanese-Americans, who had been sent to relocation camps in the mainland United States during World War II, and by Micronesians.[25]

The Congress of the United States had enacted the "Micronesian Claims Act of 1971," which made detailed provisions, after investigations, for payments of war damages in the Trust Territory of the Pacific. The statute was divided into two sections. Title 1 dealt with War Claims and the Payment to Meritorious Claimants for damages to persons, property and also dealt with uncompensated labor. Title 2 dealt with United States Usage and this essentially was to provide compensation for the taking, use, and damage to privately owned real property.[26]

The Micronesian Claims Commission worked from 1972 to mid-1976 "to solicit claims and complaints for war damages to personal and property, and to adjudicate the validity of each claim filed."[27]

Mrs. Bamba became increasingly more cognizant of how far behind Guam seemed on this issue in comparison to her neighbors, especially when the Micronesian Claims Report became public. As the implications of these successful endeavors to receive compensation began to gel in her mind, she became incensed. It did not hurt her so much that no one on Guam had pursued the issue to get recognition. What she found difficult to bear was America's pervasive negligence toward such loyal citizens. In her words, "How could the United States Government ignore us. It hurt my heart. I never felt this way before, but it's like being betrayed by someone you love" (p. 132). Her romantic idealism was tempered by the pragmatism which evolved out of her work in politics. She realized that Guamanians could not fault anyone but themselves for the lack of initiative on their part. So in 1976, the year of another cataclysm for Guam, Typhoon Pamela, Mrs. Bamba made the decision to take on the Federal Government.

She was systematic. With the reliable legal counseling of attorney John Bohn, she learned what needed to be done. She marshalled her resources and "marched into battle." She did not believe in fighting "with a sword." She preferred to approach the Federal Government in a distinctly feminine manner. But she was ready "to be radical," as she put it, if the need arose.

Cecilia Bamba was championing two causes: Land Claims and War Reparations. With determination she weighed pros and cons. She did not want to "throw herself into the fire" until she knew that she could "avoid being burned." The strategies she utilized to tackle these two projects reveal her *modus operandi* for organizing at its grandest.

The first step was to become familiar with the documents and data pertinent to the issues. Mrs. Bamba undertook her own research. As her knowledge and understanding deepened, she pondered the best alternative. The local government had conducted surveys and prepared documentary evidence on federal land acquisitions in the form of a Legislative Report as early as 1972. The problem was that island leaders did not take any subsequent initiative to follow-up on the findings contained in the Report. Both projects were important to Cecilia. She remarked:

> I am ready to pursue both if need be at the same time.
> But again I thought that this is something that deals
> with the Federal Government. I feel uncomfortable
> to go to them and ask for both at the same time.
> Someone may just chide me for asking for both at the

same time. They may ask me which one do I prefer and why don't we address one first. I would be a little embarrassed and I don't want Guam to be embarrassed because of my action. So I decided that I would pursue the land claims issue first before the war claims (p. 132).

The decision to proceed with the Land Claims issue prompted Mrs. Bamba to set a goal and improvise a plan of action. She formulated her main objective thusly: the passage of enabling legislation by the U.S. Congress to afford the Guamanian people, whose lands were taken by the Federal Government, the opportunity for redress (p. 132). Inherent complications made the task of persuading Congress more formidable. Cecilia gave herself two years to accomplish her goal. She utilized three basic strategies.

I thought the best way to convince Congress is to bring the people together that are affected and with one voice bring our plight to Congress. It means that it's not just one voice in the wilderness, but thousands of people speaking out. So I started the Guam Land-owners Associations (p. 133).

With the legal assistance of John Bohn, a proposed constitution and by-laws were prepared and the papers for a private corporation were filed by December of 1976. To facilitate the organizing process, Mrs. Bamba contacted 14 of the largest landowners and convened a meeting in January, 1977. Support from this core group was overwhelming. These charter members of the Guam Landowners Association launched a membership recruitment program with Cecilia at the lead. Working with the Commissioners they conducted village meetings to expound on the aims of the Association, its intentions and how landowners would benefit. Chilang always cautioned board members not to raise the hopes of the people unjustifiably. She enlisted elders to speak out on the value of prewar property as many claimants were descendants of landowners who had since passed away. Many villagers were skeptical at first. Some viewed the effort as another political campaign tactic. At this time, however, Mrs. Bamba had no immediate intention of running for office. She stated:

> I'm proud to say that because I was the one spearheading the project, they changed their tone and they believed that I don't do things just for self satisfaction. My track record at that time had shown them that I follow through to the end. And then, I do these things to help the people not just for my own aggrandizement. So this is what made the success of the organization really prosper and continue. I received the overwhelming confidence and trust of the landowners (p. 136).

Judging from the nearly 1,000 families who joined the Association, her assessment was perfectly legitimate. Chilang did not limit her membership drive to Guam. As President of the Guam Landowners Association since its inception, Mrs. "B" traveled to the states speaking to Guam clubs in Seattle, Santa Clara, Long Beach, Alameda, Riverside, San Diego, and Honolulu to drum up support from approximately 30,000 Chamorros who reside on the mainland.[28]

The next strategy entailed lobbying Congress. The Association proposed enabling legislation to Guam's Congressional Representative, who introduced the bill in the House. Three issues, namely tax, interest, and surplus land, caused major problems when the House approved bill reached the Senate. Cecilia journeyed with Mr. Bohn to Washington, D.C., where she became the first Chamorro woman to testify at a Congressional Hearing in support of a major bill. Her visit to the Nation's Capitol made one factor absolutely clear. Compromise was essential for passage of the bill. Mr. Bohn advised Chilang to accede to the terms specified by members of the Senate. She resigned herself to the prevailing reality. The main objective was "to get a law passed with an admission from the United States that there was an injustice" (p. 141). This realistic approach was summed up by her statement, "if you can't have a dozen eggs, you might as well settle for nine" (p. 141).

Seven months after the bill was introduced, it passed both the House and Senate. President Carter signed it into law on 15 October 1977. Title II Section 204 of Public Law 95-134 embodied a dream come true.[29]

The questions of tax on income received from claims, interest payments by the U.S. as part of the retribution, and acquisition of land declared surplus by the Department of Defense continued to trouble Mrs. Bamba. The hard-earned victory was not won without a price. Cecilia was determined to pursue these issues. She planned a two year waiting period before moving in on the Federal Government once again. The tax problem could be resolved locally once claimants were awarded compensation. As Senator, she worked with top level military officials on Guam to assure a beneficial land use plan.[30] The interest payments matter required going back to Congress.

Early in October 1979, Mrs. Bamba and Mr. Bohn traveled to Washington to meet with Senator Bennett Johnston (D, Ohio), Chairman of the Subcommittee on Interior and Insular Affairs, regarding the inclusion of interest payments in land claims settlements.[31] Together with Guam Congressman Won Pat, the two representing the Guam Landowners Association prepared to face Senator Johnston, their most outspoken opponent.[32] She recognized that Guam had little clout in the Senate. Despite such disadvantages, she came equipped with deeply rooted convictions and a well documented 85-page brief on the land claims issue, which she presented to Senator Johnston through his Administrative Assistant, Laura Hudson, a woman who Mrs. Bamba described as being, "the one that does all the reading and makes her own synopsis and recommendations to the Senator" (p. 144). She further commented that this was "a learning experience because it really showed me how those things work over there and how you can be effective; you don't have to go straight to the top. Convince the lower staff because those are the ones that can really help. The Senator would more likely listen to their recommendations (p. 144).

The Guam Delegation waited for Senator Johnston to return from his home state. His reputation for being stern and adamant frightened Cecilia, but she mustered the courage to confront him. She related her impressions of that memorable meeting:

> I was prepared to shift from a sob story ... to really being radical and tell him off. But it never came to that point because when we started he said, "I want you to know that I have read every page of the document you gave to Ms. Hudson. I am now convinced that the people of Guam should be given the opportunity to get the interest." And he said, "I promise you that I'm going to sponsor the amendment in the Senate and it will go through" (p. 144-145).

She continued:

> Actually, what he did was he withdrew the section of P.L. 95-134 which specifically said no interest. Even at that time he's trying to make me feel good because I'm a woman and of course I put on my charm, so he couldn't have the heart to be so overwhelming to me (p. 145).

Mrs. Bamba did not stop with Senator Johnston; she lobbied personally with the other Senators so that they would be familiar with the amendment when it came before them on the floor. Overnight the dreaded dragon became Guam's knight in shining armor. To Senator Bamba that was not the only incredible occurrence.

> I couldn't believe it when I came back here [to Guam], he called from his office in Washington to tell me that he already introduced the amendment. He called me again when it was passed. I never thought a U.S. Senator--here's little old me from Guam, he doesn't even know me from Timbuktu (p. 145).

In the six or more years since the enabling legislation was enacted by Congress, numerous judicial procedures have been instituted. More of the original landowners have since passed away. Certification for a class action suit was obtained. A jury trial to settle claims was scheduled. There have been repeated delays, the latest resulting from a judicial recommendation to negotiate an out-of-court settlement. Federal and local attorneys met in Washington and after tedious negotiations settled on a total award of 39.5 million dollars. News of the settlement leaked out prematurely. At the time of our interviews, Mrs. Bamba was embroiled in a controversy with three board members of the Chamorro Landowners Association who objected to the settlement amount. The number of board members had dwindled to five by 1983. One member died leaving four active. During Mrs. Bamba's absence from Guam, which coincided with the public announcement of the $39.5 million settlement, the three remaining board members convened. They voted to oust Mrs. Bamba from the presidency and dismiss the Association's Legal Counsel and Executive Director, attorney John Bohn, to demonstrate their dissatisfication with the settlement.

Mrs. Bamba explained that there was neither cause nor precedence for such action. Upon hearing of the situation, hundreds of Association members pressed Mrs. Bamba to file for a court decision on the matter. Notwithstanding procedures for electing the president in the by-laws, a hearing was held and the judge ruled in favor of the action of the three board members. Approximately 90 percent of the landowners, opposing the changeover in leadership, resigned *en masse.*

Cecilia felt betrayed and sorely disappointed but not defeated. In her estimation the Guam Landowners Association had outlived its usefulness. She stressed that individual claimants, not the organization, were parties in the litigation. In response to a majority of the landowners, Mrs. Bamba and Mr. Bohn organized a group called the Land Claimants for Settlement Alliance. Up until their deaths, they continued to advise and assist those landowners who choose to accept the settlement (pp. 146-158).

On 29 June 1986 Judge Robert Peckham "ruled in favor of a government proposed $39.5 million out-of-court settlement to pay the landowners. The next step in the process is for the judge to decide just how that money will be divided.[33] Landowners have been asked to accept or reject the recommendations of the Federal Government's staff review appraiser, who commenced his work in September 1984. Cecilia Bamba remained firm on her conviction that only the Chamorros stand to lose by further delays.

Having accomplished her major goals pertaining to Land Claims, Senator Bamba began the slow process of generating interest in and commitment to the second cause about which she felt so strongly while serving as Chair of the Committee on General Governmental Operations, Military and Veterans Affairs (GGOMVA) of the Fifteenth Guam Legislature. Her initial efforts culminated in the passage of P.L. 15-146 on 12 December 1980, which she and several of her colleagues co-sponsored, creating the Guam Reparations Commission. A legislative resolution placed the newly formed Commission under the purview of her Committee. GGOMVA staff had gathered extensive testimonies prior to her submitting proposed legislation. In her capacity as Senator, Mrs. Bamba worked to facilitate the purpose of the Commission, which was "to investigate claims for compensation accruing to the people of Guam during the period of December 7, 1941 through July 21, 1944".[34]

The five-member Commission had a life span of three years to complete the following tasks: the investigation of the number, type and extent of claims for compensation of the people of Guam against any occupying military or other government forces, and the damages resulting to the people of Guam through forced labor, confiscation of property, physical abuse, tortures, killings, rapes, and other injuries or damages to persons and property; the determination of how damages should be measured including proposed dollar amounts; the preparation of a special report on war claims by Micronesians; and finally the presentation of a full report to the Governor and Legislature of Guam no later than December 31, 1983.[35]

A preliminary survey of potential war claimants laid the groundwork for the actual filing of claims. This involved another major organizational strategy. It was essential to inform the people of the aims of the Commission and garner grassroots support. Senator Bamba was once again instrumental in working with the Commissioner's Council to set up village meetings and intensive interview sessions. Commission staff quickly discovered that there was a widespread lack of information on the part of potential claimants. An islandwide information campaign augmented efforts at the village level. Senator Bamba's office capitalized on every opportunity to promote the War Claims project. When she travelled to the United States, she spoke to Guamanian Associations in the hopes of securing their support. Her trips to Washington, D.C. included conferences with Guam's Non-Voting Delegate and the Assistant Secretary of the Interior. However, it was after she left her legislative seat that Mrs. Bamba became more personally involved as advisor to the Commission until its termination. She served as consultant to the claimants.

In July 1983 she met with the legal counsel of the House of Representatives to work out the final language of enabling legislation, which was introduced in the U.S. Congress on October 1, 1983. The still pending legislation entitled, the Guam Reparations Act, calls for a Federal Commission to investigate and award just compensation for war claims made by the people of Guam.[36]

The organizational strategies being utilized for the War Reparations project reflect the bittersweet lessons learned from the land claims efforts. Mrs. Bamba incorporated some strategies, such as lobbying, and altered them to fit the particular needs of the project. Several approaches differ considerably from those she used for the land claims. Funding for the project has been the most difficult challenge. The Land Claims project operated without funding during its initial phase. Legal fees and travel expenses were absorbed by Mrs. Bamba and Mr. Bohn with the expectation that their expenditures would eventually be reimbursed. It was only after Cecilia became Senator that she was able to push for a budget from the Legislature. When the War Reparations Commission's term expired and plans to continue the war claims project were being made, Mrs. Bamba was determined that financial matters be resolved before going any further. She proposed that the claimants be assessed a $100 contribution to cover expenses. They agreed (pp. 160-161; 137-138).

The passage of enabling legislation by the U.S. Congress is the major task at hand. Mrs. Bamba smiled knowingly as she admitted that her work was cut out for her--intensive lobbying at all levels until the Guam Reparations Act became law. She was prepared to meet the demands of organizing this massive Networking effort. Cecilia did meet with all 27 Guamanian Associations throughout the U.S. mainland and Hawaii. She drafted a resolution to be adopted by these organizations, which outlined the atrocities and the need for reparation. Once adopted, each resolution was to be sent to the organization membership's respective representative in Congress. Letters to the President of the United States, key staff, and all members of the House and Senate were also to be sent. Of her other plans, Mrs. Bamba stated:

> I'm going to set up a documentary on what happened during the war years--what it was like during the war, probably a glimpse of when people are coming out of concentration camps and identify seven or eight people representing different incidents who will relate their stories on film. This will be shown in the media all over the States, because that's what it takes. Strategy is really important (p. 19).

Mrs. Bamba was unable to see the fulfillment of this goal before her death.

Support Networks

In the previous pages of this chapter, we have been acquainted with Cecilia's life story, as told by her, through the experiences, events, and organizational activities which she has identified to be of significance or value. Her personal life has clearly been overshadowed by her activism in the public domain. While respecting her preference to focus on her public life, an accurate account of Mrs. Bamba as an organizer must include a discussion of those factors which motivated her, sustained her, and helped her to cope with the frustrations arising from her attempt to juggle important and often conflicting roles throughout her life.

One institutionalized mainstay of support that Chilang did and other Chamorros can count on is the extended family. In her roles as grand-daughter and sister she assumed the responsibility of caring for her nana and brother John. Their reciprocation allowed her the mobility and flexibility she needed as an organizer. By assuming the major share for child-care and household management, Cecilia's grandmother freed her from the minute-to-minute demands of motherhood. She utilized a culturally acceptable means of lightening her responsibility as a mother by sharing it with her grandmother. Yet, where it was culturally necessary for her to demonstrate her roles as wife, mother and grandmother, she was not remiss. As noted earlier, Chamorro women serve a pivotal role in all family celebrations, especially those linked with the Church. Cecilia managed all her children's christenings, first Holy Communion celebrations, graduations, confirmations, birthdays, marriages, etc., as well as contributing her services as expected to her own extended family, her husband's family, the families of her sons and daughters in-law, the godparents of her children, the families of her own godchildren numbering 111, distant relatives, and friends. While it may seem to a non-participant in this elaborate network of reciprocal obligations that individuals who participate in it fully may not have a moment to engage in any other activity, Chamorros have managed to shape this unwieldy cultural system into a viable structure of support.

For Cecilia, these relationships and their inherent obligations were admittedly energy-draining and time-consuming, but there was no doubt in her mind that she could not have contributed what she did without the help of close family and friends. Her support system assisted her in coping with personal tragedy. She remembered her feelings of total loss when her husband died:

> When my husband died, I thought it was the end of the world for me. It was the first impact, like half of me was gone and half of me just really doesn't function. I couldn't function the way that I should be functioning as a whole person. That's when I really noticed and recognized how much, how valuable it is to have friends. It could never be measured. I felt that lost feeling I don't care really, because half of me is gone and I'm just going to take the other half and bury it too. Even with my children, of course when you're at a loss, sometimes you think that way and you become a little selfish; you kind of think of yourself. But then I finally came to think of my children and not just of me. You have to face the world and face life.... I felt that it was my friends, those who are close to me that really gave me strength to carry on. They rallied [around me]. I really never reached the point where I'm scared to face life. I feel that there are so many there that are with me, helping me out. It made it easier. This has been the daily feeling of what I've gone through since my George died. I rely on my friends. It was at that time when I really knew how many friends I have. It just made me feel good that my husband and I, being a part of the community, were thought of like that (pp. 45-46).

Mrs. Bamba counted on her extended family to help her with family activities. When they were called they came in full force, both men and women. Chilang also relied on her children to assist her with both family and public functions. However, she rarely sought assistance from other family members for her organizational activities. For support in this area she often turned to a core of true and trusted community activists like herself.

Picking the right person to help you is very important to the success of the project. If I select persons who are going to bungle up the whole thing, that reflects on my judgment as an individual of the kinds of persons that can deliver. I resort to practically all scopes of people to help but I depend on those that I feel I can work with, who know what to do; so I can expect the work that will come out of them will be conducive to what I expect. Where at the ultimate end we'll see the success of our work (p. 61).

Asked if she had any preferences in working with either men or women, Mrs. "B" replied that she worked with both sexes; but when she has the choice, she tends to lean on women more (p. 61).

A review of Mrs. Bamba's work reveals that Networking ranked as a major organizational strategy. The contacts that she established through community service and politics augmented her network of extended family and friends as a support system which enabled Chilang to reach out far beyond home and island into national and international arenas.

Organizing: A Means of Self-Realization

Numerous explanations for Cecilia's intensity of involvement in Guam's evolution as a community could be posited from differing points of view, psychological, sociological, political, historical, and feminist. It has been the intention of this study to let the subjects define and explain their motives and work in the manner that each perceives her own experiences and meanings. Thus, for Mrs. Bamba her most important reason for getting involved in the community was linked with her roles as mother and wife.

I feel that the mother has to concern herself and be visible outside, so that whatever influence she has at home can be passed to other young women coming up. I'll use myself as a case. I am a mother of ten. When you look at, read about a mother of ten, you say that person must be so ragged. She has ten children she has to take care of. Feeding them. Clothing them, then her husband ... gee, daylight to twilight, she probably couldn't even think of herself because of rearing ten children, for yourself, to feel that you also have an identity. Not someone who is just a nurse and a maid. You also hold the power and because of that power, you have every right to go out there and look outside and also make your presence felt outside the home. It all hinges on how a person organizes her time. My motto in life is if there's a will, there's a way. I believe if a person wants to achieve something and you believe in it to the point where you are convinced it is good, nothing can stop you. You'll find time. In my case, I decided that it is the most blessed thing to have a family. And that's my priority--my home, my children, my husband. But because I also want to make sure that the outside world is conducive to what I believe is the best place for my children to roam around and my husband to be exposed, I chose to set aside time whereby I would give time to the community so that I, what I know, what I can produce as a mother, as a wife, I can impart to the other women outside to encourage others to leave the perimeter of their homes and do the same as I am doing, as wife and as a mother (p. 64).

We can see from the way she has recounted her past that as Cecilia's activities away from home increased, she continued to interpret what she did as an extension of her responsibility to her husband and children. Gradually she became aware of another dimension of meaning that organizing had acquired. She began to discover that her organizing experiences provided the opportunity for self-realization. This consciousness triggered a desire to communicate this to other women and encourage them to break through cultural and institutional barriers.

I believe that as an individual, I'd like to leave a legacy to the future, that I, as a Chamorro woman have asserted myself, have untied that bond that Chamorro women would normally live right in the perimeter of their home. I have broken that bond and I've gone out into the world. I've brought the key element that made me a good mother and a good wife to bring them out to the community so that I could share that feeling and that belief, that talent with them in the hopes that more of us will come out and work together so that ultimately everybody benefits (pp. 64-65).

Beginning with the Agana Heights Women's Group, Mrs. Bamba spent much of her adult life not only organizing but actively trying to involve other Chamorro women in community work. In the last decade her advocacy of women's involvement as active members and leaders in the Guam community went beyond the personal act of "leaving the perimeter of the home". She espoused political and institutional changes which will allow women to break through public barriers that prevent them from full participation as equal partners in community development.

Some Concluding Observations

As we conclude this case study of Cecilia Bamba, some observations bear repeating. Several factors in Mrs. Bamba's personal life served as distinct advantages to her as an organizer. Her family was a vital support system. She did not have to concern herself greatly with childcare or housekeeping as her grandmother helped her fulfill those responsibilities adequately. Her husband George supported her both financially and emotionally. He encouraged her activism and influenced its growth in many ways.

Chilang's work took her away from her family repeatedly; these absences were often in direct conflict with her perception about where a mother's place ought to be, i.e., with her children. Despite this incongruity between beliefs and actual behavior, she was able to maintain a rapport and closeness with her children throughout her life. She, her married children and their families, and her single children kept the tradition of a Sunday family gathering. Many of her children worked alongside her in her various efforts. To those who were not personally acquainted with Mrs. Bamba, her close ties with her children may not be readily apparent in the case study material. While Mrs. Bamba spoke of devoting her life to making the community of Guam a better place for her children and while they were always of first priority in her life, the commonly held misconception that a mother of ten cannot possibly do anything beyond mothering has caused her to underplay this significant aspect of her life. She has thus reacted against stereotypes and assumptions, which in fact actually intimidate women from seeing their true worth.

Her organizational work had personal value particularly as a vehicle of self-realization. Cecilia's efforts also had varying degrees of impact on the Guam community. Clearly the activities or projects she organized are not all directly related to the lives of her children. Yet she perceived the benefits of her involvement in clubs, with charity organizations, in politics, and public service as a means of bettering the quality of life for her children. Her work has directly impacted on the lives of particular segments of Guam's residents. For example, she saw a need to bridge the gap between the community and hospital and thus organized a volunteer association which serves patients and their families as well as contributing equipment and furnishings to improve the quality and environment of health care. Her beautification project and the canine control program she pushed did have islandwide ramifications. On another level, the Land Claims and War Reparations efforts have had significant impact not only for those who will benefit directly on Guam but, also as a means of educating Federal officials and the international community about the concerns and issues affecting Guam's future and its past.

Regarding the contemporary status and roles of Chamorro women, Mrs. Bamba's own experiences provide rich insight. Although she spoke of the dichotomy between the home and the "outside world," barriers seemed to dissolve with no difficulty as she extended her own "perimeter" far beyond the confines of home. The ease with which she assumed numerous and sometimes conflicting roles illustrates that such dichotomies as public and private or prescribed roles of mother and wife are not rigidly defined and at least in Cecilia's case expanded as she herself determined the need.

Much about her personal life remains to be told. The problems, difficulties, and hardships she encountered are only briefly mentioned if at all. Notwithstanding these gaps in Chilang's story, we can conclude that in her short lifetime, Cecilia Bamba epitomized the "maker and shaper" of Guam history in many ways. During our first interview session she began recollecting events in her life with the claim, "I'm just an ordinary person" (p. 1). "Maybe," I responded, "but one who has done some extraordinary things."

CHAPTER V

WOMEN ORGANIZING IN THEIR PROFESSION

Introduction

Chamorro women are increasingly entering professions that have been male dominated. In those fields which have been traditionally associated with larger concentrations of female employees such as social services, teaching, and Nursing, Chamorro women uphold the patterns of participation in the U.S. labor forces with one significant exception. Chamorro women also dominate the administrative positions in these professions and are gradually moving into top level positions in all areas of government service.

A workforce analysis conducted by the Government of Guam clearly illustrates this trend. A comparison of males and females in administrative/managerial positions in the departments and agencies of the Government of Guam for the year 1982 to 1983 reveals several unusual findings (see Appendix). Women outnumber men in these positions in the Department of Education and Public Health and Social Services, and they nearly equal the number of male administrators at the Guam Memorial Hospital and the University of Guam. Nevertheless, women occupy only 26 percent of top level offices overall. An examination of the record regarding the number of professionals and technicians in Government of Guam departments and agencies yields altogether different results. Roughly two-thirds or 68 percent of the 2,845 professionals employed by the public sector are women. Of the 709 technicians, 47 percent are women. These ratios illustrate that as Chamorro women become educated or receive training they are assuming upper level positions at a rapid rate.

The four Chamorro women organizers who are featured in this chapter are among the officials and administrators referred to above. Their educational and professional development and their ensuing organizing efforts, the types of support available to them, their family backgrounds, and personal experiences give us a more realistic understanding of the factors which prepared them for the multiple roles they have assumed.

The number of professional Chamorro women may prove surprising at first glance. Taken in historical perspective, however, one can view this seemingly recent development as a move by Chamorro women to re-establish their former status as powerful figures of authority in the public realm. The experience of the four women who have identified professional activities as most important to them can serve to expand our knowledge of this fast growing cadre of female leadership on Guam.

Two of the following case study subjects began their careers as teachers. Clotilde Gould is now an educational administrator and Pilar Lujan has been elected to public office. Carmen Pearson's career has evolved from being a social worker to her appointment as Deputy Director of the Department of Public Health and Social Services at the time of our interviews. Annie Roberto continues to serve the elderly in various capacities. While these women have different motivations for organizing and varying interests as manifested in their organizational work, their cultural training, educational experience, and personal development show many similarities. As we proceed with these case studies, it is important to look at the dynamic interaction between each subject's professional career and her organizing.

Clotilde C. Gould[1]

Clotilde Castro Gould, or Ding to those who know her well, could easily be an entertaining character in the Chamorro comic strip, *Juan Malimanga*, which she created in 1981 as part of her efforts to promote Chamorro language and culture through the news media. The witty, sometimes sarcastic, and often humorous dialogues between Juan and others depict Ding's personality in many ways. She is fun-loving and a humorous. Her outspokenness has gained her a reputation for having strong opinions and being a worthy adversary in any argument about which she feels strongly. At 56, she exhibits both the light-hearted and serious aspects of her nature with ease. These opposite qualities combine successfully in Ding's personality and are visible in her manner of working, organizing, and relating to people.

Ding claims she has been a rebel all her life. Reared by her paternal grandmother, father, and his sister as the only daughter of her never-married father, she remembers being the sole focus of attention of these three adults during her early childhood. Her aunt eventually married and had seven children. The family, including Ding's father and grandmother, all stayed together. Clotilde's father, Juan Castro Castro, was a tailor. Until his death, he assisted his sister and the eight children in their household with whatever support he could give. Ding developed a strong bond with her aunt, who treated her like a daughter in every way. She admits, though, that it must have been difficult for her aunt to deal with her rebelliousness.

She never knew her biological mother but heard that she had been an active midwife after World War II. Her aunt's seven children, who are like siblings to Clotilde, have more than adequately filled the vacuum created by the deaths of her grandmother, father, and then her aunt.

Clotilde came from a traditional Chamorro family that observed the customs of the time when she was growing up. The church was the only legitimate locus of involvement for young unmarried girls. So Ding became actively involved as a member and president of the Sodality of Mary, as a member in the church choir, as a catechist, and as a worker in a church census taken in Agana Heights, the village of her youth.

Her gaiety expresses itself in her love of music. Whether singing in the church or writing lyrics and composing musical scores as she has done in the last few decades, Ding's mischievousness comes through. A song she wrote, entitled,

I na Pinikara (Oh What a Prankish Girl), reflects her personal philosophy well. It also describes her own rebelliousness as a teenager who fooled her elders about the real reason for being an avid church goer.

Oh What a Prankish Girl[2]

1. She asked her mother to go to Church. But she didn't go there, because she followed Jesus.
Chorus: Oh what a prankish girl, Oh what a prankish girl.

2. How pitiful is this parent, because she is deaf and blind and she with her mischief caused her this suffering. Chorus:

3. Mischievous Jesus got married in order to rest. When the children started coming, he learned how difficult it could be. Chorus:

4. One day she was overcome by remorse, she even cried because she recalled what mischief she had done to all her elders. Chorus:

Ding's youthful energies were also channeled into school activities. She served as a student council representative and was a member of the high school Civic and Playhouse Clubs. Good grades earned her a scholarship to Barat College of the Sacred Heart in Lake Forest, Illinois, where she completed her undergraduate work and received a B.A. in 1954. She started college later than most because her education was interrupted by the Japanese occupation of Guam during World War II.

The groundwork for Ding's future career in the field of education was laid prior to her departure for the United States. She taught as an elementary school teacher on Guam between 1949 and 1951 and again after her return from college through 1958. By this point in her life, Ding had married Edward Gould, a Caucasian American. Clotilde laughs as she explains why she married outside her ethnic group:

One of the reasons I guess I married was because of desperation. I married somebody that is not of my own. In that, you know we were three years behind because of the war in terms of schooling; so when I went to college, I was already 21 years old. By the time I came back I was 24. There was nobody either my age or [whom] I would really like to marry. There were a lot of men but they were either younger or they were *matapang* [lackluster] or immature. I never really dreamt that I would marry anyone that was not of my kind. I also have to be very careful because I don't want to just marry my kind and be miserable. [Ding implies that she chose to be selective].[3]

Ding left Guam in 1958 to make a life with her husband Ed and eventually with their only child, Sandy. She spent the next 15 years teaching, in Kansas City for a year and then at Riverside and Pleasant Hill in California. During this period she remained active in school projects and spearheaded social activities for the Chamorro community in California. Clotilde continued to take graduate courses at state institutions in Riverside and Hayward from 1960 through 1970.

The last decade has been the most culturally meaningful for Ding. While she enjoyed her years in California, she missed home and her family deeply. These feelings heightened with each passing year. She found ways to compensate for her homesickness:

When I was in the States and I was younger, I was too busy getting excited and exploring other things, other than your own background and that's self-development. As you get older, I guess it's just natural for life to bring you back to where you came from. I guess when I was 46, that was exactly what was happening to me. Being very lonely in the States for myself and because my husband did not speak Chamorro and my daughter did not speak Chamorro, I had to find

Clotilde C. Gould

something to fill that gap, and one of those things is music. So I wrote a lot of Chamorro music.[4]

Her lyrics were recorded by Johnny Sablan, a local singer, whose popular songs are an integral part of Chamorro music today.

The circumstance which finally brought Ding back to Guam was the deteriorating health of her aunt, who had a stroke and became bedridden during Clotilde's intended short-term visit in 1972. She decided to remain on Guam to help care for her aunt. Her husband and daughter joined her, and they established their residence in the southern village of Santa Rita. She joined Guam's Department of Education as a Language Arts Consultant in 1972.

While her first year on Guam was emotionally sad for Ding, with the illness of her aunt, it served as a blessing in disguise. As a result of having worked with Chicanos in bilingual programs developed for the California school system, her main interest began to take shape. In 1973 when the Department of Education introduced the Chamorro Language and Culture Program (a federally funded program under the Emergency School Aid Act), Clotilde gladly accepted the post of Project Director. She served in that capacity until 1980 when she was appointed Administrator of Chamorro Studies and Special Projects Division in the Department of Education.

These positions have given her a forum to develop policies and projects which promote and preserve the Chamorro language and culture. This series of events also served as a catalyst for her work as an organizer. Although Ding claims that her impetus for organizing stemmed from her desire to re-establish her cultural roots, the activities she has become involved in are closely tied to her professional work.

Clotilde has coordinated many activities for the Department of Education and the Government of Guam. She has also served on the Chamorro Language Commission (1980-1983) and with the Retired Senior Voluntary Advisory Council as chairperson from 1981 to 1983. She has been appointed to numerous education committees and task forces. Among all of her professional and community activities, Ding has identified three areas that have been the most meaningful for her and to which she has devoted most of her organizing efforts.

As an educator, Clotilde has invested many years of service toward improving the quality of Chamorro education for Guam's children. Two activities have been particularly significant as hallmarks of her coordinating responsibility. In 1981 the Guam Federation of Teachers staged an islandwide strike. Clotilde did not support the strike. She joined with other educators to form the Organization of Non-striking Employees. She considered the strike anti-Chamorro as most of the striking teachers were contract hires from the States. The strike took on ethnic dimensions as the administrators were for the most part Chamorro. Chamorro parents were upset that schools threatened to close. Some viewed the strike as a blatant act of defiance against authority. Ding felt that this method of confronting a problem went against cultural tradition. Schools did remain open. Classes were taught by volunteers until the strike was settled. The other work-related activity which Ding was put in charge of was the 1983 Educational May Festival. Teachers and students competed for excellence in numerous categories in all the Guam public schools. An awards day followed the competitions. Mrs. Gould organized the entire festival through regional coordinators. What made this event a special one for her was that Chamorro oratory and spelling contests were held for the first time. The festival was so successful that the Department has chosen to make it an annual affair. Ding spoke enthusiastically of additional plans for the 1984 event which she coordinated. Contests were to include Chamorro compositions, Chamorro skits, and Chamorro readings.

One of the major benefits of the Chamorro Language and Culture Program has been the building of a community awareness of language and culture issues. This endeavor has become such an integral aspect of Ding's life that she finds it difficult to separate her organizational work from her professional responsibilities.

I like to be involved with activities that concentrate on education generally and education specifically for Chamorro children. These are all the things that every Chamorro must deal with if our people are to survive.[5]

Again, the significance of this issue must be understood in the context of Guam's colonial status. The school curriculum has been designed to meet the needs of military dependents stationed here largely to the exclusion of locally based instructional material. Ding's commitment to correct this major problem in education has been realized through the Chamorro Language and Culture Program and through the various efforts of its dedicated staff. As a result of these efforts, Chamorro music and literature have received a strong stimulus, government agencies including the courts are translating materials into Chamorro, and private businesses are using Chamorro commercials.

Ding's reputation as a Chamorro activist does not rest entirely on her professional career. It is also predicated on her active involvement in community-based and political activities. As a member of the Peoples Alliance for Responsible Alternatives (PARA) and the Organization of People for Indigenous Rights (OPIR), both of which are grassroots political coalitions, she participated in a demonstration forcing the island's daily newspaper, the **Pacific Daily News** (PDN), to formulate a liberal language policy. This led to two regular Chamorro features, *"Juan Malimanga"* and *"Fino Chamorro."* Clotilde describes her role in this effort:

I became outraged, along with several other professional associates and friends, at the arrogance of a PDN policy against using the Chamorro language. We came together to rectify the situation. We all accepted tasks equally, organized a marching rally, and published documents. Policy was changed.[6]

Later, the members of PARA joined with others in the community under an expanded acronym PARA-PADA,

Peoples' Alliance for Democratic Action, "to develop plans for a political status for Guam based on people's actual needs and historical role."[7] Clotilde assisted in organizing public awareness campaigns to defeat the ratification of the Guam constitution. Voters eventually rejected it by a ratio of 5 to 1 to show their opposition to the enabling legislation passed by the U.S. Congress which legitimized colonialism by denying the people of Guam the right to sovereignty and self-determination.

In 1981 Clotilde founded and organized the Guam Genealogical Society. She describes her work and the goals of the organization in this way:

> The Guam Genealogical Society is an organization to study, research and collect data about the history of Chamorro families and their relationships. Publication of the information is one goal. Preservation of historical and social structures of Chamorro people is another.[8]

She has spearheaded this effort because "future generations need to have information in order to develop a well-balanced historical perspective."[9] Ding conducts meetings, directs research, and is developing future plans for publication of the Society's work.

Ding Gould returned home in time to witness, participate in, and contribute to an indigenous movement that has been dubbed the "Chamorro Cultural Renaissance." Besides educational, linguistic, and political goals, other areas such as indigenous arts and crafts, local history, folklore, and Chamorro medicine have all become concerns of the movement, which continues to promote Chamorro culture and respect for the Chamorro people. Nineteen eighty-four was officially declared the Year of the Chamorro Language.[10]

Ding recalls one event in the long march over the last decade which served as a turning point for many Chamorros. In 1976 interested individuals from all fields came together to plan the first Chamorro Studies Convention. Over 500 people attended the two-day meeting held on Guam on January 21 and

22, 1977. Robert A. Underwood, chief organizer of the Convention, provides a synopsis of this important activity, which was a highlight of Ding's organizational work.

The sheer exhilaration of the event, the bringing together of educators from all the Marianas, the thrill of meeting and listening to such figures as Dr. Laura Thompson and, most importantly, the presentation of scholarly work is difficult to capture in words. There can no longer be serious questions raised about the value of studying the Chamorro people and their relationships to the world. We have reached a new plateau where we discuss how and when with a strong sense of urgency. The question of why is raised only by those ignorant of the new forces that are now reaching their mature stage.[11]

Organizing is a valuable tool for Clotilde Gould. It has provided a viable means of reaffirming her commitment to promote the Chamorro language and culture. Ding does not join organizations "just to be social." Her time and energy are concentrated on issues. Consequently, the people she seeks assistance from are usually issue-oriented. Reaching out to others is an integral part of her organizing strategy. Her staff, village commissioners, professional associates, and her very supportive husband comprise her network of support. Still, she has her preferences.

The ones that share a philosophical or cultural viewpoint are the most valuable. I work much better with people who see life in Guam in terms of issues. Those issues are Chamorro language development and continuity, cultural continuity and preservation, historical preservation, strengthening family values, and education.[12]

Ding admits that organizing can be frustrating at times, but working with people with similar commitments and accomplishing a goal are sufficient rewards to keep her active.

In the last few years Clotilde had become increasingly involved in women's groups. She explains how her interest in enhancing Chamorro culture has resulted in the women-centered focus of her current organizational endeavors.

Chamorro women have an historical destiny to fulfill. Language and cultural continuation have traditionally been responsibilities that Chamorro women have accepted since ancient times. We must assume leadership because our men are becoming culturally fragmented. Both Chamorro men and women must eventually work together if our children are to enter the future with confidence, pride, and competence![13]

Her role as an organizing member of the IWY (International Women's Year) Steering Committee for the Guam Women's Conference was a starting point for Ding. She chaired the Sub-Committee on Awards and Recognitions. It was while she was developing criteria for selection that her views on Chamorro women and their traditional roles began to crystallize. She became determined to recognize Chamorro women who were not well known, women in traditional occupations and those who had never been recognized for their silent contributions. On the day of the Conference's presentation of awards, midwives, fisherwomen, and women farmers took their places beside Chamorro women professionals and leaders. Ding's efforts to recognize the common woman were successful. She proudly describes one of "those ladies":

A woman with 24 children who farmed all her life and from the soil she fed her children while her husband was overseas. Whenever her husband takes leave and comes home, she gets pregnant. That happened 24 times until he retired. But while she was taking care of children, they ate from [the fruits of the] soil that she grew.[14]

Ding was elected to be a Guam Delegate to the 1977 National Women's Conference at Houston. Several years following the Guam Women's Conference, Clotilde and other organizers were asked by colleagues to direct a follow-up conference to determine whether the resolutions and other issues identified at the Guam Women's Conference had been addressed. This advocacy group was called the Guam Women's Task Force. Their work resulted in a published report.

When a new women's organization was being formed on Guam in 1982, Clotilde Gould was asked to join. This group called the Federation of Chamorro Women (FCW) is unique in several ways. The main objective of the organization is to "preserve Chamorro language and culture." All members are required to speak Chamorro and even the parliamentary procedures are conducted in Chamorro. This is a radical departure from the accepted format of most formal organizations on Guam, which use English as a medium of communication in conducting all business. Exceptions to this practice are the ethnic organizations on Guam. Chamorros, however, had never organized formally as an "ethnic" group. The FCW's language policy has automatically excluded non-Chamorro speakers. Whenever Chamorros organize and for whatever reason, non-Chamorro speakers have been disgruntled and some have even called the Federation's policy discriminatory. This did not stop the FCW women from organizing. The structural goal of the group is to establish member organizations in each village which can respond to the issues relevant to the women of a particular locale. These village groups form the Federation. Federation members representing the village communities on the island are charged with the responsibility of either establishing new village groups or encouraging and assisting existing informal groups to expand and join the Federation. The initial organizers envisioned a grassroots network that would feed into the islandwide Federation, which would in turn sponsor island-wide cultural projects, raise funds, etc. Ding Gould was one of the initial organizers and has served as Publicity Chairperson since 1982. She was moved to join the Federation because of its Chamorro objectives, its promise of being "issue-oriented," and her belief that Chamorro women needed to take the lead. Thus all of Clotilde's criteria for getting involved were met.

Ding is emphatic about the good that the Federation has done. Chamorro women members not familiar with conducting "official business" in Chamorro have undergone a real learning experience. Members assist each other with language difficulties.

> ... we correct each other right then and there so that there is room for improvement. And yet we feel very comfortable about doing that because we know that's one of the purposes to preserve or to encourage [the Chamorro language].[15]

Ding further discusses the work of the Federation:

> And also we would like to help Chamorro students, give them scholarships; we want to establish some funding. Right now we're doing a lot of fund-raising activities so that we can establish some funding for our own kids.[16]

But there are problems, which must be quickly addressed or the Foundation may have a "leadership" without followers. Clotilde candidly assesses the heart of the problem:

> I think the resentment now is the leadership. I think the leadership is too domineering, too overpowering, and as Chamorro women, I tell them that they have to be very careful because a lot of the members that we have, have never really come out of their domain.[17]

Ding explained that some Chamorro women who are being recruited as potential village organizers have never been active in organizing before. They are humble and are not competitive. To the more experienced organizers, meetings and luncheons at hotels and comparing notes and accomplishments in other areas may be accepted as a matter of course, but to inexperienced newcomers this type of behavior is alienating and chases prospective village representatives away. Ding blames the Board of Trustees, which is comprised of a handful of initial organizers, for being insensitive. She firmly advocates a cooperative approach to invite members and then train them in leadership skills by teaming up with an experienced organizer. She feels this method is far more characteristic of Chamorro culture and she is convinced it will succeed in establishing an islandwide network of Chamorro women activists. Unfortunately, Ding's views are not upheld by other Board members.

To compound this problem, the Board has merged efforts with another organization, the Guam Civic Center Foundation. Clotilde is concerned that the Federation of Chamorro Women has not yet been securely established, and to merge it with another organization will defeat its purpose. She expresses her feelings this way:

> I'm a little disappointed with the leadership and I'm making it known. Right now the Guam Civic Center Foundation, which is very controversial, is having some kind of fund- raising activities. The leadership [in this instance Clotilde refers to one person in the Federation of Chamorro Women] is merging our efforts and I don't think a lot of our members are participating. There was no majority decision for that kind of involvement. For that, I was appointed for entertainment, I made it known that I don't want anybody making decisions without the whole group making it and just assuming that those whom you have appointed are going to be part of it because I was never asked my opinion to begin with and therefore I don't want to participate.[18]

The disagreements do not end here. In Ding's opinion, the "leadership," as she calls them, will have to reach a compromise or alter their organizing strategies if the Federation hopes to continue as a grassroots movement.

Leadership aside, Ding has worked with many Chamorro women organizers in her educational, political, cultural, and women-centered involvements. Of these relationships, she says, "I would hope these women will remain life-long friends because I consider them sisters in a broad-based cause that will continue to become more and more crucial to Chamorro survival."[19]

Pilar C. Lujan[20]

Pilar Lujan, Chamorro educator, administrator, wife, mother, and now legislator, shares some basic commonalities with her close childhood friend and sister organizer, Ding Gould. Pilar was born in 1930 and lived her early life in Agana. She and Ding were reared in a similar cultural climate which emphasized close family ties, strict observance of Chamorro traditions, and Catholic religious practices. They both experienced World War II and the Japanese occupation of Guam as young teenagers. Both women left Guam to pursue a college education. Pilar attended Siena Heights College in Adrian, Michigan from 1951 to 1955, where she received her B.A. degree in Secondary Education. After a year of teaching in Detroit, she returned home to teach for another six years before her appointment as assistant principal of P.C. Lujan Elementary School from 1962 to 1964. Pilar again went to the United States, this time to obtain a Master's degree in Elementary School Administration from Indiana University in Bloomington. After her studies, she returned to Guam and was appointed principal of Wettengel Elementary School, a post she held for the next two years.

By this time Pilar Diaz Cruz had become the wife of attorney Frank George Lujan. At age 26 she married "a Chamorro from Sinajana, originally from Inarajan."[21] Frank and Pilar Lujan have three daughters and one son.

Although Pilar and Ding have maintained a closeness throughout their lives and have shared similar personal and professional experiences, their personalities, the nature of their involvement in island affairs, and their organizing strategies differ markedly in many respects. Pilar is quiet, reserved and soft-spoken. She exhibits a feminine and genteel demeanor regardless of circumstances. Polite diplomacy is a basic rule which she applies to her dealings with people. These characteristics, culturally associated with being a good Chamorro girl, were an integral part of her upbringing. Her father, Jose Valenzuela Cruz, and her mother, Josepha Torres Diaz, had

Pilar C. Lujan

nine children. Pilar was their seventh. She admits that her two older sisters and her brothers still spoil her to this day. Growing up in her parents' house she learned the domestic arts from her mother, whose world revolved around her family and church. Her father was quite different. He served the Naval Government in several capacities. He was also "very active in leadership roles as educator, district or community leader during the prewar, Japanese occupation, and postwar periods."[22] He served as an officer in the Chalan Pago Holy Name Society, a religious organization, and maintained an active role in politics. Reflecting on her childhood, Pilar feels that her father served as a role model who inspired her to become involved even at an early age.

> Since I was young, my father had always been a community leader, ... so he was always encouraging us to get into it .... In the eighth grade I was already taking leadership roles, Homeroom President, Student Class President .... My mother was totally different from my father; she just stayed away from everything.[23]

Pilar's village community of Chalan Pago offered its youth many opportunities to develop leadership skills. She recalls the Sodality of Mary, a civic club, a teenage club, and a choir group.[24]

The training, values, and support which were a part of her upbringing have clearly influenced her present family life, community participation, and organizational involvement. A short feature article in a Guam newspaper describes her family relationships thusly:

> Calling herself a woman of purpose, Pilar Lujan wakes up before six every morning to administer insulin shots to her sister-in-law who lives nearby. She returns home to fix breakfast if her husband, lawyer Frank Lujan has not already done so. This daily routine continues on to a light lunch and heavier supper mostly prepared by her.

150

Meals are not closely planned for this family because she prefers to cook what the family feels like eating for that day. However, when the children were all staying at home, the couple always made a point to sit down to a family supper even when they were invited out. When this happens they would talk to the children and explain where they were going, why and what they were going to do.

Talking or communicating is the main fare in the Lujan family ... . Disciplining came in the form of a talk-session, often with all members of the family and in some cases on a one-to-one basis closeted in the bedroom.

Family finances are handled jointly by husband and wife. "Those that were more convenient to be transmitted through his office were handled by him," she points out. Having worked professionally all throughout her adult life, she is used to having her own money so she maintains her own separate personal checking account.[25]

Pilar feels that her immediate family remains a tight-knit one. She also has strong bonds with her siblings and her husband's relatives and relies on them for all types of assistance. Her sisters are especially helpful. Pilar maintains that her egalitarian relationship with Frank has been particularly important in minimizing the strain between her family life and obligations and an active professional career.

Brought up in a strict religious atmosphere, she tries to convey to her children the values she was taught. Much of Pilar's voluntary work is centered in the Catholic parish of Our Lady of Peace in Chalan Pago. As a young girl she belonged to a church group called *Apostot* (Apostles) and later joined the Sodality of Mary for young single women. When she married, she became a member of the Confraternity of Christian Mothers. She also belongs to the Our Lady of Peace Parish Council and serves as a Lay Eucharistic Minister of Chalan Pago. In these capacities she has performed numerous volunteer services for her church community. Her involvement in a secular village organization, the Chalan Pago-Ordot Family Association, extends her strong sense of shared responsibility with other members of her residential community. Pilar and her husband joined the Association as a means of nurturing a connection with neighbors and fellow parishioners at a social level. She says the group's main purpose for organizing was:

> to have all those families together to help one another in time of need. [When a member of the association dies] a big amount of money [dues collected] is given to the survivors of the deceased member. And every night of the rosary they either say the rosary and also come and serve the food or [assist in some way].[26]

In addition to the "Christian ideals" which form a central motivation for Pilar's voluntary efforts and community involvement, her activities are often shaped and determined by a keen professional earnestness. This developed when she was attending college in the United States. The exposure to success-oriented strategies and competition transformed her understanding of future possibilities for herself. She recalls how her educational experiences became a turning point in her life:

> Because it was painful to me, when I came back I was a totally different person. Before, I was very modest. I was holding back all the kinds of things that I know I wouldn't go up to you and say I know this. But, when I came back from a mainland institution, I was really able to go up and say I can do this and that, where before I could never do that. And I think it was partly our upbringing because that stress was to be modest, to be humble, not to brag and all this. And when you say something about yourself, it's like bragging or being egocentric. But, I learned it differently. And so when I came back I said, Hey, I'm not going to sit back and let the opportunities go by. So, I'd apply for the job. And every time there was a position open in the upper level, I went for it.[27]

Many of Pilar's organizational affiliations and efforts are directly related to her professional work in the field of education. Her experiences reflect a progressive development from teaching through administrative positions, including Associate Superintendent of Curriculum and Instruction and Acting Director of Education to her Chairpersonship in the first elected Guam Territorial Board of Education. She has also served in PTA's, on school accreditation teams, and has chaired the Electoral Council for the Catholic Board of Education. Some of Pilar's efforts have entailed Chamorro language development. Besides serving on numerous education committees and maintaining membership in professional organizations, she also chaired the Chamorro Language Commission from 1973 through 1980. As a licensed educational consultant, she continues to engage in projects that promote Chamorro language and culture. These endeavors have included Chamorro language instruction at the University of Guam.

To balance her propensity for professionally related involvements, Pilar has deliberately sought out other kinds of organizations to create a well-rounded core of activities to which she devotes the time she has set aside for community voluntarism. She belongs to several women's organizations with a wide range of foci: Christian Mothers--religious, International Women's Club of Guam--social, League of Women Voters--political, Soroptimists--community, and the American Association of University Women (AAUW)--professional. Her work with the AAUW has been the most personally meaningful. Membership in this organization has provided the impetus for the women-centered activities which she has organized.

When Pilar first returned home after obtaining her M.S. degree, a colleague from the Department of Education sponsored her membership in the AAUW, which had been established on Guam several years before. She wanted to continue "growing and learning" and viewed the AAUW as an ideal forum for "keeping abreast with what was going on as well as becoming involved in community affairs."[28] Long before the Women's Conference in Houston, Pilar had her initial introduction to women's rights issues. There was growing concern among AAUW members that women were receiving inequitable treatment in the field of education. Pilar recalls her first club assignment:

> I was assigned first to look into women's rights. Just how much women were paid and whether or not they are being discriminated [against]; that's one of the very first issues I had to deal with. I was never a feminist or a woman liberator, but I was kind of made more conscious because I never really thought of myself as someone who would go out and promote women's equal rights because I never felt that I was discriminated [against] in any way. Sure enough, I did find that there were some inequities . . . ; so I was driven with much more interest to deal with the problem.[29]

Pilar became president of the Association in 1977, the year the Women's Conferences were held on Guam and in Houston. As an offshoot of these meetings, Pilar organized an AAUW forum on the Equal Rights Amendment and issues which had been raised in Houston. Pilar favors the AAUW because of its issue-orientation and programs, which are personally enhancing as well as being beneficial to the community. Most of the Association's 60 members are non-Chamorro, but Pilar feels a strong sense of camaraderie with other professional women, regardless of ethnic identification.

Perhaps the most significant advantage of her AAUW involvement has been its awareness-building aspect, which has served to alert Pilar to the barriers and issues that Guam women face. Since she claims to have had no personal experience with discriminatory practices nor does she feel oppressed in her home life, her club activities and relationships were critical to her involvement as the parliamentarian and member of the Coordinating Committee of the First International Women's Year Conference on Guam in 1977 and later as a Delegate to the National Conference. Pilar subsequently became President of the Guam Women's Issues Task Force, which sponsored a women's workshop on equality in November, 1981. Speaking as chairperson of this event, Pilar stated:

> Solutions to sex discrimination will be discussed. . . . Women are becoming much more aware that the issues affecting them affect all of society. They know they must take more important roles.[30]

An interview with Pilar Lujan on workshop activities which was published in the **Pacific Daily News** also reported that:

> The women's group explains that it does not consider itself to be a "feminist" organization.

> Lujan says the need for participation in society is universal between men and women.

> "However, some women must be encouraged to take a more assertive role in making decisions which affect their lives," Lujan explained.[31]

Pilar Lujan is now serving her fourth consecutive term as a Guam Senator. This "new role" provides Senator Lujan with the opportunities to promote women's rights. Early in her first year in office she challenged the Executive Branch to nominate more women to boards and commissions. Senator Lujan made her views public through the media. The **Pacific Daily News** carried this story:

> One of Guam's four female senators criticized the lack of women nominated to boards and commissions. ...

> Sen. Pilar Lujan said the female nominations have been just token appointments and said the governor's record in that area is a dismal one.

> "Women make up more than half the electorate," Lujan said. "And there are so many qualified women who aren't being used to their fullest."

According to the senator's records, of the 50 names which have been sent to the Legislature from January to March 9 for confirmation to boards and commissions, only nine are women.

Guam law says that each board and commission must have representation of both sexes.

"I am not asking that women be selected indiscriminately regardless of their qualifications. There are many women on our island who could and would serve ably on the government's boards and commissions," Lujan said.[32]

In the traditionally male-dominated arena of political office, Senator Lujan (Democrat) feels that her colleagues, most of whom are men, treat her as an equal. Unlike Senator Cecilia Bamba, who viewed the Legislature as a microcosm of the male-oriented, dog-eat-dog world of society at large, Pilar describes her experience differently. Citing Guam's endorsement of the Equal Rights Amendment, she points out:

And if you recall, I think Guam was the first one that went right out, and it was all male senators other than two women--Katherine [Aguon] and Cecilia Bamba--and they passed the E.R.A. There was no hesitancy; they were all out there supporting the movement. So I think that is a great demonstration of our people, that they really never thought of us as sexual inferiors. I say they over there [17th Guam Legislature], they actually treat us [equally]. I don't feel any conflict about those men because we are all colleagues together. They are all our colleagues; they don't really look down upon us. I think in the past they have had some reservations about some of the women senators. In this particular Legislature, I don't think that any of the women can honestly claim that they have been treated [as] less of a colleague than the men.[33]

Whether the above statement is an accurate assessment or a romantic tribute to her colleagues, Senator Lujan nevertheless recognizes that her experience is not necessarily true for all of Guam's women. Her organizational work, especially that related to women's rights, manifests this awareness.

Questioned about the process of organizing, Pilar comments that she derives satisfaction from working with people and contributing to a better community. Still, there are some problems in attempting to organize through formal strategies such as meetings and other structured activities. She offers a cultural explanation for such difficulties:

> Just trying to get people together here. Because you know, our setting here; it is very difficult to run if it interferes with our culture. That's the reason why I have not been very active in AAUW [recently] because of the funerals and the wakes that I have to attend on Saturdays. And it's happening to the other women as they find themselves zooming to higher roles in government. They find that they are also obligated to go to all these social functions. They have been very apologetic for not attending the meetings. But I can really understand what they are going through. So that's the biggest difficulty now trying to get the people together.[34]

The pattern of extending familial obligations islandwide is referred to by all the case study subjects who hold elective offices or whose husbands are in those positions. It appears that Pilar views difficulties from the standpoint of the organizer's availability to participate. Many Chamorro women express similar reasons for not joining formal organizations. Familial obligations remain a priority even for women active in the public sphere. In fact these obligations escalate the more involved a woman becomes in public affairs.

Pilar admits that she has not given specific consideration to organizing strategies. She simply does what seems to her to be effective in achieving her organizational goals. When asked about whom she relies on to assist her, it is clear that she unconsciously depends on a large network of support beginning with her siblings, husband and his family, colleagues, organization members, commissioners, priests, neighbors, friends, and a growing number of islandwide supporters. She vows to utilize Networking as a deliberate strategy in her next campaign.

Carmen L.G. Pearson[35]

The enviable rise from social worker in 1966 to her appointment as Deputy Director of the Department of Public Health and Social Services is a brilliant chapter in Carmen Leon Guerrero Pearson's story. Life was not always so pleasant or successful for Carmen. Hardships during her childhood and the struggle to keep her first marriage from destroying her and her two sons contributed to Carmen's pragmatic outlook. These difficult experiences helped to prepare her for the professional roles she has assumed in nearly two decades of active work on Guam. Current circumstances and a happy second marriage to Wes Pearson, "a Caucasian from Fresno," have brought significant changes in Carmen's life.[36]

Carmen's parents, Pedro Cruz Leon Guerrero and Benita Rojas had six children before and during World War II. Carmen, their youngest, was born on November 5, 1943 during the Japanese occupation of Guam. Two of her siblings died in the course of the war, and her father passed away when she was only a month old. Carmen's mother was forced by the loss of her husband to muster her resources to provide a livelihood for her four living children. *Tan* Benita became a cleaning and ironing lady in order to support her family. Her only active involvement besides her work and home responsibilities was membership in the Christian Mothers' Association. Carmen remembers her childhood: "I felt we were poor in terms of materialistic things but we were rich in spiritualistic matters. We are blessed with a "real" Christian mother to guide us."[37] She continues:

I recall, of course, during my day we did not have
television going on. And one of the things that *Nana*
would do in the evenings after dinner is that she
would gather the four of us and talk to us occasionally
about how important it is to have strong family ties
and especially in her case because she became a
widow early in her life. And she found that she really
needed the network and support from relatives in
terms of just basically everything. And I remember
during those days my mom really did have to work
very hard. She literally washed and ironed people's
clothes in order to feed us. But the one thing she
really stressed is the importance of the family, the
importance of the church in reference to the family,
and the community as a whole.[38]

Carmen's mother continues to play a central role in the
Pearson household today. This gives Carmen the freedom and
support she needs to pursue an active career.

I don't think that without my mom at this stage, I don't
think I would be into as many activities as I am today.
Nana helps me in the sense that she keeps the home
fires burning; by that I mean when the kids come
home from school, she's there. Of course the two boys
are always hungry and so *Nana's* always got food on
the table and she helps in the sense that in the mornings when I'm getting ready for work and most everybody is gone by then, she comes in with a cup of
coffee. To me that's a real big help. It's not because I
want to drink coffee; it's her presence. She irons my
clothes to this day and I really tell her not to but she
does it. She wants to help that way. She straightens
up the house as by the time I get home I'm exhausted.
On the weekdays she does this; then on the weekends
she goes to the ranch.[39]

Tan Benita has since remarried, but she continues to nurture
her adult children as she sees the need.

Carmen L.G. Pearson

Carmen, her brother, and sisters were brought up in a traditional Chamorro environment. Church and school were pivotal to her development as an organizer. She attended both public and private schools before departing in 1962 to work her way through St. Mary's College in Los Angeles. Assessing her motivation for her organizational efforts which began with a B.A.in 1966, Carmen writes,

In retrospect, I believe that in 1959 when Sr. Wilhelmine, F.S.P.A., asked me to compete in a speech contest [island-wide] in reference to "helping your community," this was the real origin in my enthusiasm [for] organizing.[40]

Although her organizing efforts in the profession of social work have blossomed in the past five years, Carmen traces her involvement back to her adolescence.

I was active, I would tend to think, in my formative years as a teenager in reference to being a member of the Sodality and church organizations. But, ... it was really after my divorce and my remarriage that led me to become even more active in organizations although I did belong to some in the early years of my first marriage. My first husband [a Chamorro] was very possessive of my time and did not want to see me get totally involved and immersed in community work or organizations or things like that. So therefore I relegated a lot of my time with my family.[41]

The period between her return to Guam from St. Mary's and her remarriage was extremely painful for Carmen and eventually for her two sons. Besides preventing Carmen from actively participating in community work, her first marriage involved the trauma of being an abused spouse. Her repeated efforts to seek counsel and unsuccessful attempts to salvage her family life gave Carmen firsthand knowledge of the pain and suffering which abused victims must combat daily. It took years for her own wounds to heal. Gradually she was able to put her divorce behind her. Throughout this period she continued to work, first as a social worker, and later in various government positions through 1978. She then decided to pursue a M.S.W. degree from the University of Arizona. Her second marriage has been an entirely different and supportive experience.

Carmen returned to Guam once again to her position as Community Development Agent in the Cooperative Extension Service at the University of Guam. She vacated this position in 1984 upon her appointment as Deputy Director of Public Health and Social Services. Her involvement as a Community Development Agent has served as a springboard for her recent organizational work. She had previously volunteered with the American Red Cross and became President of its Board in 1982. She was also President of the Santa Barbara School PTA. For four years she chaired Project Help and Sanctuary, an assistance and counseling program for runaway teenagers. Memberships in the Community Development Society of America, the Pi Lambda Theta, and the American Society for Public Administration also offered Carmen new perspectives as a professional. The contacts she made, coupled with the need to respond to the problems encountered by abused victims, prompted her to aid in the formation of the Guam Task Force on Family Abuse and Sexual Assault. This effort has been her most meaningful organizing experience. She describes how and why she took action.

In 1981, a stewardess was killed in Tumon (a tourist center on Guam). Shortly after that, there were a series of other rapes occurring in the community. There was a big concern among the residents. . . . No one had addressed the issue of community education which is creating community awareness about sexual assault, because a lot of people don't even want to talk about [it]. We first got started when I started sending out letters to various agencies that we preliminarily meet to discuss some of the issues and concerns of the community. We talked first about the rape problem and then other people at the meeting were saying,

162

"but we've got problems also in spouse abuse and child abuse and neglect."[42]

With a core group of representatives from other helping agencies, the next step was to develop an outreach plan.

The Task force members met with the Bishop (Flores) to address their concerns. After about six months of planning, the Task Force members called the principals of public schools and the parish priests to inform them of their community awareness program. An overview of issues concerning child abuse and neglect, spouse abuse, and rape (sexual assault) was discussed. Task Force members facilitated the discussion as those were tied in with PTA meetings. A list of agency resources were identified and passed out at these meetings for future contacts. The initial members of the Task Force composed of professionals from different helping agencies plus community volunteers whose backgrounds were: psychologist, social worker, marriage counselor, community edu cator, and victims themselves. The response from the community turned out to be overwhelming in the sense that requests were made by participants in the village workshops to address future sessions either in the homes or in various agencies. A slide/tape series entitled "Violence in the Family" was purchased by the CDI [Community Development Institute] at the UOG [University of Guam] and shown to numerous groups and organizations.

... In addition, an outgrowth of the Task Force is the Counseling Advocates Reaching Out (CARO) A group of 60 individuals who were trained to assist local victims of sexual assault. The CARO group is now being used by the Family and Juvenile Courts as well as other agencies.[43]

In assessing her own contributions to the Task Force, Carmen writes:

> I was the principal organizer in the sense that I facilitated several planning meetings with other helping agencies. I also conducted an assessment via the Commissioners as to what they felt was the priority in their villages. I was able to have many interested people volunteer their expertise.[44]

She now serves as a consultant to the Task Force and CARO.

While strategies were being developed to generate awareness of the problems of abuse in the community, cultural traditions and attitudes were given great consideration. Thus the approach used was always non-threatening and planners attempted to encourage the use of the Chamorro language whenever possible.

Carmen's subsequent community involvement as Chairperson on Special Constituents for the Guam Women's Issues Task Force in 1981, and as an appointed member of the Guam Advisory Council on Vocational Education, as well as Chairperson of the Guam Health Coordinating Council, reflects her current areas of interest. She has incorporated into her work strategies which proved effective in organizing the Task Force. Although her interest is not restricted to female victims or clients, Carmen describes her work as being predominantly women-centered.

This orientation is not surprising, for throughout Carmen's life women have served as a major source of support and inspiration to her, beginning with her mother. Although Carmen is keenly aware of the trauma of being victimized as a woman, she has had strong female role models at home and in the community that have encouraged her to deal with setbacks successfully. In her estimation education has been the most enriching force in her life. Through it many doors have been unlocked. Carmen recalls that when she first proposed to go abroad for her undergraduate degree her mother objected.

Nana said, "Hey, you want to leave so you could date in the States, right." She was an old lady, very very old-fashioned. I said, "*Nana*, no. I've looked at you as an example and I love you dearly and I know you want me to learn from this experience. *Nana*, I don't think I want to be poor forever." I said, "you know you did not get a chance to get your education because of the time you were in. You were an orphan and during that time the war was going on and you couldn't pursue your education if you wanted to. In this day and age, a high school education is not enough anymore." I, in a way had to educate my mom about how important it is for me to go and get my education. And here she thought I just wanted to get out of her hands, because I wanted to date and this and that, and that I wanted to be free. It's really not that. It's really because I wanted to get a better education so I could get a better job. My education taught me to be financially, socially, and emotionally independent.[45]

Carmen did pursue a graduate education and upon receiving her M.S.W. in 1979 returned to Guam to assume leadership roles in a variety of professional and volunteer-related activities.

Annie P. Roberto[46]

"Aging is not a synonym for uselessness."[47] Social worker Annie Pangelinan Roberto has dedicated years of her life to demonstrate the veracity of this rallying cry. Her interest in and concern for the elderly of Guam, is deeply rooted in her childhood.

Annie Pangelinan was born to Maria Duenas Iriarte and Tomas Manuel Pereira Pangelinan on September 2, 1934 in Agana, where her extended family resided until after the Second World War. She was the oldest of four children. She and her two brothers experienced the Japanese occupation as youngsters; their sister was born after the war. Annie was brought up by her parents, grandparents, unmarried aunts, and uncles. She spent most of her time as a child with her maternal grandmother, who became the major influence and source of inspiration for Annie's subsequent work with the elderly.

Born into a strict Catholic family, Annie's upbringing closely parallels the experiences of her sister organizers in the preceding case studies. Like Cecilia Bamba, Clotilde Gould, Pilar Lujan, and Carmen Pearson, Annie Roberto's youthful experiences revolved around her extended family, church, and school. She actively participated in organizations such as the Sodality of Mary, Girl Scouts, the Spanish and Civic Clubs in high school, and in the Book of the Month Club. She also acted in school plays.

This type of involvement continued when Annie left Guam in 1953 to pursue a B.A. from Bowling Green State University in Ohio. She was active in the Newman Club and the International Students Association during her college years. Annie values her education and attributes a growing sense of independence to her college experience. Going abroad and managing on her own "boosted self esteem," she developed a confidence which has made her feel more useful to her children.[48]

After attaining her degree, Annie remained in the United States, where she met her husband, a Chamorro serviceman from the village of Santa Rita.[49] Annie was married at age 25. The Robertos resided in several places in the United States and on Guam for the first fifteen years of their marriage. During this period they had four of their five sons, who range in age from 23 to 6. Annie's dual roles as wife and mother were a full-time occupation for nearly two decades. Activities outside her home were limited to her serving as a catechist and tutor in several school districts.

The Roberto family returned to Guam permanently in 1975. At this time Annie decided to go back to teaching. She taught at local junior high and elementary schools at different times for a total of eight years.

After the birth of her fifth and youngest son, she and her husband were divorced. In spite of the hardships of being a single parent, Annie is determined to provide guidance and create a stable Christian family life for her sons. She devotes many hours to their training and seeks to:

> ... bring them up in a manner to be responsible, law abiding, and independent, to respect excellence and a good education; for through education, their inheritance, they can make their way through life.[50]

Part of this effort includes teaching her sons to cook, wash clothes, and clean house so that they are equipped to survive on their own. Annie has continued to upgrade her own education by taking over 130 credit hours of coursework at the University of Guam.

Annie's parents have joined her household located in Barrigada. Since her divorce, she has filled her life with meaning and new direction in several ways. Her family, including her parents, come first. Discussing issues of importance to her, she states:

> For me, those that have a direct bearing on my children are very important to me. Because of my position now as being the only parent, it especially magnifies that need. Because I have very young family, anything that affects children, their education and their health, their recreation, I consider them as very important.[51]

Annie has translated these beliefs into action through her involvement in her children's school activities. From 1978 to 1981, she served as a board member of the Father Duenas Parents-Teachers Guild and as Secretary of the B. P. Carbullido Elementary School PTA in 1982.

Faith has sustained Annie Roberto in times of trouble and has prevented her from wallowing in despair. The breakup of her marriage has been a painful "cross to bear."

Annie P. Roberto

Annie describes how her religious training as a Catholic has given her the courage to persevere:

> We tend to be philosophical about some things. Because of the way that we've been brought up in our faith, we don't lose hope, maybe, as easily as some people. We have that faith to hang on to. So that when we can no longer solve our problems through reason, we could fall back and say, I'm sure that God has a plan for me that I don't see yet. I think that has been a sustaining power on us, for those who are practicing their religion.[52]

Her religious commitment is further manifested in her service as a member of the Barrigada Parish Council since 1981; in the six years she has spent teaching Christian Doctrine every Saturday morning; in weekly Charismatic Prayer Meetings, which she says contribute to her spiritual growth and prepare her for her other church work; and most recently as a counselor with the Christian Conciliation Service, a group that uses Christian principles to provide meditation service for couples who seek help. Annie's religious philosophy has prompted her to reach out and assit those who are in need.

The most meaningful and gratifying of volunteer activities that Annie Roberto has undertaken have been directed at the needs of the elderly. Annie has acquired a special understanding of the ways and views of elders through her close relationship with her maternal grandmother, who played a central role in her childhood. Annie's father, a retired Navy musician, and her mother, who worked as a hospital attendant, entrusted the responsibility of Annie's upbringing to *Tan* Maria's mother.

This decision had a profound impact on Annie. Her grandmother practiced the traditional professions of healer or *suruhana* and of prayer leader or *techa*. Under her tutelage, Annie learned to speak, read, and write in Chamorro. She was introduced to a daily regimen of prayers often said in Chamorro, or in Spanish or Latin. She also learned how to cook. Annie was strictly disciplined by her grandmother, a "diligent woman," who practiced a "never waste time" philosophy.[53]

Perhaps the most significant outcome of the years as her grandmother's apprentice and companion has been Annie's knowledge and appreciation of Chamorro practices and the respect and concern she feels for the aged. She describes this influential period in her life:

> My grandmother made voluntary activities a daily part of her life, and she would always have me tag along with her. So I have been exposed to that kind of work during my growing up days. She was always doing things for people as a *suruhana*. She was always going out trying to relieve people of their physical discomforts. She would go out and look for medicinal herbs. If someone came to her with a particular ailment, she would go out the next day or however long it would take and she would collect all the herbs that are necessary for that particular problem. And if the patient wouldn't be able to come to her, she would go to the patient's home and apply the medication, massage the person, say prayers for the person. She would have me involved in a small way; for instance, as she goes out collecting these herbs she would point out to me what the name of the plant is, what it's used for, how many leaves, or what part of the plant is useful for what particular ailment, and how to go about preparing it. And sometimes when she's getting ready to apply these things to the patient she would say to me, okay, you boil water for me and she would be saying prayers over the sick person or she would have me ground the herbs. And in some small ways I shared in her daily experiences with her volunteering her services. She was called on a lot to say *Nobenas* and I would follow her. Before we go to each *Nobena*, she would go through it. She would rehearse her songs. And, if there was a part in the prayer that needs answering, she would have me answer those.

That's how I learned to say rosaries and *Nobenas* when I was very young because I had to do a lot of the answering in addition to family evening and morning prayer services. When there's a member within the community who is sick or dying, she was called on a lot to pray over that person. On all of these trips that she made in the role as a *suruhana* or *techa*, I would go around with her.[54]

I asked Annie whether she currently practices these traditional customs passed down from her grandmother. She admits:

Not the application of medicine, which again is a contradiction on my part. At the time I saw them as something good ... it made people happy. She was about to revive some of them to the point where they felt good. But, when it came to me personally being ill, I told her I would rather die than take any of those medicines. The reason for that is I cannot take anything orally, not liquid medicines. I'll take tablets, capsules, injections but not liquid medicines. I would gag and throw up and so I said, "forget it." But I love the massaging part. And I believe in the value of that. I find it to be highly therapeutic, very relaxing. And the rubbing of the ointment, coconut oil, and that type of thing. I believe in the value of that. As far as the native medicinal herbs, I don't apply that to myself and I don't apply that to my children. But I respected her ability to administer them.[55]

Evidently Annie has not carried on the professions of *suruhana* nor *techa* as they were traditionally practiced by her grandmother. Nevertheless, both her career and voluntary activities reflect how she has transformed these traditional roles into modern forms of activism. Her church work mirrors the roles the *techa* performs, and her involvement as a social worker parallels the "psychological and emotional" healing practices of the *suruhana*.

It is not an accident that when Annie sought to establish a career following the dissolution of her marriage, she gravitated to the field of social work specifically to serve the elderly, using the skills that she learned early in life. Right after the divorce she began job hunting. Someone mentioned that the Retired Senior Volunteer Program (RSVP) was losing its director. She decided to "give it her best shot."[56] Annie Roberto became RSVP Director in 1979. She felt that working with seniors would be constructive and worthwhile. Her position gave her the incentive to identify ways in which able elderly could contribute to society and at the same time gain meaning and satisfaction from being involved.

This main task proved to be quite a challenge. The RSVP had been experiencing difficulties in getting local seniors to volunteer and then in sustaining their interest once they became involved. Annie undertook to examine the root of the problem. Guam's elderly were simply uninterested or lacked the skills necessary to participate in the types of voluntary activities which were successful in similar programs among other communities in the United States. The numbers of volunteers dwindled to the point at which the continuation of the program was jeopardized.

Annie labored over the best possible course of action to salvage the program. Aside from administrative concerns, an attractive project was required. Prior to becoming director, Annie had visited geriatric wards in several American hospitals and became personally acquainted with the desolate condition of infirm senior citizens. The situation on Guam was no different. In the interview Annie referred to an article which depicted the sad state of affairs for the elderly housed in the Extended Care Facility of the Guam Memorial Hospital. The writer conveys the loneliness and undesirable conditions which Annie resolved to address:

"*Kanta, kanta* (sing, sing)", the nurse coaxes.

The aged woman, tied into her bed, slowly stirs. She gasps to honor the nurse's commands and strains are heard of a Chamorro song from long ago.

Like her song, she is forgotten.

She is 1 of 33 elderly patients awaiting death within the drab confines of the Guam Memorial Hospital (GMH) Extended Care Facility.

Sometimes the wait is long. It is uneventful, and its results are always the same: "They will all die here," says a nurse assigned to the ward.

And what remains of life is "plain boring," says Dr. Sitkin, GMH administrator.

The ward serves as a Nursing home. It is full to the brim ... with a waiting list. A visit to the ward indicates that the Chamorro elder has lost his traditional role, victimized by Guam's cultural upheaval into "the modern world."

Their position of prestige as the family elder is vanishing before the aged's eyes. Instead, in many cases, they find themselves seldom visited or even vitually discarded.[57]

Initially, Annie casually inquired if a group of seniors from one of the Nutrition Centers for the Aged would like to visit the Extended Care Facility. They agreed and arrangements with the hospital staff were made. Annie relates:

I took at least 12 people and we went over there. All of them without exception were moved by what they saw. They had a chance to talk to some of the patients who were injured and they found out that some of them had friends who they thought had died a long time ago. Some of them even discovered that they had relatives and old neighbors that they had way back, and so they decided they wanted to come back and see these people again. And they wanted to come back not just to visit, but they wanted to find out if there was something that they could do to brighten the lives of these people. So, that was the best thing for me for taking them there because from that first trip there, they themselves came up with ideas they wanted to do.[58]

The casual visits eventually became a daily routine for different groups of seniors, who engaged in a variety of activities including singing, chatting, preparing delicacies and other forms of celebrating, praying, and even sewing gowns for the patients. Annie estimates that of all the projects RSVP undertook during her tenure, the geriatric ward visitations were the most rewarding for over a hundred volunteers that she gradually recruited. The project was also unusual when compared with other national programs for the elderly which were typically designed to make "seniors feel younger by putting them with children or productive people, but the trend was never to put them with their own age."[59] Guam provided a new model which was acknowledged by the State Program Director during his visit to the island as the only one of its kind.[60]

Other projects for senior volunteers were developed. Aside from the voluntary involvement of seniors at schools to teach various clerical tasks, they also planted indigenous medicinal plants at the University of Guam under the direction of the Department of Biology, participated in a genealogy workshop, and assisted in the production of a film entitled, "Climbing the Family Tree," which was aired in ten segments on public television.

Annie Roberto continues to volunteer privately at the geriatric ward. Although she no longer holds the position of RSVP Director, her current work as a social worker for the elderly keeps her in touch with many of the *manamko* and older resource persons that she has established rapport with through the years. Her profesional affiliations reflect her interests and ongoing commitment to carry on the work which she organized for RSVP. She has been a member of the Western Gerontological Association since 1979 and was appointed to the Guam Council of Senior Citizens from 1981 to 1983. She currently holds membership in the Chamorro Genealogical Society and the Guam Association of Social Workers.[61]

In addition to her professional involvements, Annie is also active in the Guam Symphony Society, the Guam Women's Club, the Civic Center Foundation of Guam, and most recently the Federation of Chamorro Women.[62] Of the latter she states:

They were looking for Chamorro women who were civic minded and where there could be a lobbying force for Chamorro women ... We should also take pride in our island. We shouldn't just take pride by paying lip service but also do something real, be a positive force in the community.[63]

Annie Roberto's activism gained momentum at a turning point in her life. Marriage, her chief occupation for over 20 years came to an abrupt end. Increasing numbers of women share a similar fate. Many are ill-equipped to deal with the pressures of single parenting and employment. Others, like Annie, are determined to survive. Annie utilized her skills acquired through an informal apprenticeship with her grandmother and through formal education to become "a positive force in the community." Commenting on her organizational work to date, she says:

Well, for one thing, it has made us aware I think that there are a lot of older people that are still useful. And we should tap these people for their resources.[64]

There are also personal reasons which motivate Annie to organize and volunteer.

I do voluntary work quite a bit on a personal basis when I have time. Well, it's not just a humble experience but it makes me, I guess, more appreciative of my life. I think there are times when I find myself feeling unfortunate or deprived of some things. And then I go over there [the geriatrics ward] and I see that there are people more unfortunate. That would boost my morale, make me feel better of myself when I'm feeling low and start feeling pretty sorry for myself. I go there and I see that my problems are nothing compared to their problems.[65]

She also comments:

> Insofar as my professional work is concerned, personal development is something that I put a big emphasis on. But also the emotional satisfaction that I get out of knowing that I've done something to brighten somebody else's life. And that's important to me ... I guess also the fact that I'm a mother, I like to believe that some day some of the things that I do for other people will be extended to my children when they find themselves in that position where they could use the help of somebody. You know that saying, the good you do to somebody will be returned to you not necessarily by the same person. It's something nice to believe in, to hold on to, that what you do in this world, the services that you've rendered are not really going to be a loss or unappreciated but that it will come back to you also in some way, shape, or form.[66]

The reflective mood captured in the above disclosures of Annie's thoughts characterizes her personality quite well. She is quiet and reserved, often pensive. She describes herself as being private, not social. Annie is not in the habit of throwing large parties or attending them unless this is obligatory. She remarks:

> Our family is just the same way. We don't go to any *fiestas* or have any *fiestas*. I just feel that since I have no plans to reciprocate, I really have no business accepting those invitations. So, if I want to go out for dinner, I just take myself out to dinner or call up an old friend, a lady friend, someone I'm comfortable with. And I've done this from time to time ... . Other than that, if somebody gets married and it's a very close member of the family or a very, very old friend, I'll go and attend the wedding reception. Normally what I do is give my contribution, extend my best wishes and just leave and go home.[67]

Nevertheless, when she needs assistance, Annie's natal family and close friends are on hand to provide whatever help is required. Her mother helps with childcare and household responsibilities. Annie describes her as:

> a very thoughtful type person, very solicitous and sensitive of other people's needs. So, when she sees and thinks that you might be able to use help she'll offer before you ask. And sometimes if she sees that something needs doing, she'll just go ahead and do it.[68]

The rest of her family is supportive in "a quiet sort of way."[69] This support system can be called upon whenever the need arises. For the most part, however, Annie prefers doing things on her own. This, she says, is a personal idiosyncrasy.

Some Concluding Observations

The case studies presented in this chapter illustrate a few noteworthy trends that are becoming increasingly prevalent among Chamorro women professionals. Education is a key factor in the lives of the preceding four subjects. They all began their careers with degrees obtained from American universities. All of them sought to further their education in the middle of their careers, after marriage and rearing their children. They consider their educational experiences to have been highly influential in the development of self-confidence and independence. Their scholastic training led to desirable career opportunities for each of them.

The professional careers represented in the case studies, i.e., educator and social worker, are traditionally female and have often been characterized as an extension of maternal roles into the public domain. While this depiction is by no means entirely false, Clotilde Gould, Pilar Lujan, Carmen Pearson, and Annie Roberto have defied the norm by going all the way to the top in these professions. Clearly, these women utilized the "so-called" female professions as a springboard for their activism and community leadership. The adaptive or creative strategies they employed to shape their professional careers and advance their personal and community goals and commitments further illustrate their effectiveness as organizers. An added incentive for their involvement, and one which has provided a substantial source of energy and commitment, is the personal satisfaction these organizers derive from their work. This discredits such popular notions as the "vacuous" volunteer or the selfless social "do-gooder", images that tend to trivialize the "public" work that women do.

The manner in which they have transformed traditional customs, values, and practices into workable modern strategies highlights their role as transitional figures in Guam's history. They have adapted and expanded traditional roles as they have seen fit, thus enabling themselves to transcend cultural limitations while at the same time actively preserving the Chamorro cultural values and practices which they accept. Their versatility and willingness to employ new coping mechanisms without breaking away from old ways has served to their great advantage.

Another factor, one which is evident in all of the case studies contained in this study, is the widespread support system available to each organizer. Clotilde, Pilar, Carmen, and Annie have drawn on their networks for assistance with childcare, household help, and occasionally for their organizing. As we turn to the next series of case studies, the utilization of these support networks will be examined more directly.

CHAPTER VI

WOMEN ORGANIZING THROUGH FORMAL

AND INFORMAL NETWORKS

Introduction

Chamorro women typically organize informally. To examine their organizational behavior strictly through their participation in formally structured groups would not only distort the nature of their involvement in the community, it would also ignore a substantial part of their contribution. The absence of Chamorro women in many formally structured organizations--like the AAUW, Guam Women's Club, Business and Professional Women's Club--has led some to conclude erroneously that Chamorro women lack organizational skills, public commitment, or the ability to work in groups. The five case studies presented thus far prove otherwise. Chamorro women do indeed join religious, political, social, professional, civic, and charitable organizations. Nevertheless, the number of Chamorro women represented in a wide range of secular formal organizations established on Guam, frequently with ties to parent organizations in the United States, is few. Several reasons have been offered by case study subjects themselves for the dearth of Chamorro female participation in such associations. Cultural and familial obligations preventing women from regular attendance at meetings is often cited as a cause for not joining. Another inhibiting factor is the dominance of non-Chamorros in these organizations. Church groups comprise the only formal affiliation for most of Guam's adult Chamorro female population. The activists participating in this study are exceptions.

Several factors influence participation. Younger women who have been exposed to formal organizations at school and through girls' clubs later become active joiners with greater frequency than those who have not. Professional women join organizations as a means of self-development. Local women rarely--though this is beginning to change--organize for themselves at the formal level. Of 57 women's organizations on Guam listed in the **1983 Directory of Women's Organizations on Guam,** only the Federation of Chamorro Women has been organized by Chamorro women for themselves.[1]

Hence, it is imperative that we look beyond formal organizations to more fully appreciate how and in what contexts Chamorro women organize through networks. Evidence that a rich organizing tradition is commonly neglected when only formal organizations are considered by researchers exists.[2]

One could point to a situation which arose on Guam in 1977 as a classic example. A well-financed pro-casino gambling campaign--backed by the Guam business community and off-island investors--was defeated by public referendum. This was due in large part to the efforts of the Christian Mothers of Guam who organized an islandwide anti-gambling movement. Reactions ranging from incredulity to grudging admiration were registered by the gambling proponents, who underestimated the organizing skills of a "handful of righteous women" working hand in hand with the clergy and the Governor. The first case study in this chapter features Elizabeth Arriola, one of two Chamorro women co-chairing the anti-gambling movement.

The existence of informal women's groups elsewhere organized around issues or to serve particular collective needs has been unequivocally established by much of the literature emerging from feminist studies. Kinship ties and other socially structured relationships have traditionally linked women together to form powerful support systems which could be drawn on for various types of assistance. The significance and potential of "female-bonding" and "sisterhood" have been largely overlooked by scholars until recently.[3] In fact all of the nine case study subjects were themselves unaware of the extent to which they utilized their own support systems as an effective organizational strategy.

Nevertheless, I contend that Chamorro women have developed highly successful strategies for carrying out culturally prescribed roles, such as the orchestration of all family celebrations, gatherings, and obligations. The managerial and organizational skills which have evolved with regard to the performance of these female tasks are manifested in all the case studies herein presented. The utilization of socially-structured informal and formal networks provides the central foci of the following case studies.

The next four subjects tap different subgroups of their support systems in their efforts to organize. Elizabeth Arriola, as pointed out earlier, used an islandwide, formal network to co-organize the anti-gambling movement. Ernestina Blas used an alumnae network to organize a tribute to the Sisters of Mercy on their 150 years founding anniversary. Geri Gutierrez employs familial and other social networks to organize informal activities. Delgadina Hiton sought assistance from village/neighborhood groups when she organized Brownie and Girl Scout troops in her locale. The experiences and strategies employed by these women may give us further insights into the nature of informal groups and social networks comprising the Chamorro women's support system and into how these serve as vehicles for organizing.

Elizabeth P. Arriola[4]

Senator Arriola, most widely recognized for her stand on issues affecting the family, fits the archtypal mold of a

Chamorro woman organizer quite well. She is a middle-aged mother of eight and a grandmother of two, who shares a number of common experiences with other case study subjects, particularly her peers.

The daughter of Vicente Borja Perez and Maria Guerrero Pangelinan, Elizabeth Perez was born on November 19, 1928. The oldest daughter in a family of six boys and three girls, Elizabeth was brought up by members of her maternal family.

> While my mother was having her other kids, I stayed with my grandmother and my aunt, who got married late in life, from about six months until I was 12 years old. So they influenced me a great deal. And she was the aunt who helped all over the place, not just my mother but the others also. She's still alive.[5]

Elizabeth has pleasant memories of childhood. Speaking of her mother's family she remembers:

> My mother's brothers were all brought up in the ranch. And the ranch is like an estate with my grandfather and all the sons tilling the soil and bringing the produce home. That's what I remember of them; it's really a happy type of thing. Them bringing all the produce and I being brought up by my grandmother and my aunt; it's like I was just there to get all the prize things from the ranch.[6]

Mr. Perez died when Elizabeth was only 11 years old leaving his wife with nine children to support. Shortly after her father's death, Elizabeth returned home to help her mother, who worked as a seamstress.

Like other Chamorro women organizers of her age cohort, Elizabeth had a strict Catholic upbringing. She experienced World War II as a teenager. Her education was also interrupted by the Japanese occupation.

In 1948 Elizabeth graduated salutatorian from George Washington Senior High School and then left Guam to pursue a Bachelor of Arts degree from Rosemont College in Pennsylvania. She was listed in **Who's Who Among Students in Colleges and Universities.** She holds a teaching certificate from the State of Pennsylvania and has subsequently attended a graduate class on drug education at the University of Guam.[7]

When Elizabeth returned to Guam in 1952, she embarked on a teaching career at the Academy of Our Lady of Guam. She was eager to expand her professional horizons. One opportunity which occurred shortly after her return was the formation of the AAUW Guam Chapter. Although Elizabeth is no longer active in the Association, she was one of seven or eight teachers who were charter members.[8]

At twenty-five years of age, Elizabeth married attorney Joaquin C. Arriola. The Arriolas established their residence in Tamuning where their three daughters and five sons--ranging in age from twenty-eight to ten years old--have been reared. Throughout his married life (the Arriolas are separated) Mr. Arriola was engaged in an active political career. He currently maintains a private legal practice.

The arrival of her children interrupted Elizabeth's teaching career. She recalls:

When I started having my children, I just quit. At that time, Loling, [here, the subject refers to me, the interviewer, by my nickname] I didn't think anyone was qualified to take care of my kids; so I stayed home. Every once in a while, like when they need a substitute for like a week, sometimes I make the effort to go. But I really didn't go back [to teaching] until maybe four or five years ago. That's when the kids are big now.[9]

Elizabeth P. Arriola

Elizabeth focused her time and attention on her family. Maternal obligations prevented her from becoming actively involved in community work. She points to another reason for her minimal involvement during this period in her life. In discussing whether her husband encouraged her to be active in the community she says:

> He was in some ways [supportive] and in some ways not. Because when you take in a lot of these things you're pretty much away from the family. But I always try to do what I was doing without being away from home for too long, or I wouldn't be away from home when he's there and all the kids are there in the evening. I try to have meetings in the afternoon. I know that he would not say, but I just feel that somehow [or maybe it's just me] that he is not very happy when I'm doing a lot of this. that's why I never do a lot at one time.[10]

The twenty plus years Elizabeth spent as a homemaker were not void of public service. On the contrary, she served appointed terms on both the Territorial Board of Education and the University Board of Regents. In addition, she has held office and membership in the PTA's of Father Duenas Memorial High School, Academy of Our Lady of Guam, Bishop Baumgartner Junior High School, Cathedral Grade School, and St. Anthony's and remains active in school projects involving her children. Elizabeth also contributed her services as a member of the Diocesan Board of Education.

Although her volunteer work was sporadic due to the priority she gives to the care of her family, she nevertheless found the time to engage in fundraising for schools, the Catholic Church, and charities. It was difficult to maintain regular membership in organizations, but she did join and contributed what she could to the Guam Memorial Hospital Volunteer Association, Beauty World (Guam) Ltd., Guam Beauty

Association, and the American Cancer Society. Elizabeth often assisted with church decorations and other parish projects.[11]

Organizing has been an integral part of Elizabeth's life since here childhood years. She recalls when she first started organizing:

> I think maybe even in grade school and early high school, I was always a president or secretary or something in the class. That's how it got started. Then when I came into the bigger things, it's always like I would become a member first and then graduate up that way.[12]

Elizabeth assumed a low-key posture while she was bringing up her children. Her activities were related to either her husband's work or her children.

Mr. Arriola, a successful politician served for many years in the Guam Legislature and was a Speaker of the House. As his spouse Elizabeth was called upon to organize political functions and participate in activities of the Democratic Party. In fact she became the first President of the Women's Democratic Club of Guam. For the most part, however, her involvement was limited to assisting her husband with his election campaigns.

The past decade has marked a turning point in Elizabeth Arriola's life. In the late seventies she returned to teaching, partly because her children no longer needed constant care, partly for personal reasons. Marital problems forced her to take stock of her life. She attributes her ability to cope to her faith:

> I always feel that my talent whatever, what little thing I have, my mind, whatever, is all a God given thing. And without acknowledging that, I wouldn't feel safe to venture out into anything. And now I think this is the sustaining thing with me.[13]

In the last few years Elizabeth's involvement in formal organizations has increased. She now belongs to the Citizens for a Decent Community, the Curcillos in Christianity, and the Christian Mothers Association in her parish.[14] Following her formal profession as a member in 1977, Elizabeth became the Tamuning representative to the Christian Mothers Islandwide Board. Subsequently elected President, she was asked by the Bishop of Guam to co-chair the Anti-Gambling Campaign with Mrs. Remedios Cruz. She remembers the role she and other Christian Mothers across the island played:

> Well, I remembered vividly when the Bishop called and asked if I would be willing to co-chair the campaign. And of course at that time I said, oh my gosh this is a big thing. It's too much, too big. But then, I think knowing in my own heart that I felt very strongly against this type of thing [gambling], I just was very glad. I didn't think there was going to be this big opposition that finally surfaced .... I knew then and there that it was going to be the Christian Mothers that was going to be the core of the organization.[15]

The established network of Christian Mothers in every parish in all of Guam's village communities was utilized to educate families concerning the detrimental effects of legalized casino gambling. The fear that organized crime would gain a foothold on Guam spurred a battalion of crusading mothers to urge their own families, relatives, neighbors, and friends to vote against gambling at the public referendum scheduled in April 1977. Mrs. Arriola and her colleagues organized a rally at the Agana Cathedral to initiate their campaign activities. She recalls that women including herself took over the pulpits on that day to plead for support from Sunday mass-goers. Political campaign strategies, such as home to home visits, were employed by the women. Mrs. Arriola, commenting on the success of the campaign, states:

You see what happens ... I think that's what makes it a
winner, because the church is there. And anytime you
are hitting faith and morals together, the other side is
bound to go down, especially I think in a Catholic
place like Guam.

Elizabeth prevailed on members of her support system, including her relatives, old classmates, political associates, teachers,
community activists, and most especially mothers like herself,
who were determined to protect their families.

Mrs. Arriola, Mrs. Cruz and the Christian Mothers
mobilized an extensive grassroots movement to resolve a problem which they defined as threatening to their families and to
the community. Long-established networks were tapped in a
very short period of time. This groundswell of support over-
came the opposition, despite its substantial budget and the
efforts of a consultant firm whose track record included legislation which legalized gambling in Atlantic City, New Jersey.
Mrs. Arriola and her network contributed significantly to the
efforts of numerous individuals and organized groups representing the churches, government, and the community which led to
the success of the anti-gambling campaign in the spring of 1977.

Besides the impact it had on the community, the anti-
gambling campaign marked a transition in Elizabeth Arriola's
own life. Her involvement became a catalyst for her subsequent
role as an island lawmaker. The negative effects of modernization on the moral climate of the island have been a growing
concern of Elizabeth's. She remarks:

Faith on Guam is very strong. But I'm getting a little
worried about the younger people. In other words, we
as homemakers and as wives and mothers, we have to
work harder to instill our children with the same type,
if not more so, of faith and religious convictions.
Because, today there's so many, many more

enticements out there to let us forget about faith and religion.[16]

Given the opportunity to organize, Elizabeth realized that she could and should do something to strengthen the moral fiber and improve the quality of life on Guam. She ran for public office in 1982 and is still serving in the Guam Legislature.

Senator Arriola assesses her primary motive for becoming a politician:

I really want to serve the people of Guam in the capacity not so much different as in the Christian Mothers or my other functions from other organizations. I just feel that you reach them more.[17]

While in office, she has introduced and supported legislation to strengthen the family and improve health and education.

Organizing has increased Senator Arriola's awareness of the values and resourcefulness that Guam's women have to offer each other.

When you organize, especially women, there are very many common things that we share. We have common problems, common joys and satisfactions. You learn a lot from them, how did they approach this problem within their own family.[18]

Female support groups which outlive specific organizational activities have continued without conscious effort. Still, their full potential has remained relatively untapped. At more informal levels, however, Elizabeth describes how such networks operate:

I see this working all the time. You have a charitable project. You tell it to one lady in the block, the next lady in the next block, and pretty soon this whole area will be aware of what's going on. In that way I think we help a lot. Who knows we may have the original ideas that we just somehow implant in the men's minds. And then they pick it up. The support always comes back. It's the women who support the men and their ideas. I've always had that feeling anyway.[19]

As we will see later, in the case study on Geri Guttierez for example, Chamorro women are often a valuable source of power "behind the throne." This was also true for Cecilia Bamba.

Ernestina T. Blas[20]

"When I die, I don't think that the Chamorro culture would cry."[21] This startling pronouncement was Tina's way of prefacing her remarks on how she views her Chamorro identity. For Tina Blas, personal identity is based neither on gender nor on culture. Rather, she sees herself simply as an independent person without any strings attached. She admits that she has been "westernized to a certain degree," but perceives her actions as neither Chamorro nor Western. She does not think in these terms. In her words, "I just do it because I do it."[22] Whatever the circumstances--whether sitting at her desk as a Staff Development Officer with the Department of Public Health and Social Services, managing her home and family, serving on community projects, or visiting her relatives in Agat--Tina asserts her independence.

Born in Saipan, now capital of the Commonwealth of the Northern Marianas, on March 1, 1944 to Antonio Pangelinan Tenorio and Ignacia Castro de la Cruz, Ernestina was the third of five Tenorio children. Her father, a carpenter, and his wife moved their young family to Guam after the United States reoccupied Guam in 1944. Both *Tan* Ignacia and *Tun* Antonio left their siblings in Saipan when they migrated along with other Chamorro families. Tina remembers that her family survived on their own in Guam, relying on neighbors and distant relatives to help for *fiestas* and other large family functions. The Tenorios eventually established their nuclear household in the southern village of Agat. It wasn't easy because relations between the pro-American Chamorros of Guam and Saipanese Chamorros, who were used by the Japanese to oversee Chamorro prisoners and workers on Guam, were antagonistic. This created immense hostility between Marianas Islanders evidence of which is still felt today.

Tina recalls a childhood incident which depicts her personality well even at such a young age:

My parents never left the island until I returned to Guam after getting my college education. That is when we went back to Saipan together. Thereafter, they made more frequent trips. They were very poor; my father worked to provide. And they put a lot of emphasis on providing us with our education. We really could not afford a Catholic education. But, they provided us a Catholic education. I remember, I make it a joke nowadays; you know I talked a lot even when I was a small kid. And if you may recall, the Mercy Sisters would charge 25 cents everytime you speak Chamorro or you chew betel nut or you chew gum. When we go to school, we go with our sack sandwiches for lunch and 10 cents for soup. I used to laugh at them because it doesn't matter how much they fine me, I cannot pay. So they finally caught up with me and made me write, I will not talk.[23]

In spite of the many pranks she conceived as a student, she did graduate from the Academy of Our Lady of Guam and proceeded to Milwaukee, Wisconsin where she obtained a degree in Nursing from Alverno College. Going abroad nurtured Tina's independent spirit and provided numerous opportunities to learn beyond the classroom. While in the United States she acquired the American value of self-reliance. Tina values her college experience and recognizes it as a turning point in her life.

For four years I struggled very hard to become a very independent person .... When I went away, I didn't have them [parents] to tell me what to do; so it's got to be me finding out my own path. It was difficult all those years that I was trying to find my way; I just became so independent. You better believe it was a lot of discovery. Which a lot of our women don't have an opportunity to do because they don't go away and they don't have to think for themselves. They will always be within the family. That could be the difference, and that's why I'm so ... really I don't know ... all I do know is it's me; it's coming from me.[24]

Her sense of self-confidence had developed while she was away from Guam. When she returned in 1967, Tina began speaking out and taking leadership roles. She describes this transformation:

I used to assist; I would just give my ideas and let somebody else run the show. By sitting back and watching I learned a lot and that is where my strength comes in .... I didn't really become a leader in the sense of being the person responsible for the specific task until I returned to Guam, and it started with my own commitment to make sure that there is a Guam Nurse's Association.[25]

This determined attitude has manifested itself in much of Tina's personal and professional life. Her career as a registered nurse and health professional was not compromised by her marriage at age twenty-seven to a widower, Frank F. Blas. Tina describes her husband as being:

Very active. Involved in community affairs through membership in District Commissioner's Council. Active in business organizations such as Guam Chamber of Commerce and the Marianas Business Alliance. Was actively involved with Jaycees before

40 ... . Regular church goer; one of the liturgy readers ... . Active in politics; elected four times as Senator to the Guam Legislature, and now serves as Lt. Governor of Guam, Life Member National Republican Party ... . Life Member, Air Force Association; Member Board of Director's, Guam Girl Scout Council.[26]

Frank and Tina, Frank's two older children, a grandchild, and a son and daughters from their own marriage live in Barrigada Heights. While she may be an independent career woman, Tina's number one priority is her family. She refuses to sacrifice the needs of her family for anything. She says:

I want to believe I am the manager of the house. I shop for food on a regular basis, cook at least one good meal a day, wash and iron clothes. I supervise the house cleaning done by the children. I provide support to family members. Nurse them when ill. Plus an array of other roles played by most mothers in any given household.[27]

Tina wants her children to:

Complete their college education; be responsible, mature and good citizens of Guam; be good practicing Roman Catholics; and be good parents to their children, if and when applicable.[28]

She has persistently budgeted her time and community involvements so that these do not compete with her responsibilities as a wife and mother.

Tina relies on her mother or sister for assistance with childcare from time to time. As soon as her son and daughter were old enough for day care, however, she relieved her family of the responsibility which she feels is hers to cope with. While Tina is a dedicated wife and mother, her manner of fulfilling

Ernestina T. Blas

these roles often defies convention. Perhaps the best example of how she personally challenges accepted norms is evident in her role as helpmate to her politician husband.

Here on Guam, when a spouse is active in politics, the opposite sex automatically becomes a very public supporter of that particular spouse who's running or who is elected into office. With me, I was never actively out there campaigning on behalf of my husband. It was something that Frank and I discussed before the first year that he decided to run for a senatorial seat back in 1972 or 1973. I had told him that being what I am, very honest, very vocal, I say what's in my heart. And I told him that I would be a terrible public supporter because I may be contradicting him, his belief, his point of view in some of the public issues. So, I told him that I would be his wife; I would take care of the family while he takes care of those other things. Even with public social functions, I rarely accompany him. He'd go unaccompanied primarily because I felt that my family needed me more than to accompany him to those functions. I have been criticized, let me tell you, I have been crticized by very close friends, relatives, very strong supporters of Frank because I'm not out there. At times to some I had responded my true feelings; to others, those I don't know very well, I just say yes, I have to try a little bit harder.[29]

Devotion to her career and family has not precluded Tina Blas' involvement in community affairs. However, she selects the activities carefully and weighs the value of her input prior to committing herself. She remarks:

Because I am a goal-oriented person, whatever activity I engage in, it must have a goal wherein objectives are developed and monitored to maintain my full support and active participation. Otherwise, I would resign from such. For me to become involved in any organization, I first must feel my way to see if I would be comfortable with the people and their goals. In this regards, my interest varies from time to time, depending on the availability of activities. When involved, however, I devote as much time as it takes to meeting stated objectives.[30]

These involvements span a range of interests. Past activities include membership in the Johnny Sablan Fan Club (Secretary), Sodality of Mary (Secretary, President), Young Territorial Party of Guam, Agat Youth Club (Advisor), Guam Nurses' Association (Secretary, Director-at-Large, Chairperson-Nurses Week), American Nurses Association, Guam Board of Nurse Examiners (Vice-Chair and Chairperson), American Cancer Society Board of Directors (Chairperson--Awards Banquet, Volunteer); and the Carbullido Elementary School PTA (Vice-President). Tina was also appointed to the Board of Trustees of the Guam Memorial Hospital. In that capacity she served as Secretary, Vice-Chairperson, and chair of several standing committees.[31] Tina is currently a member of the University of Guam Division of Nursing Education Advisory Committee, the Secretary of the San Vicente School PTA, the Treasurer of the Guam Council of Senior Citizens, and the newly elected Treasurer of the American Cancer Society.[32]

Most of Tina Blas' organizational work relates to her career as a health professional. Tina approaches whatever activity she is charged with organizing systematically. She describes several basic strategies which she employs:

I do my own thinking and then I put it down in writing because I cannot depend on my memory at any one time. If it's not in my calendar, then I'm sorry, you're not scheduled to be with me. But if it's down in my calendar, then I know my activities and I can follow it beautifully.[33]

Tina feels very strongly about "going by the book." Through her observations of committees at work, she has learned the true value of the written record. She says:

> My main problem is having people that are not truly committed to the end result. Part of my strategy is constant communication through meetings. However, before and until we accomplish the particular task, there is that continuation of meetings. In most instances, I like to record those meetings maybe not in the form of a real in-depth reporting meeting minutes but at least a recording of the essential decisions made during those meetings. That's basically why I do it; there's a constant follow through, knowing what further steps need to be done. That's my strategy in making sure that everything is followed through to the end.[34]

Working with people who are committed is very important to Tina. Discussing the difficulties of organizing, Tina uses an analogy to depict her views:

> Sometimes when the bottom falls out it becomes very difficult. Those are the things that concerns me when I accept something. That's why when I get people working with me I want them to be in full support and become involved. If you don't, one pedestal breaks then the whole shebang breaks down. You have to have a solid foundation in order for it to be effective.[35]

Tina cites the one exception to her usual organizational activities as the most successful event she has ever organized and as evidence that a solid foundation spells success. The activity was a tribute to the Religious Sisters of Mercy on the 150th anniversary of their founding. The Academy of Our Lady of Guam alumnae sponsored a mass and brunch to honor all the Mercy Sisters on Guam on December 6, 1981. While this activity differs in scope and nature from others discussed in the study, it provides one example of the way in which informal female networks, formed to accomplish particular tasks, can continue to exist as support groups for women even after specific objectives have been achieved. What makes this occasion such a special organizing endeavor for Tina can be better understood by looking at how it came to be, those who were involved, and why it was a personally satisfying experience.

Sometime in November 1981, Lina Calvo McDonald called Tina and told her she was contacting Academy alumnae in hopes of persuading representatives from each graduating class to help organize a tribute to the Sisters of Mercy. Lina asked Tina to represent her class of '63. The Sisters of Mercy had established the Academy of Our Lady of Guam and had been an integral part of the training and discipline of Academians since the first students enrolled in 1949. Tina agreed to help, feeling that it was a worthwhile cause. At an initial planning meeting Tina reports:

> They decided to have me become their Chairperson.
> I looked around very shy at first. I didn't really want
> to accept it because I didn't know most of the people
> that I was going to work with. But the strong voices
> coming from Lina, Faye Carbullido and of course
> Jane Aguon [a very close friend of Tina's] gave that
> solid foundation to accept the role because I felt that I
> had the support I needed.[36]

This core group of alumnae planned the Eucharistic liturgy and a luncheon, and they collected donations for gifts. Through a network which grew out of the initial planning meetings, Academians were contacted to participate. The celebration was a very moving tribute to former teachers. It also provided an opportunity for alumnae from all walks of life to re-establish bonds. From the grapevine the committee learned that the new Mercy Convent Chapel in Agana was in need of a tabernacle and sanctuary lamp. The Sisters received these and on a more practical level were also given serving platters.

For Tina Blas, the significance of this effort was magnified by the working relationships she established, especially with the core group of planners. She told me that they continue to keep in close contact. Nevertheless, when I asked Tina if she utilizes Networking as a regular strategy in her organizing, her first response was, "no." Tina prides herself on being self-sufficient. She does not like to rely on others. Depending on a support system seemed to go against the independent stance upon which she prides herself.

During the course of our discussion on Networking as a strategy, Tina acknowledged that she did not consciously think of it as a strategy but conceded that it is an effective means of achieving objectives.[37] She admits that a first step in organizing any project involves contacting the right people to get the job done.

That is basically how I do it. It is not that I think of it consciously. It is subconscious. I'm sure it is there because my mannerism in implementing any kind of task requires that kind of activity. But it is not a conscious effort.[38]

Tina has made it a practice not to involve her family in her organizational work. She does have a few close friends, like Jane Aguon, on whom she can count. Reflecting on how she has expanded this small group of reliable people, she states:

Now there have been a few instances wherein I would discover the talent of specific individuals, and I would encourage that individual to join me in other things and continue to tap their talents in that way.[39]

She notes that they are "mainly women."[40]

While Tina vows to make more conscious use of Networking as an organizational strategy, she does not view her network as a female support system. She replied in this way to the question, Are any of the activities you have organized women-centered?

> Yes, but at the time of involvement, I did not feel nor was consciously aware that they were women-centered activities. I became involved in organizations, functions, etc., based on their objectives and my personal assessment that I can be an active contributor to the success of the event and/or group experience.[41]

Tina Blas sums up her philosophy on the gender issue with another pronouncement: "I think by now you can pick up the fact that I'm not a women's libber at all. I fight for equal recognition for tasks accomplished, but I still like to be treated as a lady."[42] Tina--and for that matter, most Chamorro women--equate women's liberation with a loss of femininity or female identity. This is a main reason why Chamorro women choose not to identify themselves with the Women's Movement.

Geraldine T. Gutierrez[43]

> I feel that I've done a lot of organizing on my own very small scale that I think an average community organizer has not had the experiences to undertake. Truly I do not feel that my organizing has made any earth-shaking impacts, but I feel that a lot of earth-shaking good has come because of my organizing. That may sound contradictory, but it really isn't. What I'm trying to say is that I'm not up there on the top of organizing, but a lot of big organizers I don't think would have gone through with such flying colors without small organizers like myself and the tremendous effort of the people that work with me.[44]

Geraldine Joyce Chance Torres Gutierrez shares the strong Chamorro-Catholic heritage of young women on Guam who grew up during and after the Second World War. What distinguishes Geri from many Chamorro women in her age cohort is her orientation towards organizing. While there are those of Geri's age, like Carmen Pearson and Tina Blas, who are organizers at the structured/formal level, few have had the extensive experiences that Geri has had of organizing culturally prescribed or other informal activities. Usually such responsibilities are reserved for the "well-seasoned" older Chamorro woman.

Her personal background accounts for part of Geri's penchant for a form of organizing which is deeply rooted in the Chamorro system of reciprocal exchange and obligation. Geri is the third and youngest daughter of Felix Calvo Torres and Hannah Ann Flores Chance. Born on April 5, 1943, Geri, a fragile child, struggled for survival at a time of war and Japanese military occupation. Like all others who experienced World War II, the Torres family had its share of pain.

Don A. Farrell, writing on the events leading up to the defeat of Japanese forces and the reclaiming of Guam by U.S. military forces in 1944, describes an incident which altered the course of Geri's life.

The Manengon Death March

On July 12 [1944], the Japanese Command ordered that all the Chamorros be rounded up and herded into concentration camps on the eastern side of the island ... . Throughout the night they marched south then turned toward Barrigada. Arriving in Barrigada village early in the morning ... the marchers continued to Mangilao ... in the evening they headed for Maimai valley, where they were to spend several days before being ordered to move on to Manengon Valley, inland from Yona. Young men carried their grandmothers on their backs. The trails from Yona village to Manengon quickly turned to mud as the summer rains

201

Geraldine T. Gutierrez

began. Bare feet slipped, and women carrying babies fell to the ground. Japanese guards pounced quickly, slapping and kicking them to force them back into the line. Mrs. Hannah Chance Torres, carrying her baby daughter Geraldine, was beaten to death by a Japanese guard. Miss Mariquita Calvo Torres took the baby in her arms and made her way along the trail with the others.[45]

Mariquita Calvo Torres (Souder) is Geri's father's sister and my mother. Felix, Geri's father, and his three daughters moved in with his own parents, Jose M. and Maria C. Torres. After the war, the Torres family established their home in Agana Heights. Grandparents and aunts all played a role in bringing up Geri and her sisters. A close-knit extended family provided Geri with love, security, and guidance. Two of her kinswomen filled the maternal role, *Nana*, her paternal grandmother, and her Aunt Mariquita.

One thing I have to say about *Nana*, she was very very fair. She always made it a point to tell me about my grandmother, my grandfather [maternal grandparents], about my mother. Constantly she would tell me what a beautiful, beautiful person she was. I don't think a day of my growing up has ever gone by without *Nana* in one way or another giving me a reminder. If I did things well and she felt I was a credit to the way my mother was, she would bring it up; and if I didn't do things so well, she would tell me how my mother would have done it. My mother was always a constant shining example in my life.[46]

She continues:

Well, my father's family have always been very supportive, everyone. I'm especially close to my Aunt Tita [Mariquita]. She has really been like a second mother to me. At the time my mother was killed she was not yet married, she was still single. She was still living with my grandparents and my father. She played a very important and influential role in my family. As a matter of fact her children I regard as my own brother and sisters, not cousins. That is how close the relationship is. My father's family are very very close ... his sisters and brothers, and now that they're deceased, their wives and children. Even the children of my cousins are so close they're like sisters and brothers to my own children. I constantly pray that this closeness is always in the family because I don't think we could exist or we could have survived a lot of the trials and tribulations without the family being so clannish.[47]

"Growing up after the war was so different compared to the experiences my children have today," says Geri. "And memories can take forever to relate." She emphasizes that she learned from each member of the family. For example,

Tata, my grandfather, was a very generous person. He always told us what makes giving truly beautiful and meaningful is when the right hand gives not even the left hand should know about it. Also, that the true spirit of being Christian is being truthful. He would say, a person is only as good as his word. All of the family were very religious. We were taught the value and traditions of a good Christian family. Things like this I could never forget.[48]

"The strict upbringing of young ladies," is one example of how different things were. "We couldn't go out anywhere without a chaperone; you remember, Loling, I frequently had to take you with me," Geri recalls with amusement.[49]

Her two older sisters went to the United States for high school and college. Geri, on the other hand, attended St. Francis School, then went to high school at the Academy of Our

Lady. She graduated in 1961 and later took one year of course-work at the University of Guam. Just as Geri was prone to helping *Nana* with social obligations and family activities, she also assisted her father with paper work and book keeping for his retail business, from the time she was 13 years old. Geri's high school years marked a period of significant training. Besides being exposed to business operations, she learned the art of organizing through responsibilities delegated to her by *Nana*.

> Even before I was married, I used to help *Nana*.
> Family activities would be at her house [by this time
> *Tata* had passed away], and she would take care of the
> cooking and everything. But then she would rely on
> me to organize things, and this was when I was in high
> school. I think one of the main reasons I got involved
> was because none of them drove and I drove. I always
> ended up helping them. I think that has been very
> instrumental to me. Sure, at the time I looked on it as
> a pain. I didn't realize how much it would help me in
> later years, especially married to Carl.[50]

These apprenticeships helped to prepare Geri for her future roles, some of which were passed on to her when *Nana* died while others resulted from her marriage to Carl T.C. Gutierrez. Twenty-year old Geri married Carl, a Chamorro, who was serving as an Airman in the U.S. Air Force at the time. The couple stayed with *Nana* and Geri's father at the family home, which was given to Geri as a child.

During their early years of marriage, Geri worked in various accounting and book keeping positions for both private firms and the Government of Guam. Her participation in the labor force was interrupted for two years when, between 1966 and 1968, the first two Gutierrez children, a daughter and son, were born ten months apart. Geri resumed employment from 1968 to 1972, at which point she and Carl decided to establish their own business. Carlton Construction Company was opened, later followed by Carla's Beauty Shop. Geri became Vice-President and was responsible for office management.[51]

After *Nana's* death in 1973, with the help of her aunts Geri assumed a central role in keeping the Torres family traditions alive. One such tradition is *Nana's Nobenan Niño*, the novena to the infant Jesus at Christmas.

Every year we still have the novena at the house and at the last day of the novena [nine days], everybody gets together. It's a beautiful and very spiritual tradition and it is a reason, or an excuse if you want to call it that, for the family to get together. I hope that even if I should pass away, that my children and my grandchildren would carry it on because I truly feel that there's a very special need for a family to pray together.

This house is the official family house; so it is right that our family christenings, weddings, showers, other celebrations, and rosaries for the dead are held here.[52]

Felix Torres had by this time remarried and was again widowed. Another addition to the Torres family was Geri's half-brother Vincent. In 1975 Carl and Geri had their last child, another daughter.

A major turning point for the Gutierrez family occurred when Carl became interested in politics, a move that expanded Geri's organizing repertoire to include the political arena. Carl served as a two-term Speaker of the Guam Legislature. He is serving his eighth term as Senator and was President of the Constitutional Convention. "Being married to an active politician has placed added demands on whatever skills I have as an organizer," says Geri.[53]

The locus of Geri's organizing is her home. Managing a large household--at least three times the size of her nuclear family at any given time--operating the family business, and

organizing functions causes Geri to "change hats" constantly.
She describes what challenges a typical day might bring:

> A lot of the organizing that I do is family- oriented.
> They are functions that keep the family together like
> weddings, holiday get-togethers, wakes .... I entertain
> at an average of twice a week. If two weeks go by
> without my having a party of at least forty or fifty
> people that's a rare happening.
>
> Now that Carl is Speaker, we frequently host Legisla-
> tive functions here; only I don't have an official staff.
> It's not unusual for Carl's secretary to call me close to
> noon saying the Speaker is on his way home with
> fifteen guests for lunch. My motto is to be prepared.
> Of course a function for a thousand or more people
> takes a couple of days to organize. We also have
> fundraisers, some for political candidates, also for
> non-profit organizations. Right now I'm involved in a
> church fundraising. Our church needs a new roof.
> We've been serving meals every Sunday morning after
> mass. I prepare food and take it over. The biggest
> fundraisers we've had here have accommodated two
> to three thousand people. You know, Loling, this
> house is like Grand Central Station; there's something
> going on all the time. Aside from that, the payroll for
> Carlton employees might be due, the kids have
> projects, not to mention my obligations.[54]

Being involved in community projects is another aspect
of Geri's busy schedule. She has been active in formal organizations since her childhood. Past memberships have included the
Sodality of Mary, Girl Scouts, Territorial Party Youth Organization, and many school clubs. She has been active in the PTA's
of all the schools her children have attended. In addition, she
has been a Christian Mother since 1968. Voluntary work for
the American Cancer Society and the Guam Memorial Hospital
Volunteer Association augments her community service as

Chairperson of the Board of Directors of Awareness House and Training and Development Systems Incorporated, a non-profit organization which provides training and other needed programs for drug and alcohol rehabilitation. During election years, Geri actively campaigns for Carl. She has served as a member of the Provisional League of Women Voters and as Precinct Vice-President for the Democratic Club of Agana Heights.

Commenting on her community involvement, Geri remarks:

> It's only natural that I am involved. I come from a family of dedicated community volunteers. Although my mother died at age 27 she was an active businesswoman. Dad tells me she participated in fairs, fundraising projects, was a member of the Christian Mothers in Sumay. She sponsored and managed the Women's Athletic Club of Sumay. My father has always been active. Both Tita and *Nana* were involved. Tita, Carl, and other relatives are actively engaged in community work.[55]

> I organize activities for various reasons. Like for fundraisers, I organize them to meet a goal, to help out a friend or to help out the church, and political activities to help out a candidate. It doesn't necessarily have to be a fundraiser. I've organized just meetings where I just try to get people to come and listen to political candidates or just family functions to get family members together.

> ... It doesn't matter what activity, the strategy is basically the same.

> ... I may not seek out the same people, but I organize basically the same way. I decide who needs to be called in; I delegate responsibilities and follow through to make sure they're going to be there.[56]

> To try to organize something and to say that you're

going to do it all yourself is a nice thought, but it just doesn't work.[57]

As a rule there is a majority of the people that help me that I can call on for any type of activity.[58] I think that Networking as a strategy will be most useful to whomever is intelligent enough to realize that people need people. That's what it boils down to.[59]

I asked Geri to elaborate on who these people are and how she has developed her network. While she says it is hard to decide how to classify a particular individual because so many are relatives as well as *komadres* and the like, still there are "sub groupings" which she turns to depending on the activity to be organized.

First, there is the family--my father, sister, and brother when the need arises, Tita, and her family, Auntie Chong and her clan, Auntie Lina, Auntie Luisa, Auntie Cynthia and their families, cousins, and extended relatives on my paternal side especially regarding a family function.[60]

From my mother's side I get moral support more than anything because the only maternal family I have now is my grandmother who is 88 and my mother's sister who is getting along in years also. They're there with all the love I need; they're always there plugging for me in the most important times.[61]

Geri can also count on the support of friends from childhood.

I have a lot of childhood friends that are very supportive of me and my husband in his political life. Until this day, this is one reason why I enjoy campaigns. I enjoy going house to house. In fact a lot of politician's wives dread that. I actually enjoy it because I run into more people that I went to school with and they're so supportive. But, for a lot of the little things that I do have at home, I do have two very special friends that

I've gone to school with since I was in kindergarten.
We've kept in touch over the years. I think that
Vivian, Rosie, and I are just as close as before, if not
closer. We're really in the sense like sisters. We have
daughters of the same age and they're also close. And
that's really helpful plus our husbands are compatible.
And I think my family members have also taken them
in as family members.[62]

Another "sub-group" is comprised of Carl's relatives.

My husband's brothers are very close to Carl, especially Ralph. He and his wife are always there. He
comes from a very large family. His mother and sisters are very supportive of him politically. Mostly, I
rely on them for political functions or large family
activities. Carl's friends are there generally for political functions.[63]

Komadres and *kompadres* are also a significant source
of support. Geri and Carl have over a hundred godchildren. In
addition each of their children has Baptism and Confirmation
godparents. Some are closer to the Gutierrezes than others. Of
this "sub-group" Geri says:

A few of them are related to me. But most of them
are close friends. Some are very special, like *koma-
dren* Tita Paulino, who are really like family to me.
They are supportive of Carl and I in everything we
need support in. They are always there. They're there
to help put things together; they're there to clean up
afterwards and there to help financially.[64]

She points out that there are literally hundreds of other people
who are part of the Gutierrez network of reciprocal exchange
and obligation upon whom she can rely, usually for political
support or community work. Among them she lists the parents
of her children's friends, neighbors from Agana Heights as well
as Santa Rita where her father operated a market, business

associates, political acquaintances, and supporters of Carl.[65]

How does Geri utilize this network of support to organize?

> The minute I find out I've got to organize something, what goes through my mind is who's going to be responsible for this. Mama Tita is going to be taking care of decorating the table. Vivian is going to take care of the pastries. Rosie will be making the procurement after I take an inventory of what is needed. Uncle Pepe will prepare such and such, and so on down the line. The minute I plan a party all these things run through my mind and I've got everything down pat, just who's going to be responsible for what. To be an organizer you've got to be able to delegate responsibilities and to rely on people.[66]

"Absolutely" is Geri's response to the question, do you consciously use your support networks as a strategy for organizing? After planning out the tasks and identifying who is best suited for each thing that needs to be done, she elicits help.

> I never sit back and wait for people to come looking for me. I always appreciate it when people let me know that I'm needed. It's a good feeling and whenever I need anything, I never for one moment hesitate to let them know. My husband and his position in politics makes it just impossible for me to go day to day without these families. It's one thing right after the other. Nothing is planned long range. Even feeding a thousand people we can get together in three or four days. I could never do it without family and friends. There are just no words to express to you how much these people do for me. Of course I rely on different groups depending on what work I have, but there is always my circle of reliables that I turn to regularly.[67]

Assistance comes in many forms. Besides actually being present to help in the preparation of things, one can give *chinchule'* either in the form of money or food items--a case of chicken, couple cases of drinks, a ham, freshly caught crabs, vegetables from one's ranch. The possibilities are numerous. For this reason giving a party is not such a financial burden as everyone pitches in.[68]

The key to using such a system skillfully and advantageously lies in understanding the essential responsibilities and obligations linked to the benefits. Effective reciprocation is what makes the system work. Geri reciprocates the assistance given to her without fail.

It's a people to people network. It's reaching out and exchanging. I reciprocate. When these people have functions at the house, I'm not only there to help them, but quite a number of the things that are being prepared are prepared at my house by people that I employ or those I asked to come help me to prepare things. It's really a give and take proposition.[69]

Geri views organizing in this traditional way as a means of preserving Chamorro culture. She notes:

That is what the Chamorro culture is all about, the tremendous family togetherness.[70]

Compared to other organizers her age like Carmen Pearson or Tina Blas, Geri's preference for traditional organizational strategies may appear unusual. Her appreciation and utilization of this style of organizing may in part be due to her constant exposure to older women organizers in her family. She also spent her formative years, as a young adult, on Guam while Carmen and Tina went abroad for a secondary education where they acquired Western styles of organizing.

When I commented, during the interview, that her organizing seemed to revolve around food, Geri replied:

I don't know, maybe it's because I like to cook. I enjoy cooking. It is also the heart of the culture in a sense. At my house the kitchen is where we do our communicating. Many family problems are solved while chopping vegetables. It is especially nice because Carl likes to cook too.[71]

There are other advantages to organizing that she mentions:

For one thing you are overseeing everything. You can affect the outcome. There's also the good feeling you get when a goal to assist charities or the church is met. It's worth all the trouble you have to go through even if you end up having more corns under your feet than the whole state of Iowa.

I feel a sense of responsibility toward the community. I'm not always going to be around. My children are going to be in situations when we're not going to be around them. Or God knows we're not going to be on this earth forever, and for some reason I feel in my heart that somebody is going to look after my kids. I am convinced of that. As the good book says, "Whatever you sow, so shall you reap." I feel that if I try my best, my children will benefit.[72]

Because Geri and Carl are so active, I asked her to share perceptions on how her organizing has affected her family life. She says:

For all that I do, I still operate most of my activities from my home. A lot of times organizers feel that anything they do for their community takes away from their family life. I'm very fortunate that my children have grown up with this happening around them constantly and are part of it.[73]

At the same time, Geri observes changes in the way her own children view this system, which is so central to her life.

What saddens me is I see a change there. Even my
children, they're exposed to this all the time yet
they're not as willing to go early to somebody's party
to help as I myself remember doing as a little girl.
Maybe it's because when we were growing up, we
didn't question what our parents asked us to do or
expected of us half as much as our children do today.
I think it's a little loss of the culture as you go along.[74]

With increasing exposure to modern values and practices, young
people on Guam have a wider range of lifestyles and strategies
from which to choose. Their growing emphasis on personal
independence influences their perceptions about traditional
ways, which they consider restrictive. These differences in attitude between women in Geri's generation or older and those in
her children's generation illustrate the widening conflict between tradition and modernity in the lives of Chamorros.

Finally, she discusses her work in terms of what she
identifies as the top priority of most Chamorro women:

Chamorro women take pride in their homes and their
families. No matter what professional capacity they
have, their role of being a housewife, a mother, a
homemaker is still very very important and uppermost
in their lives. Chamorro women are also good organizers. Chamorro men very often tip their hats and
take the bows, but it's always the women that do the
organizing. They are fantastic organizers. Civic
minded, very community oriented. Let's face it,
Chamorro women are involved in every aspect of life.
We take such tremendous pride in what we do. I don't
feel that there are women anywhere in the United
States or in the world that take this kind of pride as do
Chamorro women.[75]

Delgadina P. Hiton

*Yangin taya affamaulekmo, ni un fan-apasi ti unmada-
lalak. Eyu mas impottanti i para unguaiya i bisinumo, i
para un gayafamulek taotao, un gaytiningo sa yangin-
taya lokui tininigomo, taya balimo.*[77]

You cannot buy with money what can be gained by
caring for people, especially your neighbors, says Delgadina
Perez Hiton. Having lived for seven decades, *Tan* Del insists
that relationships among people are the only enduring thing a
person can count on. Houses come and go. She uses her own
experience as an example. In Agana where she spent her youth,
the family lived in a thatched roof home which was destroyed by
American bombardment in 1944. After the war she lived in a
tin roof house, then from 1954 to 1962 in a quonset hut.
Typhoon Karen destroyed that too. In 1962 the Hitons built a
cement block house, which is her home today. Bonds with
people do not change so easily. This philosophy pervades Mrs.
Hiton's work as an active volunteer in her village of Yona.

Reared by "old fashioned" parents, she never imagined
while she was growing up that she would be doing the things she
does now, at her age. "A girl could never think of continuing
her education even if she wanted." Once she reached me-
narche, *Tan* Del's parents, Joaquin and Ana, "pulled her out of
school to care for her younger brothers and sisters." She was
the eldest living daughter of fourteen children.[78]

Delgadina had to quit school when she was in the fifth
grade. She learned to sew when she was ten. *Tan* Del remembers her youthful years as a continuous cycle of cooking, sewing,
and washing for her family. At night she went fishing to help
supplement the family diet.[79]

Girls had no alternative; they were homebound and
sheltered from the outside world. Mrs. Hiton is pleased and

relieved that time has changed this situation. "Nowadays women are free. Free to pursue an education, free to work and earn a salary, free to become what they want." She notes that women have entered such fields as medicine and politics. "Before, even if you wanted to go to school, you could only go up to the eighth grade. Now you can become a doctor."[80]

Tan Del married a Hawaiian, Nathaniel P. Hiton. They have three children and ten grandchildren, who are all grown. After the children were married and went off to live on their own, *Tan* Del decided she would do something she desired to do all her life. Encouraged by a public announcement in the paper inviting adults to return to school to pursue a high school diploma, *Tan* Del resolved she would take advantage of the opportunity and "nothing would stop her." She graduated from Trade School at the age of 60.[81] *Tan* Del proudly showed me the class ring she wears.

She admits going back to school took much courage, but her husband was very supportive. In addition she was highly motivated. "One has to believe in what you're doing. Look at my sister. She started going to school with me, but everytime her husband came back from work they told him she's at school. He asked my sister why she is going back to school to become President or Governor? He stopped her from going." *Tan* Del says she would not have stopped if she were in the same position as her sister. She remarks that if her sister really wanted to go, she should not have listened to her husband.[82]

Mr. and Mrs. Hiton had a very special relationship. Up until his death, they worked as a team. Both were active and they participated in many projects together. Mr. Hiton was a crane operator. When he was not working, he devoted many hours to the Holy Name Society, the Knights of Columbus, the Lions Club, Elks Club, Charleston Lodge Masonary, and to both the Girl Scout Council and Boy Scout Council.[83]

Delgadina P. Hiton

Mrs. Hiton's current activities are primarily church related. She has been active in the Christian Mothers Association in Yona since 1949. Besides serving in offices and attending meetings, *Tan* Del also decorates the *karosa* (float) for the annual procession of the village Patron Saint. She decorates the church for First Fridays and helps out with cleaning, cooking, and serving foods at special gatherings. As a *techa*, she leads the rosary in honor of Our Lady of Fatima in her block. In 1981 she was "professed" into the Third Order of St. Francis. Both religious groups visit the sick, plan programs for the patients in the Extended Care Facility at the hospital, and help out members especially when a death occurs. One practice observed through the years has been group rosaries at the home of the deceased or at church.[84] Mrs. Hiton says that women should make church related work their priority. In her own life she goes by the motto, "serve the Lord first, then your neighbor."[85]

Responsibilities as a mother and a wife plus her church work occupied Mrs. Hiton fully throughout the time her children were growing up. She has always tried to be a helpful neighbor and speaks very highly of the camaraderie that exists among the villagers of Yona.[86] It was not until 1970 that *Tan* Del expanded her involvement in the community in response to her granddaughter's desire to become a Brownie.

She remembers the early 70s as a turning point in her life. *Tan* Del went back to school. She and Mr. Hiton also decided that since Yona did not have a Brownie troop they would organize one. They jointly "led" the initial troop of 32 seven to nine year old girls through eleven years of scouting from Brownies, to Junior Scouts, Cadettes and then Senior Girl Scouts. Mrs. Hiton points to this period of organizing as the most personally meaningful. Her reason:

I started it because my granddaughter wanted to join the Girl Scouts, but because she is under age, I organized the Brownies for her.[87]

In addition, *Tan* Del felt that her newly acquired education together with what she learned and valued as a Chamorro woman could be imparted to the young girls in her neighborhood. So she and her husband contacted neighbors with young daughters who might be interested in joining Troop 32. Recruitment was successful. With the support of parents, these young girls were guided by Mr. and Mrs. Hiton. Outings, arts, crafts, visiting the sick, and attending island celebrations were all part of the program designed to teach youngsters civic responsibility, obedience, and discipline. Mrs. Hiton spoke of the responsiveness of "her scouts" in attending village functions and rosaries for the dead. Whenever there was a need, the scouts were ready to assist. *Tan* Del emphasizes that "one is never too old to learn." With the scouts she has done and seen many things that she never had the opportunity to do during her childhood. Witnessing "her scouts grow up to be responsible citizens on Guam" is more than adequate compensation for her efforts. She has numerous photographs and samples of the handiwork that she taught the girls of Troop 32.[88] Her work with the scouts helped her to cement relationships with families in the neighborhood. *Tan* Del points out that the respect and helpfulness that she and her husband attempted to instill in the scouts under their leadership are still evident today.

Tan Del does not think of the strategy she uses to organize at the village level as Networking. Nevertheless, her descriptions of the church and community activities she engages in provide ample evidence that neighborhood support systems actively operate in the village of Yona. The community joins together to help those in need especially during times of hardship.

Tan Delgadina Hiton's life gives quiet testimony to the strength, faith, and community-mindedness of Chamorro women. Despite the difficulties in her personal life due to a rigid upbringing and the hardships of war, she persistently strove to improve herself and has worked ever since in small ways for the betterment of her community. *Tan* Del speaks of one regret. "If I could, I'd rather work for pay. For housework you get nothing. At least you could look forward to a pay check every two weeks if you worked outside. Cleaning and washing gives me only one thing, tired limbs. In that sense, being seventy has its limits."[90]

Some Concluding Observations

Chamorro women organizers, as exemplified by my nine case study subjects depend on elaborate support systems, the core of which is the extended family. However, they are in most instances unaware either that they actively participate in Networking on a daily basis or that they systematically, though unconsciously, employ Networking as an organizing strategy.

Whether recognized or not, the Networking process is a common feature of social interaction. Webster's Ninth New Collegiate Dictionary defines Networking as the exchange of information or services among individuals, groups, or institutions. The Chamorro system of reciprocity employed by Chamorro women organizers easily accords with this definition. The support systems that the case study subjects described have additional significance in that they serve as concrete manifestations of essential aspects of Chamorro social structure. These subjects further demonstrate how kin-related and other social networks can be utilized in organizing.

The women's movement has contributed to a growing awareness among women that female networks are a vital resource which should be maximized for personal, political, or economic reasons.[91] Viewed in this context, the culturally established social networks which form a central part of the Chamorro woman's support system offer exciting possibilities. Recognizing the potential of such networks is a first step towards maximizing collective advantages.

Recently, Chamorro women in the United States have attempted formally to organize a Chamorro Women's network. Dr. Faye Untalan-Munoz, chief organizer of Famalaoan Inc., began contacting potential members nationwide as well as on Guam in 1980. By 1981 the network, which had grown to include 200 regular members all of whom were Chamorro women, held its first national conference in Long Beach, California. The goals of Famalaoan Inc. are: "community visibility, leadership development, advocacy and promotion of Chamorros, access to resources and power structure, and as a forum to promote cultural traditions."[92] This is one example of how the well developed traditional strategy of Networking can be adapted to serve modern needs.

Carol Kleiman in **Women's Networks** describes what she calls the "new wave of the eighties, women's networks."[93]

The past ten years have aroused the hunger among women to work with each other, says Dr. Rosabeth Moss Kanter, professor of sociology at Yale University. 'We hunger for contacts with one another. Women have left the isolation of their kitchens and are seeking the sisterhood they once had.' For women got together for sociability and comfort long before the network explosion of today .... But what is new today is the formation of networks with the expressed purpose of women helping women.[94]

Chamorro women have continuously participated in an unbroken tradition of informal Networking to help each other with family responsibilities and obligations. In fact their kitchens are often the "locus of operation" for kin and other social networks. It is here where young Chamorro girls get their sex education by eavesdropping on conversations about sexual practices among adult female relatives. Besides providing emotional reinforcement, these networks have been relied upon for childcare, physical and monetary assistance at family functions, community work, and organizing at all levels. The potential of this system of resources for serving specifically female-defined needs is immense. Chamorro women have yet to transform their informal strategies into formally organized women's networks for the specific purpose of helping women.

CHAPTER VII

NEW PERSPECTIVES ON THE CHAMORRO
FEMALE EXPERIENCE

The formulation of new perspectives on the historical and contemporary experience of Chamorro women on Guam marks another beginning. I do not pretend to conclude with a definitive statement on the position of Chamorro women. Rather, I offer insights from my own vantage points as a Chamorro woman and a feminist. What follows is the cumulative product of both my academic search for answers to the questions raised at the outset of this endeavor and of my personal search for a way of grappling with gender/culture contradictions. These last pages of the study focus on four inter-related themes.

The Historical Position of Chamorro Women:
Making Sense of Outsiders' Perspective

Etienne and Leacock offer this insight:

It is critical to clarify the fact that egalitarian relations between women and men are not an imported Western value and that, instead, the reverse is true. Egalitarian relations or at least mutually respectful relations were a living reality in much of the world in precolonial times, which was far from the case in Western culture.[1]

We know virtually nothing of how Chamorro women in the past perceived their own experience. Nevertheless, a reconstruction of "herstory" based on diverse accounts was attempted in Chapter III. These "outsiders'" observations have provided some insights about the roles and significance of Chamorro women in their culture.

Females--particularly elder women in the clan, who were married and mothers--were powerful in all spheres of ancient Chamorro society. Through a matrilineal kinship system, women exercised control over family life, property, and inheritance. They assumed a central role and possessed strong bargaining powers in their marriages. They were active in commerce and wielded great influence in district governing councils. Their esteemed status was also reflected in rituals, legends, and ceremonial events.

The high status Chamorro women enjoyed began to change with the introduction of Christianity and Spanish colonization of the Marianas. Both men and women were forced to relinquish many rights. The woman's responsibility for preserving the language, values, and cultural practices of the Chamorro people became crucial for Chamorro cultural survival. A virginity cult, double-standards, and patriarchal attitudes relegated women to the domestic sphere and subjected them to their husband's authority. These changes must have created tremendous internal struggle for Chamorro women, who once had control over their own lives. Nevertheless, the ancient Chamorro system, though subverted, was not obliterated by Spanish colonizers and missionaries.

Colonialism did succeed in lessening the direct involvement of women in island affairs. Their "formal" authority in the home was curtailed. The "demure Spanish lady" became a model whom all Chamorro girls were encouraged to emulate. New codes of behavior for good wives and daughters were promulgated by parish priests and taught at schools established for girls as early as the 1670s. Missionaries and Spanish administrators, then, institutionalized profoundly different role expectations with corollary gender-specific activities. As a result, the sexual division of labor became increasingly more specialized.

American control over Guam worsened the effects of colonization. The Chamorro practice of matrilineal descent with its concomitant privileges for women was officially abolished by U.S. Naval officials. By the first quarter of the twentieth century, many of the customs and values which favored women in ancient Chamorro society had been radically transformed. More restrictions and the imposition of yet another colonial system furthered the overall decline of status for Chamorros. Though women were adversely affected, they were nonetheless able to maintain control in the prescribed private domain of the family. By contrast Chamorro men lacked control in the public domain.

An essential component of Americanization has been modernization. Socializing forces such as an American system of education and the media, especially television, have been instrumental in remaking female "ideals" in the eyes of contemporary Chamorro women. A host of unfamiliar images have challenged their historical position of power. The more Chamorro women have accommodated to the expected roles of a good American housewife, the more alienated they have become from the beliefs and practices that have worked to their advantage in the past. This alienation caused by the clash between traditional and contemporary American culture is symptomatic of modernization and is becoming an increasingly characteristic reality for younger Chamorro women. Ironically, progress may prove to be the most significant threat thus far to the historically advantaged status of Chamorro women.

Contemporary Realities and Challenges: Insiders' Perspectives

Sherna Gluck reminds us that:

> No matter how we process the recorded interview, we must remember that we have created a unique "document" one which above all is oral/aural .... With our foremothers we are creating a new kind of women's history, a new kind of women's literature. To this task we should bring the sensitivity, respect, tremendous joy and excitement that comes from the awareness that we are not only creating new materials, but that we are also validating the lives of the women who preceded us and are forging direct links with our own past.[2]

The Chamorro women organizers participating in this study have spoken in a medley of voices. What they have shared about themselves lends continuity to "herstory." More importantly, these Chamorro women have recounted their perceptions about values and traditions which are important to them, cultural practices that they observe, and contributions which they have made. While this record has barely scratched the surface, it is a beginning step in bringing women out of hiding.

The in-depth case studies presented herein do afford readers a closer look at the Chamorro female experience from the perspectives of nine organizers. Despite the negative effects of modernization on their status, these Chamorro women have perpetuated many of their traditional cultural roles and have transformed them to meet modern circumstances.

Although the experiences of Cecilia Bamba, Clotilde Gould, Pilar Lujan, Carmen Pearson, Annie Roberto, Elizabeth Arriola, Tina Blas, Geri Gutierrez, and Delgadina Hiton cannot be generalized to include all Chamorro women, these subjects do represent a discernible segment of Guam's Chamorro female population. Typically, they are well-educated professionals over 40 years of age, who are married and have more than the average number of children. They come from large natal families with whom they keep close ties. Many of these women have been gainfully employed throughout their adult lives. They are residentially mobile. These women observe traditional cultural practices and have strong extended family relationships, especially with their maternal relatives. Their grandmothers, mothers, and other female relatives have served as role models in their lives. They are active at all levels of community life; many hold memberships in various religious, community, professional, and political organizations. Their concern for the welfare of their families, especially their children, has prompted these women to work toward reforms, support issues, and develop programs that improve the quality of life on Guam. Their values and behavior are influenced by their strict traditional upbringing. Yet, they have readily accommodated to change or directed change as they considered it necessary for the survival of their children and for the benefit of their families.

The personal testimonies of these Chamorro women organizers have contributed considerably to our knowledge of the actual experience of these women during both the traditional and modern periods in Guam history. As transitional figures, their lives were distinctly different from their mothers' lives, and different still from the lives of their daughters. For example, most of the subjects' mothers were housewives who had never been gainfully employed, nor were they highly educated. Their mothers' activities outside the home were limited to church work.

These women have been at the vanguard of change. Clearly their lives reflect both traditional and modern elements. These have been blended and are manifested in their organizational work. In their community activism they seek modern solutions but are motivated by traditional values.

The active involvement of Chamorro women organizers provides ample evidence of the continuity of traditional female roles on Guam. These Chamorro women, like their historical counterparts, placed great value on their maternal and marital roles. They managed their households, fulfilled family obligations, taught the Chamorro language and customs to their children, and were responsible for the religious training and moral well-being of family members. These responsibilities required subjects to be adaptable and innovative. Their familial responsibilities also took them outside the home, as they sought solutions to problems.

The record attests to their contributions as makers and shapers of island events and policies. For many subjects their own experiences reflected problems in the community, which became issues of concern leading to their activism. Some subjects were divorced; one was an abused spouse. They felt the effects of the generation gap between themselves and their children. These experiences eventually led to much of their advocacy work.

The subjects' background, personal faith, and involvement in religious activities illustrate the continued importance and influence of the Catholic Church in the lives of Chamorro women. Church activities and membership in church organizations provided most of the subjects with their first opportunities to organize. Through these nascent organizing efforts, they developed skills and strategies which they eventually applied to a wide range of organizational work. Aside from providing the training ground for their later activism in the community, the Church has also played a dominant role as the biggest institutionalized supporter of the values and traditions which subjects work to preserve through their organizational activities.

Another major influence for subjects was education. While a few subjects received only minimal education, most were very well-educated. They attributed their organizing styles and interests to their educational experiences. Those organizers who had received post-secondary education at American universities reflected the values and strategies they were exposed to in their work and in their attitudes.

Women who were educated on Guam showed a distinct preference for more traditional forms of involvement. Many who were educated in the United States adapted modern organizational strategies. Education also affected the types of involvement engaged in by women. Professional women tended to organize islandwide activities at a formal level. In contrast, women with less education more frequently organized informal activities at the village level.

Several factors of significance emerged from the material provided by Chamorro women organizers. Their lives illustrated the continuity of the roles Chamorro women have assumed throughout history. As in the past, the Catholic Church has been instrumental in shaping their values, providing a venue for training, and lending tremendous support to women. In addition, education has been of prime importance to their work. Subjects' motivations for organizing evolved out of their own experiences. As family values began to decline with modernization, these women saw the effects in their own families and in their relationships with their children. They experienced separation and divorce in their own lives. These and other problems stemming from the realities of their existence, coupled with their sense of responsibility for the preservation of Chamorro cultural traditions, provided the greatest impetus for their organizing.

Organizers clearly recognize that they could not have made their contributions to the community nor could they have engaged in their organizational work without the support and assistance of family members--their parents, siblings, other relatives, husbands, and children--friends, and professional associates. These networks of support were vitally important.

So much so, that they constituted the primary organizational strategy employed by Chamorro women organizers. In their accounts, subjects illuminated the nature of these relationships, which are central to their family life and work.

Two relationships were particularly significant to subjects, their relationships with their husbands and with female members of their family--either their mothers, grandmothers, or aunts. Strong female models in the family served to strengthen subjects' images of themselves as women. Most of the subjects could rely on their mothers, grandmothers, or sisters to assist them with childcare and household responsibilities. From these women they learned many of the traditional values and practices, which subsequently prepared subjects for many of their professional and organizational interests.

Undoubtedly, Chamorro women organizers enjoy a favorable status in the community as activists. Their relationships with their husbands also give us some insight about their status in relation to their male counterparts. Overall, marriage freed subjects from the restrictions imposed by their strict Catholic upbringing. However, through marriage subjects acquired enormous responsibilities. These were not strictly confined to husbands and children. As is customary, once married, subjects were expected to manage their families' participation in the reciprocal system of exchange and obligation among kin. As their responsibilities grew, so did their networks of support, which they drew on for assistance. The varying nature of the relationships with their husbands that organizers described reflects the wide range of husband-wife relations in Chamorro society. Some organizers felt that their possessive husbands prevented them from participating more freely in community life. Subjects often cited this as one reason why more Chamorro women are not actively involved in island affairs. While these stressful marital relationships did exist for some organizers, most of the subjects described their husbands as being extremely supportive and encouraging. Many husbands assisted with childcare. Others encouraged their wives to become partners in business and politics. One clear-cut pattern emerges from the case study material. With the exception of the two women who were divorced, all of the subjects attributed much of their successful involvement in island development to the support of their husbands. Apparently these subjects had strong, positive, egalitarian relationships with their spouses. Other subjects worked through their husbands to effect changes in public policy or community life.

In describing their relationships with their husbands, Chamorro women organizers help to clarify the male-female relations on Guam. Subjects were able to deal successfully with apparent contradictions between those roles stemming from their position of strength and power since ancient Chamorro times and the more recently instituted "Western traditional" subordinate roles, which also differ from their modern roles as independent women and activists in the community. Though these and other roles seemed to be contradictory, they were able to compartmentalize different roles in their lives and fulfill diverse expectations with relative ease. While this adaptive strategy may prove unacceptable to modern women who strive for consistency between their behavior and their beliefs, traditional women, as exemplified by the case study subjects, manipulated their roles and relationships to their advantage. They insured their freedom to participate actively in the public domain by emphasizing traditional values and traits. Thus, they were able to re-enter public life with only minimal struggles.

From the lives of these Chamorro women organizers, we gain a better understanding of the Chamorro woman's position in society. Subjects unequivocally establish that Chamorro women continue to be an active and influential force in Guam history. Modern trends have increasingly affected the cultural foundations which have shaped their contemporary status and roles. These transitional women serve a vital role in narrowing the gap between the past experience of Chamorro women and future possibilities.

Understanding Feminism in the Chamorro Context: Mixed Perspectives

Cesara asserts that:

As surely as I am alive at the writing of these words, I know that many women, one by one, will embark on the lonely journey of passing through their own valley of the blind, and one by one, they will find themselves questioning who they are, and discover that who they are is not to be found in any existing theory. Then, they too, will have to come out of hiding.[3]

Acknowledgment of the ancient cultural heritage of Chamorro women and of the subsequent effects of colonization constitutes the first step in the process of developing an understanding of feminism in the Chamorro context. Chamorro women have much in common with colonized women elsewhere, who have held esteemed positions in their indigenous cultures.

Ann M. Pescatello concludes her study of females in Iberian families, societies, and cultures with observations that are particularly relevant to the Chamorro woman's historical experience.

1) With such shifts from matriarchal to patriarchal power appurtenances such as bridegroom contributions of service degenerated into a bride price, and female promiscuity became subject to penalties as a hedge against lowering the value of a woman in these arrangements.

2) Laws and attitudes developed and spread with the patriarchal family, as did practices that seemed crucial to maintaining the external lines of authority and

patterns of behavior within a society. Yet, in practice, as we have seen, the female retained, almost consistently throughout time and in almost every place, a power often of equal disposition with the male ... in the figure of the mother and thus as "head" of the household, she has been the central figure of the family and thus in society.[4]

Pescatello points out that in pre-modern Western societies the family was the most significant social unit. It served as the center of nearly all social, political, and economic functions. The female was a major figure in these familial contexts. In contrast modern societies have caused the decline of female influence.[5]

3) To the extent to which societies acquire the ideas and the apparatus that we have associated with the post-Reformation, modern, industrial, capitalist, bourgeois culture is the extent to which the importance of the family, and thus of the female, declines in the public sphere. All of the functions that once had been the purview of the family have become subsumed by society's institutions. The personal control of the female has been eroded by the impersonal control of bureaucracies.[6]

The material presented in this study illustrates the validity of Pescatello's observations for the Chamorro case. In addition to causing the decline of female status, Spanish and American colonization profoundly affected the Chamorro psyche. A sense of disconnectedness with their ancient Chamorro past is directly linked to this colonial experience and is manifested in the aforementioned limited vision of history held by most Chamorros today.

Due to this narrow perspective, modernization has erroneously been viewed as a liberalizing force for women. The Chamorro female experience provides evidence to the contrary.

The position of contemporary Chamorro women has been shaped by centuries of struggle and adaptation. Whether or not Chamorro women today are consciously aware of their history, which predates what they define as "traditional," it nevertheless provides a legacy that has influenced their perceptions. Furthermore, an understanding of this historical heritage helps to illuminate some prevalent views about feminism held by the Chamorro women in this study.

The nine case study subjects privately and openly expressed anti-feminist sentiments, which have been echoed by other Chamorro women in their age cohorts. Their opinions are often summarized by the statement, "We don't need to be liberated." As women in transition, their life experiences reflect both traditional and modern trends. Yet, their reactions to the principles of feminism appear conservative. Their verbally expressed anti-feminist sentiments cannot be understood if taken at face value.

Terms such as feminism, the women's movement, women's liberation, freedom of choice, control over one's own body, and the attendant theories and academic constructs created to describe the female experience have to a great extent emerged from the specific experiences of Western, middle-class, educated women. Applying the "personal is political" philosophy of feminists to the Chamorro female experience, it becomes immediately apparent that at least for Chamorro women represented in this study, the popular cliches and images associated with the above conceptualizations do not necessarily reflect their experience.

Hence, some Chamorro women's perceptions about feminism and their reactions to it are influenced by different realities. Case study subjects remarked that they did not feel oppressed as women. Some noted that sexual discrimination did not exist on Guam. Others clearly expressed their desire to be treated like a lady. All of the organizers admired traditional feminine qualities and refused to identify with a philosophy which, they felt, espoused an androgynous existence.

Obviously, misconceptions about feminism abound and are perpetuated by patriarchal institutions on Guam as they are elsewhere. However unaware these Chamorro women may be of the diverse positions taken by Western feminists, their reactions are colored in part by the historically advantaged status Chamorro women have enjoyed. Thus, for some Chamorro women, there are other forms of oppression which need to be addressed.

With the development of consciousness regarding colonial oppression and the continuous effects of cultural imperialism, some Chamorro women are skeptical about feminism because it can become another imperialist tool. Cecilia Bamba articulated this position cogently.

There are other points of divergence between popular feminist views and those of the subjects. Social goals differ markedly. Unlike many American feminists who seek to radically alter established institutions and build a new society, some Chamorro women feel that traditional institutions through which women are able to wield power and authority should be preserved.

A classic point of departure between many Western feminists and most Chamorro women relates to fundamental differences in their attitudes about motherhood. Feminists generally view the child-bearing role as the source of female subordination. In contrast, the centrality of mothers in Chamorro culture and the power and authority linked with the maternal role make it difficult for Chamorro women, such as those in this study, to view motherhood as a source of oppression. Rather, it has been a traditional source of power and prestige for them. The socio-cultural context which assured the powerful position of mothers on Guam is changing. The experiences of younger mothers may be more akin to those of modern American women than to the experiences of middle-aged Chamorro women.

Subjects prefer not to be called feminists or women's libbers. Though their experiences and views do point to serious disagreement and conflict with the underlying assumptions of feminism (as they know it), Chamorro women organizers have been strong advocates of women's rights, the particulars of which reflect their own needs. Case study materials also show that their activism often converges with the types of advocacy engaged in by Western feminists. This suggests that just as female status is relative to culture and circumstance, the interpretations of the female experience, women's needs, and potential strategies, and solutions are also relative. In other words, while the end results may be similar, the means may vary.

I contend that the subjects of this study became active in the public sphere as their family life and status were threatened. Whether or not they attribute their activism and advocacy roles to a feminist consciousness, best represented by the philosophy "personal is political", their motivations for organizing clearly illustrate a grassroots commitment to feminist ideals. In attempting to preserve the Chamorro culture and insure a wholesome future for their children and the extended family, these women have instituted social reforms. They left the traditional confines of their homes and have re-entered the social-political mainstream without abandoning domestic values. They emphasized feminine traits in their approach to organizing. Despite their reluctance to be identified as feminists, these women are not estranged from feminist goals.

Modernization has had a homogenizing effect on traditional cultures. As modern trends become more characteristic of the life-style and values of young Chamorros, female perspectives on feminism will also change. It is highly probable that the daughters of these organizers will have different views. When Chamorro women begin to define their sense of worth in terms of personal autonomy, another major turning point in the Chamorro female experience will have occurred.

Concluding Recommendations: Future Perspectives

In the preceding pages I have tried to convey to readers a deeper understanding and appreciation of the Chamorro female experience. Through this endeavor, I have become more intimately aware of the necessity for Chamorros to document our experience as we see it and live it. Future possibilities for research are consequently enormous. Nonetheless, it may be more fruitful to limit my concluding recommendations to future perspectives relative to Chamorro women organizers.

Building on the data collected for this project, in-depth case studies of Chamorro women organizers engaged in traditional activities, organizers representing younger age cohorts, unmarried organizers, and less-educated and non-professional organizers would enhance our understanding of the diversity of experience among Chamorro women organizers. Comparative studies with other groups on Guam would be a next logical step. Such studies could explore possible similarities and differences between Chamorro women organizers and non-organizers, between female and male Chamorro organizers, and between organizers of different age groups and educational experiences.

Colonization and modernization have altered the ancient Chamorro social order beyond recognition. The emergent cultural imperatives have affected Chamorro men and women in different ways. These differences could be better understood through research designed to compare and analyze the roles, experiences, and perceptions of Chamorro women organizers with those of their husbands and/or brothers. The actual status of women can only be realistically measured relative to the status of men. Such a research endeavor could provide invaluable insights in this regard.

At another level, the status of Chamorro women is reflected in their roles as wives, mothers, managers of family finances, teachers, and as key figures in their communities, in the church, and within their extended families. The experiences of Chamorro women organizers show that modernization has effected changes in these traditional roles. The structural and cultural contexts which have legitimized and perpetuated a favorable status for Chamorro women are also being transformed by modernization. Against these shifting patterns, the lives of contemporary women of different generations have been diversely affected.

A cross-generational study comparing subjects with their daughters would highlight the nature and consequences of change between generations. This type of study could also explore the similarities and differences in perceptions about gender roles between subjects and their daughters.

Other research possibilities can be generated based on the strategies, involvements, and organizational activities of Chamorro women organizers. At a more practical level, I suggest that Chamorro women organizers can contribute significantly to Guam's future through a collective application of their activism. Chamorro women can and should transform the power they derive from traditional sources into viable modern strategies, it they are to recapture their former strength and favorable position in society. This will enable them to continue to effectively participate in and shape the direction of Guam's future development.

Recognition is a first step towards using any source of power in support of a cause. Chamorro women must themselves become conscious that the leadership positions they now hold can be employed constructively to achieve social, economic, and political goals, which they may collectively strive to attain.

The power of women to shape change is irrefutable. History provides ample evidence. Laura Thompson in her 1947 study of the first decades of American administration on Guam noted:

> The task of administrators in Guam would be easier, however, if they would bear in mind the importance of women in the Chamorro scheme for living, a fact which could be utilized much more than it is in the determination and implementation of policy and program, especially regarding the improvement of native welfare.[7]

The potential Thompson spoke of remains largely untapped even today. Nevertheless, a sterling record of successful organizing on the part of Chamorro women is woven through centuries of history. For example, they have been the most vociferous proponents of language rights, cultural conservation, preservation of the extended family system, and controlled economic growth. They united to fight against casino gambling and capital punishment and won. They have continuously organized to improve the quality of life on Guam for their children.

When viewed together, these seemingly isolated efforts take on new meaning. They manifest the rudiments of an informal, and as yet loosely structured, Chamorro women's movement. One that is rooted in the actual experience and needs of Chamorro women themselves. One might ask at this point what the underlying motives of an organized Chamorro women's movement would be.

Cultural survival has been the cornerstone of the Chamorro woman's position in society. Her multiple and often conflicting roles as culture-bearer, preserver of traditional values, and facilitator of change especially on behalf of her children, have involved her in all areas affecting her family life. Accordingly, she has contributed significantly to the island's development at many levels. The survival of Chamorro culture is of great concern to Chamorro women and undoubtedly provides a major motivation for organizing. The women in this study demonstrate this. In line with cultural survival, the protection and maintenance of the extended family as the most significant unit of society are also of fundamental importance to them. These concerns would most likely form the bedrock of an organized movement by Chamorro women.

In my opinion, the goal of political self-determination provides a unique challenge and opportunity for Chamorro women to coalesce and organize. The question of sovereignty is the key political issue in the Pacific in the 1980s. The former Micronesian territories held in trust by the United States have determined their relationships with each other and with the American Federal Government. Women have not been passive observers of these developments by any means. At the Pacific Women's Conference in Suva, Fiji in 1975, women from all quarters of the Pacific spoke out on issues of political rights, colonial oppression, and the nuclear waste issue. A call to action, a growing sentiment among many women's groups in the Pacific, was articulated by a New Zealander.

It may be said that Maori women are liberated in our own society. We are a powerful and effective voice among our own people. In the broader context of Pakeha society, however, our struggles are the struggles of all our people--to free ourselves of the burden of racism which threatens to engulf us. As we strive to liberate our men and children, so too, we liberate ourselves.[8]

A former Guam Senator, Mrs. Concepcion Cruz Barrett once said in an address to a women's political convention:

I am confident that properly organized women will continue their climb to political success. The time may come when men will say, the hand that rocks the cradle, rules the world.[9]

Perhaps it is too ambitious to aim for the world just yet. But an organized effort by Chamorro women in support of a political status alternative that would create the socio-economic environment conducive to the values and beliefs that are meaningful to the Chamorro people is not such a far-fetched possibility.

Guam is at the threshold of a new era in its political development. The people of Guam are finally coming to terms with our historical experience as a colonial territory, first as a Spanish colony then as an American colony. As such, they are demanding a change in their political relationship with the United States. A large segment of the island's population are on food stamps and a large percentage are welfare recipients. This dependency on sources outside of the family's ability to sustain itself economically, which is unquestionably a bi-product of the U.S. government's need to maintain control over economic and political development on Guam, has had a dramatic effect on how Chamorros perceive themselves, how they are perceived by American administrators (wards of the Federal Government), and the kind of self-image that is communicated to upcoming generations. A cultural identity crisis, loss of pride, and a dependent community are not the only problems the people of Guam face today. Crime, divorce, prices, housing costs, water and power rates are escalating at an alarming speed. The status of women and their ability to regain the strength and power that they have possessed are intrinsically related to the broader problems which Chamorros must resolve. To avoid the continued control and domination by outside forces which the people of Guam have experienced for nearly five hundred years under colonialism, Chamorros need to adopt a future course which will allow for economic self-sufficiency, humanitarian goals, and a climate in which the Chamorro language and culture can flourish.

This is where a women's movement could be crucial. Using the existing network of leadership and resources at their disposal, Chamorro women educators could mobilize the education system as a means of consciousness raising and awareness building of important issues facing the community both in the schools and through out reach programs. Female politicians and government administrators can collectively influence public policy. Most importantly, grassroots organizers can channel their activism to effect desired changes.

I view these possibilities as major milestones in achieving feminist scholar Ulla Olin's suggested role for women as co-managers of the public family. The organized involvement of Chamorro women is bound to affect Guam's social, economic, and political future. It will also testify to the quality and kind of leadership Chamorro women have to offer in the public sphere.

Table 61

Government of Guam Workforce Analysis for 1982-1983

Department/Agency	Administrators Officials		Professionals		Technicians	
	M	F	M	F	M	F
Dept. of Administration	6				68	83
Agency of Human Development	4	1	4	4		
Dept. of Agriculture	5	1	13	4		
Bur. of Budget & Mgt. Res.		2	14	7		
Bureau of Planning	5	1	6	3	2	2
Civil Service Commission	2	1	3	3		
Dept. of Commerce	4		8	4	2	4
Dept. of Corrections	2		6	2		
Dept. of Education	43	53	394	1,492	21	32
Dept. of Labor	9	3	11	15	6	2
Dept. of Land Mgmt.	5	1	5	17	10	
Dept. of Law	4	1	16	4	2	
Dept. of Parks & Recreation	5	1	3	1	3	
Dept. of Public Health and Social Services	8	23	11	46	14	33
Dept. of Public Safety	88	4	2	3	6	1
Dept. of Public Works	19	1	44	11	15	4
Dept. of Revenue and Taxation	12	4	12	3	1	2
Dept. of Voc. Rehab.	2	1	5	7	1	5
Dept. of Youth Affairs	5	1	3	4	4	4
Guam Airport Authority	8	2	2		2	3
Guam Community College	6		94	57	18	6
Guam Economic Dev. Agency	2		4	3		
Guam Educational Telecommunication Corporation	2			1	3	
Guam Election Commission	2					
Guam Energy Office	3		2	1		
Guam Environmental Protection Agency	3		10	4	11	
Guam Health Planning	1	1	3	3		
Guam Housing & Urban Renewal	9	1	2		16	18
Guam Housing Corporation	3	1				
Guam Memorial Hospital	9	8	38	136	42	53
Guam Power Authority	25	1	25	4	32	14
Guam Public Library		1	2	4	4	18
Guam Telephone Authority	7	2	7	7	52	10
Mental Health & Substance Abuse	3		7	2	1	
Office of Civil Defense	2		4	1		
Port Authority of Guam	11	3	6	2	10	10
Public Utility Agency	20	1	12		9	
University of Guam	16	10	125	84	20	30
Veterans Affairs	2					
Total	362	130	903	1,942	375	334
Percentage of M/F Employees within Occupational Categories	74%	26%	32%	68%	53%	47%

Source: Government of Guam, Civil Service Commission

CHAPTER NOTES

Chapter I

[1]This book is a revision of a previous work by the author entitled, New Perspectives on the Chamorro Female Experience: Case Studies of Nine Contemporary Chamorro Women Organizers, which was submitted as a doctoral dissertation in American Studies at the University of Hawaii, Manoa in 1985.

[2]See Alice Yun Chai, "Towards a Holistic Paradigm for Asian American Women's Studies: A Synthesis of Feminist Scholarship and Women of Color's Feminist Scholarship," **Working Paper #51** (1984); Leslie B. Curtin, **Status of Women: A Comparative Analysis of Twenty Developing Countries** (1982); Barbara Alpern Engel, "Introduction: Feminism and the Non-Western World," **Frontiers** (1984); Devaki Jain, "Can Feminism Be a Global Ideology?" **Quest** (1978); Sharon W. Tiffany, **Women, Work and Motherhood, The Power of Female Sexuality in the Workplace** (1982).

[3]Nancy Schrom Dye, "Clio's American Daughters," **The Prism of Sex** (Madison: The University of Wisconsin Press, 1979), pp. 16-17.

[4]Dye, p. 19.

[5]Tamara K. Hareven, **Anonymous Americans: Explorations in Nineteenth Century Social History** (Englewood Cliffs, New Jersey: Prentice-Hall, 1971), p. x.

[6]Dye, p. 19.

[7]Works consulted for a perspective on Women's History include: Rosemary and Joseph Agonito, "Resurrecting History's Forgotten Women: A Case Study from the Cheyenne Indians," **Frontiers** (1982); Mary Ritter Beard, **Women as Force in History** (1962); Nancy Cott, **The Bonds of Womanhood, "Women's Sphere" in New England**, 1780-1835 (1978); Nancy Cott and Elizabeth Pleck (eds.), **A Heritage of Her Own: Towards a New Social History of American Women** (1979); Natalie Zemon Davis, "Women's History in Transition: the European Case," **Feminist Studies** (1976); Nancy Schrom Dye, "Clio's American Daughters: Male History, Female Reality," **The Prism of Sex** (1979); Jo Feeman (ed.), **Women: A Feminist Perspective** (1979); Sherna Gluck, "What's So Special About Women? Women's Oral

History," **Frontiers** (1977); Mary S. Hartman and Lois W. Banner (eds.), **Clio's Consciousness Raised: New Perspectives on the History of Women** (1974); Abby Wettan Kleinbaum, "Women's History: Old Formulas Out," **New Direction for Women** (1984); Gerda Lerner (ed.), **Black Women in White America: A Documentary History** (1973), **Teaching Women's History** (1981), **The Female Experience, An American Documentary** (1977), **The Majority Finds Its Past** (1979), "The Necessity of History and the Professional Historian," **The Journal of American History** (1982); Jane Lewis, "Women, Lost and Found: The Impact of Feminism on History," **Male Studies Modified** (1981); Ruth Pierson and Alison Prentice, "Feminism and the Writing and Teaching of History," **Feminism in Canada: From Pressure to Politics** (1982); Mary Ryan, "The Power of Women's Networks: A Case Study of Female Reform in Antebellum America," **Feminist Studies** (1979); Jane Tibbetts Schulenburg, "Clio's European Daughters: Myoptic Modes of Perception," **Prism of Sex** (1979); Barbara Sicherman et al., **Recent United States Scholarship on the History of Women** (1980); Hilda Smith, "Feminism and the Methodology of Women's History," **Liberating Women's History: Theoretical and Critical Essays** (1976); Catherine Stimpson, "Gerda Lerner on the Future of Our Past," **Ms. Magazine** (1981); and Judith Walkowitz, "Politics and Culture in Women's History: A Symposium," **Feminist Studies** (1980). Barbara Sicherman et al. provide an excellent review of sources on the history of women by American scholars. See also Joan Kelly, **Women, History and Theory, The Essays of Joan Kelly** (Chicago: The University of Chicago Press, 1984).

[8]Gerda Lerner, **The Majority Finds Its Past Placing Women in History.** (New York: Oxford University Press, 1979), p. 14.

[9]Lerner, **The Majority** ..., p. 10.

[10]Ibid.

[11]Ibid., p. 11.

[12]Ibid., p. 12.

[13]Ibid., p. 13.

[14]Lerner, **Teaching Women's History**, p. 20.

[15]For a more in-depth discussion of these approaches, see Gerda Lerner, "Placing Women in History: Definitions and Challenges" in **The Majority Finds Its Past**, pp. 145-159.

[16]L. L. Langness and Gelya Frank, **Lives: An Anthropological**

Approach to Biography (Novato, California: Chandler & Sharp Publishers, Inc., 1981). For further discussion of the use of life/oral history as a methodology, also see Lynn Z. Bloom, "Listen! Women Speaking," **Frontiers** (1977); Susan H. Armitage, "The Next Step," **Frontiers** (1983); Willa Baum, **Oral History for the Local Historical Society** (1975); Cindy Cohen, "Building Multicultural and Intergenerational Networks Through Oral History," **Frontiers** (1983); Cullum Davis et al., **Oral History From Tape to Tape** (1977); Amelia R. Fry, "Suffragist Alice Paul's Memoirs: Pros and Cons of Oral History," **Frontiers** (1977); Norman Hoyle, "Oral History," **Library Trends** (1972); Joan Jensen et al., "Family History and Oral History," **Frontiers** (1977); Corrine Azen Krause, "Grandmothers, Mothers and Daughters: An Oral History Study of Ethnicity, Mental Health and Continuity of Three Generations of Jewish, Italian and Slavic-American Women" (n.d.); L.L. Langness, **The Life History in Anthropological Science** (1965); Oscar Lewis, **La Vida** (1966); Ann Oakley, "Interviewing Women: A Contradiction in Terms," **Doing Feminist Research** (1981); Barbara Rubin and Doris Freidensohn, "Daughters Interview Mothers: The Questions," **Women's Studies Quarterly** (1981); Margaret Strobel, "Doing Oral History as an Outsider," **Frontiers** (1977); Sherry Thomas, "Digging Beneath the Surface: Oral History Techniques, **Frontiers** (1983); and Mary Sheridan, "The Life History Method," **Lives: Chinese Working Women** (Bloomington: Indiana University Press, 1984).

[17]Langness and Frank, Lives ..., p. 1.

[18]Ibid., p. 24.

[19]See Claire Robertson, "In Pursuit of Life Histories: The Problem of Bias," **Frontiers** (University of Colorado, Women's Studies Program, V.2, N.2, 1983), p. 63 and Kenneth Fuge, "Problems of Oral History in the Pacific," Paper presented at Third National Conference sponsored by the National Association for Asia and Pacific American Education, Honolulu, Hawaii, April 24, 1981, for a more detailed discussion of the merits and difficulties in using life histories to study nonliterate peoples.

[20]Excellent examples of such studies include: Sue Armitage et al., "Black Women and their Communities in Colorado," **Frontiers** (1977); Alice Chai, "A Picture Bride from Korea: The Life History of a Korean American Woman in Hawaii," **Bridge: An Asian American Perspective** (1978), "Korean Women in Hawaii 1903-1945," **Women in New Worlds** (1981), "The Life History of an Early Korean Immigrant Woman in Hawaii," **The Woman**

Studies Program Working Papers Series (1978); Robert and Jane Hallowell Cole, **Women of Crisis: Lives of Struggle and Hope** (1978); Mary Elmendorf, **Nine Mayan Women, A Village Faces Change** (1976); Sherna Gluck, **From Parlor to Prison, Five American Suffragists Talk About Their Lives** (1976); Youngsook Kim Harvey, **Six Korean Women, The Socialization of Shamans** (1978); Virginia Kearns, **Women and the Ancestors, Black Karib Kinship and Ritual** (1983); Jane Holden Kelly, **Yaqui Women Contemporary Life Histories** (1978); Akemi Kikumura, **Through Harsh Winters: The Life of Japanese Immigrant Woman** (1981); Frank Linderman, **Pretty Shield: Medicine Woman of the Crows** (1972); Alice and Straughton Lynd, **Rank and File, Personal Histories of Working Class Organizers** (1973); Anica Vesel Mander, **Bloodties: A Woman's History** (1976); Yolanda and Robert F. Murphy, **Women of the Forest** (1974); Denise Paulme (ed.), **Women of Tropical Africa** (1974); Marjorie Shostak, **Nisa, The Life and Words of a ¡Kung Woman** (1981); Amrit Wilson, **Finding a Voice, Asian Women in Britain** (1978); and Beverly Hungry Wolf, **The Ways of My Grandmothers** (1980).

[21]Sherna Gluck, "What's So Special About Women? Women's Oral History," **Frontiers** (University of Colorado, Women's Studies Program, V.2, N.2, 1977), p. 3.

[22]Lynn Z. Bloom, "Listen! Women Speaking," **Frontiers** (University of Colorado, Women's Studies Program, V.2, N.2, 1977), p. 1.

[23]Tamara Hareven, **Anonymous Americans...**, p. ix.

[24]Hareven, p. 99.

Chapter II

[1]For more detailed information on the history of Guam, see Charles Beardsley, **Guam Past and Present** (1964); Paul Carano and Pedro C. Sanchez, **A Complete History of Guam** (1964); Francisco Garcia, "First History of Guam" (translated from the Spanish and serialized in the **Guam Recorder**, (1936-1939); and Laura Thompson, **Guam and Its People** (1947).

[2]"Its Creation, *Nanajuyong*", **Guam U.S.A., Gateway to Micronesia** (Agana, Guam: Guam Visitors Bureau, n.d.), p. 5. Other versions of this legend are available in various anthologies and history books on Guam. The basic components, however, are similar in all accounts. There is another legend of creation which attributes the origin of people to the work of the god

of winds, waves and fire, Chaifi. This legend includes concepts such as hell or *sasalaguan* and the human soul, which indicate some Christian influences; hence the rationale for my selection.

[3]Douglas Oliver, **The Pacific Islands** (New York: Doubleday and Company, Inc., 1961), p. 334.

[4]Antonio Pigafetta, **Magellan's Voyage**, V. I (translated and edited by R. A. Skelton; New Haven and London, Yale University Press, 1969), p. 60.

[5]"Characteristics of the Natives of Guam when the First Settlement was Established by the Spanish," the **Guam Recorder** (January 1930), p. 188.

[6]Jane H. Underwood, "Population History of Guam: Context of Microevolution," **Micronesica**, V. 9, No.1 (July 1973), pp. 16-17.

[7]Underwood, pp. 15, 20.

[8]Paul Carano and Pedro C. Sanchez, **A Complete History of Guam** (Tokyo: Charles E. Tuttle Company, 1964), p. 86.

[9]Carano and Sanchez, p. 175.

[10]I disagree with the position Carano and Sanchez have taken in their dated work. Describing Guam's cultural evolution up to this point in its history, they stated:

"Because Guam is isolated from the rest of the world by vast stretches of the Pacific Ocean, its history, at least until World War II, was one of physical and cultural stagnation" (p. 1).

This view perpetuates the notion that the significant aspects of our history are linked to Guam's strategic role in military operations of the Second World War, the Korean War, and Vietnam. It also supports the erroneous conclusion that we have no "real history" outside of our relationship with Western powers.

[11]Carano and Sanchez, see pp. 267-318.

[12]Department of Commerce, **Guam Annual Economic Review 1981** (Agana, Guam: Government of Guam, August 1981), pp. 28-29.

[13]Department of Commerce, p. 50.

[14]Robert A. Underwood, "The Role of Mass Media in Small Pacific Societies: The Case of Guam", **Panorama, The Guam Tribune** (Agana, Guam: V. 1, No. 47, Part II, August 26, 1983), pp. 12C-13C.

[15]Robert A. Underwood, Part I, August 19, 1983, p. 5A.

[16]Bureau of Planning, Government of Guam, **Guam Comprehensive Development Plan** (Agana, Guam: Government of Guam, 1978), pp. 71-72.

[17]The Organization of People for Indigenous Rights (OPI-R) is a political grassroots organization which was formed in 1981 in response to political status changes being called for by the Chamorro population on Guam. OPI-R is devoted to facilitating all means by which Chamorro self-determination can be exercised. The group has represented Chamorro aspirations and indigenous views in numerous forums including the United Nations Committee Hearings on Decolonization and Non Self-governing Territories.

Chapter III

[1]Laura Thompson, **The Native Culture of the Marianas Islands**, Bernice P. Bishop Museum Bulletin 185 (Honolulu Bishop Museum, 1945), pp. 15-16.

[2]Anita Johnston, "The Ethnic Identity Experience of Chamorro Women," Diss. The California School of Professional Psychology, 1980, p. 46.

[3]Thompson, **The Native Culture**. . . , p. 16.

[4]Douglas Oliver, **The Pacific Islands** (New York: Doubleday and Company, Inc., 1961), p. 335.

[5]Francisco Garcia, "Life and Martyrdom of the Venerable Father Diego Luis de Sanvitores, First Missionary to the Mariana Islands and the Happenings in these Islands from the year 1668 until the year 1681," trans. Margaret M. Higgins, in the **Guam Recorder** (April 1937), p. 39.

[6]Des Graz Manuscript, trans. Robert D. Craig, pp. 17-18. This document is located in the Guam Room of the Nieves Flores Memorial Library, Agana, Guam.

[7]Des Graz Manuscript, p. 23.

[8]Antoine-Alfred Marche, **The Mariana Islands 1887-1889** trans. Sylvia E. Cheng and ed. Robert D. Craig (Guam: Micronesian Area Research Center, 1982), p. 4.

[9]Des Graz Manuscript, p. 17.

[10]William E. Safford, **A Year on the Island of Guam Extracts from the Notebook of a Naturalist on the Island of Guam, 1899-1900** (TS), p.61.

This document is located in the Guam Room of the Nieves Flores Memorial Library, Agana, Guam.

[11]Laura Thompson, **Guam and Its People** (Princeton, N.J.: Princeton University Press, 1947), pp. 259-261.

[12]Thompson, **Guam and Its People**, p. 262.

[13]Charles Beardsley, **Guam Past and Present** (Tokyo: Charles E. Tuttle Company, 1964), pp. 65-66.

[14]Marjorie Driver (trans. and ed.) **Fray Juan Pobre de Zamara and His Account of the Mariana Islands 1602**, MARC Working Paper #40 (Guam: Micronesian Area Research Center, 1983), p. 35.

[15]Francisco Garcia, "**Life and Martyrdom ...**" (May 1937), pp. 18-19.

[16]Charles Le Gobien, **History of the Mariana Islands** (Paris: n.p., 1700), pp. 8-9.

[17]Larry A. Lawcock, "Guam Women: A Hasty History," **Women of Guam** (Guam: The Guam Women's Conference, 1977), p. 11.

[18]Le Gobien, **History of the Mariana Islands**, p. 124.

[19]Francisco Garcia, "**Life and Martyrdom ...**" (April 1939), p. 41.

[20]Sister Joanne Poehlman, "Culture Change and Identity among Chamorro Women of Guam," Diss. University of Minnesota, 1979, p. 70.

[21]The Civil Code of the Territory of Guam 1970 (V.I, Section 64), p. 17.

[22]The Civil Code ... (V.I, Section 103), p. 24.

[23]The Civil Code ... (V.I, Section 156), p. 34.

[24]The Civil Code ... (V.I), pp. 13-40 and (V.IV), pp. 238-249.

[25]Personal interview with Anthony Ramirez, 22 July 1983.

[26]Marjorie Driver, "The Account of a Descalced Friar's Stay in the Islands of the Ladrones," **The Guam Tribune**, Panorama, 19 August 1983, p. 3A.

[27]Driver, **Fray Juan Pobre ...** , p. 31.

[28]Francisco Garcia, "**Life and Martyrdom ...**" (May 1937), p. 18.

[29]See Beardsley, **Guam Past and Present** (1964); Teresa del Valle,

Social and Cultural Change in the Community of Umatac, Southern Guam (Agana, Guam: Micronesian Area Research Center, 1979); Faye Untalan-Munoz, "Family Life Patterns of Pacific Islanders," Women of Guam (1977); and Laura Thompson,Guam and Its People (1947).

[30]Poehlman, "Culture Change ...," p. 60.

[31]Genevieve Ploke, "Guam Productivity Is Tops in the World," Pacific Profile V.II, January 1964, p. 12.

[32]Poehlman, "Culture Change ...," p. 72.

[33]Poehlman, p. 80.

[34]William Haswell, Remarks on a Voyage in 1801 to the Islands of Guam (Historical Collections of the Essex Institute, 1917), p. 167.

[35]Personal interview with Anthony Ramirez, 22 July 1983.

[36]Poehlman, "Culture Change ...," p. 146.

[37]Poehlman, p. 146.

[38]William C. Repetti, "Miscellany," The Catholic Historical Review (The Catholic University of America Press, V. XXXI, N.4, January 1946), p. 435.

[39]Felipe de la Corte, A Report by Governor Felipe de la Corte of the Marianas, 1870 (TS), p. 116. This document is located in the Guam Room of the Nieves Flores Memorial Library, Agana, Guam.

[40]Des Graz Manuscript, p. 19.

[41]Lawcock, "Guam Women ...," p. 11.

[42]"Whalers in Guam in 1850," Guam Recorder (July 1925), p. 140.

[43]Beardsley, Guam Past and Present, p. 79.

[44]Safford, A Year on the Island of Guam, pp. 142-143.

[45]Guam Women's Conference, Final Report-Nihi Ta Fandana Famalaoan Guam (Agana, Guam: Guam Women's Conference, 1977), p. 25.

[46]Driver, "The Account of a Descalced Friar's Stay ...," p. 3A.

[47]Ann Marie G Pobutsky, "Suruhanas: Women Herbalists of Guam," The Guam Tribune, Panorama, 8 July 1983, p. 4A.

[48]Driver, Fray Juan Pobre ..., p. 41.

[49]Lawcock, "Guam Women ...," p. 7.

[50]Lawcock, p. 7.

[51]de la Corte, **A Report** ..., p. 49.

[52]Poehlman, "Culture Change ... , pp. 62-64.

[53]Thompson, **The Native Culture** ... , p. 27.

[54]Marche, **The Mariana Islands** ..., p. 2.

[55]Frederick J. Nelson, "Lieutenant William E. Safford, Guam's First Lieutenant Governor" (n.p., n.d.), p. 10.

[56]Laura Thompson, "The Women of Guam," **Asia and the Americas** (September 1944), p. 415.

[57]Safford, **A Year on the Island of Guam**, pp. 35, 38, 54, 58, 78, 85, 98, 122, 131, 139, 174.

[58]Thompson, **The Native Culture** ..., p. 18.

[59]Lawcock, "Guam Women ...," p. 7.

[60]Le Gobien, **History of the Mariana Islands**, p. 117.

[61]Francisco Garcia, "Life and Martyrdom ...," (May 1939), p. 79.

[62]Beardsley, **Guam Past and Present**, p. 163.

[63]Lawcock, "Guam Women ...," p. 10.

[64]Laura Thompson, "Crisis on Guam," **Far Eastern Quarterly** (V. 1, November 1946), p. 7.

[65]Safford, **A Year on the Island of Guam**, pp. 38, 70, 77, 149, 175.

[66]"Women in Guam Politics", **Women of Guam** (Guam: The Guam Women's Conference,1977), p. 20.

[67]See Nani Fernandez, "Nuclear and Independent Pacific Conference Vanuatu-1983," **All She Wrote** (Honolulu, Hawaii, Nov./Dec. 1983), p. 11; Sally Aquino, "Anti-Nuclear Strategy discussed in Vanuatu," **The Guam Tribune**, 29 July 1983, p. 56; and Shannon Babauta, "Guam Grabs Attention at Vanuatu," **Pacific Daily News Islander**, 21 August 1983, p. 5.

Chapter IV

[1]Francisco Garcia, "Life and Martyrdom of the Venerable Father Diego Luis de Sanvitores, First Missionary to the Mariana Islands, and the Happenings in these Islands from the year 1668 until the year 1681," trans

Margaret M. Higgins, in the **Guam Recorder** (April 1937), pp. 38-39. Also entitled, "The First History of Guam."

[2]Cecilia Cruz Bamba was also known as Mrs. "B", Chilang, and Senator. These names have been used interchangeably for diversity as well as to reflect the numerous ways she was referred to on Guam while she was alive. I knew Mrs. Bamba for as long as I can remember. She and I were close friends. She was also my mother's long-time trusted friend. I worked with her in several capacities, as both a volunteer and her employee while she was Senator. I viewed the in-depth interviews for my dissertation as an opportunity for another kind of encounter. During six marathon sessions varying from five to ten hours in length, which were held at my family home, Casa de Souder on Cuesta San Ramon, in October and November of 1983, Cecilia Cruz Bamba's life story unfolded.

Every Monday for six consecutive weeks, we sat across from each other at a small table in the living room and explored her life in relation to her community work and organizing. The **Cecilia Bamba Transcript** resulted. This transcription is a verbatim record of the six taped interviews. The transcriptions for each interview have been arranged in chronological order by interview date. Each page of the transcript has been numbered consecutively from 1 to 174 for easy reference. Citations from the verbatim transcript will take the form of a page number(s) enclosed in parentheses following each quotation.

[3]**Profile of Senator Cecilia Bamba** (Agana, Guam: unpublished, n.d.), pp. 1, 6. This vitae was obtained from Mrs. Bamba during our interview sessions in October, 1983.

[4]Cecilia Bamba's **Preliminary Survey Questionnaire**, I/9-3/83. This questionnaire was distributed to all subjects included in this study.

[5]**Preliminary Survey Questionnaire**, I/9-3/83.

[6]**Preliminary Survey Questionnaire**, I/10-3/83.

[7]**Preliminary Survey Questionnaire**, I/11-3/83.

[8]**Profile of Senator Cecilia Bamba**, p. 1.

[9]**Profile of Senator Cecilia Bamba**, pp. 5, 6, 9.

[10]Listings of the numerous bills and resolutions Senator Cecilia Bamba introduced are available in the four issues of *Tolai Mensahi*, a quarterly newsletter which she published for her constituents while in office.

[11]"Senator presents UN Ambassadors with Special Report," *Tolai Mensahi*, #2 (Agana, Guam: Cecilia Bamba, n.d.), p. 4.

[12]Profile of Senator Cecilia Bamba, p. 8.

[13]Mark Shapiro, "Bamba's Puerto Rican Speech," **The Guam Tribune**, 28 April 1980, p. 4.

[14]Profile of Senator Cecilia Bamba, p. 10 and *Tolai Mensahi* #3, p. 5.

[15]Profile of Senator Cecilia Bamba, p. 11.

[16]Profile of Senator Cecilia Bamba, p. 10.

[17]Profile of Senator Cecilia Bamba, pp. 2, 3, 4.

[18]"Advisory Council on Women's Concerns Called," *Tolai Mensahi* #2, p. 3.

[19]Profile of Senator Cecilia Bamba, pp. 7, 8.

[20]"Sisters of the Pacific Islands," **The Asian-American Journal**, April, 1980, pp. 30-31.

[21]Preliminary Survey Questionnaire, I/14-3/83.

[22]Profile of Senator Cecilia Bamba, p. 7.

[23]Profile of Senator Cecilia Bamba, pp. 4, 5.

[24]Profile of Senator Cecilia Bamba, pp. 9, 10.

[25]Guam Reparations Commission, **Final Report** (Agana, Guam, 7 November 1983), pp. 2, 3.

[26]Guam Reparations Commission, **Final Report**, pp. 3, 4.

[27]Guam Reparations Commission, **Status Report** (Agana, Guam, 1 December 1982), p. 9.

[28]Profile of Senator Cecilia Bamba, p. 11.

[29]Stat. 1) **62 PL 95-134**. 15 October 1977.

[30]"Positive response by Air Force Command on Guam's Land Use Plan," *Tolai Mensahi* #2, p. 1.

[31]"Bamba lauds Bennett Johnston and Won Pat for Acquisition of 6% Interest in Federal Land Claims," *Tolai Mensahi* #2, p. 1.

[32]The actual designation for "Congressman" is Non-Voting Dele-

gate. While Guam's representative carries the title of a Member of Congress, Guam has no vote and bears little if any political clout.

[33]Suzette Kioshi-Nelson, "Appraiser to Value Land Claims," **Pacific Daily News** (Agana, Guam), V. 15, No. 182, 31 July 1984, p. 1.

[34]"War Claims Responsibility of Legislative Committee," *Tolai Mensahi* #3, p. 6.

[35]Guam Reparations Commission, **Final Report**, Exhibit 7, pp. 1, 2.

[36]Letter to all War Claimants from Mrs. Cecilia Bamba dba Oceania Consultants, regarding proposed Guam war claims reparations, Agana, Guam, not dated.

Chapter V

[1]Clotilde Gould spent two full mornings in November, 1983 (8th and 15th) at her office in the Department of Education's Administrative Headquarters in Agana sharing her story. She fended off occasional interruptions with a friendly gesture or "later please." Ding is well liked by the people with whom she works. That has become increasingly evident to me as I've worked with her in the various issue-oriented activities she was involved in and through the ease and friendliness which characterized the interviews conducted for this study. Ding's responses to the **Preliminary Survey Questionnaire**, a personal resume, a DOE publication on its Division of Chamorro Studies and Special Projects, reports, brochure, programs, and newspaper articles comprise the data base for this case study.

[2]"*I Na Pinikara*," music and lyrics by Clotilde Gould and English translation by Laura Souder. This song was provided by Ding during our first interview session, November 8, 1983.

[3]Clotilde Gould Transcription, pp. 18-19.

[4]Clotilde Gould Transcription, p. 22.

[5]Clotilde Gould's **Preliminary Survey Questionnaire**, I/17-3/83.

[6]Clotilde Gould's **Preliminary Survey Questionnaire**, I/18-3/83.

[7]Clotilde Gould's **Preliminary Survey Questionnaire**, I/18-3/83.

[8]Clotilde Gould's **Preliminary Survey Questionnaire**, I/19-3/83.

[9]Clotilde Gould's **Preliminary Survey Questionnaire**, I/19-3/83.

[10]"Chamorro Language Year Proclaimed by Governor," **The Guam Tribune** (March 23, 1984), p. 53. For a comprehensive study of Chamorro language issues, see Mary L. Spencer, **Chamorro Language Issues and Research on Guam: A Book of Readings** (Mangilao: University of Guam, 1987).

[11]Robert A. Underwood, Chamorro Studies Convention: Evaluation and Summary (Unpublished report, Agana, Guam).

[12]Clotilde Gould's **Preliminary Survey Questionnaire**, I/16-3/83.

[13]Clotilde Gould's **Preliminary Survey Questionnaire**, I/20-3/83.

[14]Clotilde Gould Transcription, p. 4.

[15]Clotilde Gould Transcription, p. 8.

[16]Clotilde Gould Transcription, p. 8.

[17]Clotilde Gould Transcription, p. 11.

[18]Clotilde Gould Transcription, p. 10.

[19]Clotilde Gould Transcription, p. 10.

[19]Clotilde Gould's **Preliminary Survey Questionnaire**, I/20-3/83.

[20]Senator Pilar Lujan and I have been friends for several years. We worked together on several major projects while I was Special Assistant to the Governor for Cultural Affairs. We were also co-organizers of both the Guam Women's Conference and Guam Pre-White House Conference on Libraries and Information Services in Washington, D.C. Our prior relationship paved the way for a relaxed interview of three hours duration on November 23, 1983 at Senator Lujan's legislative office. Uninterrupted, I was able to obtain the basic information used for this case study. **The Preliminary Survey Questionnaire** with an attached resume also comprised a significant source of data. Supplemental information in several feature newspaper articles on Pilar Lujan was used to augment interview material.

[21]Pilar Lujan's **Preliminary Survey Questionnaire**, I/9-3/83.

[22]Pilar Lujan's **Preliminary Survey Questionnaire**, I/4-3/83.

[23]Pilar Lujan Transcription, p. 14.

[24]Pilar Lujan Transcription, p. 15.

[25]"Pilar Lujan", **Guam Shopper's Guide** (Thursday, August 5, 1982), p. 6.

[26]Pilar Lujan Transcription, p. 28.

[27]Pilar Lujan Transcription, p. 13.

[28]Pilar Lujan Transcription, p. 1.

[29]Pilar Lujan Transcription, p. 2.

[30]Focus "Equality of Women's Conference," **Guam Shopper's Guide** (Thursday, November 12, 1981), p. 6.

[31]Jolene Krawzcak, "Lujan: Government Needs More Women," **Pacific Daily News** (March 15, 1983), p. 3.

[32]Jolene Krawzcak, "Lujan: Government ...," p. 3.

[33]Pilar Lujan Transcription, p. 18.

[34]Pilar Lujan Transcription, p. 8.

[35]My first encounter with Carmen Leon Guerrero Pearson took place while we were young girls. She had accompanied her mother to our family home where her mother did some ironing for my mother. Many years later, Carmen and I met while both of us were conducting sessions for the Navy's Family Service Center Orientation program for newcomers to Guam. Subsequently Carmen agreed to participate in my study. She consented to become a case study subject and on October 14, 1983 we met at my home, once again, for a lengthy interview which lasted eight hours. Carmen brought newspaper articles, a written overview of the Task Force on Family Abuse and Sexual Assault and minutes of meetings. These materials supplement her PSQ responses and interview transcript. Collectively they comprise the data base for her case study.

[36]Carmen Pearson's **Preliminary Survey Questionnaire**, I/9-3/83.

[37]Carmen Pearson's **Preliminary Survey Questionnaire**, I/6-3/83.

[38]Carmen Pearson Transcription, p. 2.

[39]Carmen Pearson Transcription, pp. 3-4.

[40]Carmen Pearson's **Preliminary Survey Questionnaire**, I/13-3/83.

[41]Carmen Pearson Transcription, p. 14.

[42]Carmen Pearson Transcription, pp. 21-22.

[43]Carmen Pearson, "An Overview of the Task Force on Family Abuse and Sexual Assault." This document, an ESCAP Report, and the ALEE Impact Study were provided by the subject.

[44]Carmen Pearson's **Preliminary Survey Questionnaire**, I/19-3/83.

[45]Carmen Pearson Transcription, p. 45.

[46]Annie Roberto and I never met prior to our first interview session on October 22, 1983 at the Nieves Flores Memorial Library in Agana. During our initial encounter Mrs. Roberto and I established rapport and shared views on a number of issues. I took the opportunity to tell her about the dissertation and we went through the PSQ to clarify background information. We met on two other Saturday afternoons on October 29th and again on November 12th. The material used in this case study was gathered at these three meetings and is supplemented by Annie's PSQ responses, several issues of the **RSVP Quarterly** and other background materials on the RSVP program together with an article on the Geriatric Ward at Guam Memorial Hospital.

[47]"Project Director Attends Gerontological Society Conference in California," **RSVP Quarterly** (V. 1, N. 1, May 1980), p. 2.

[48]Annie Roberto's **Preliminary Survey Questionnaire**, I/9-3/83.

[49]Annie Roberto's **Preliminary Survey Questionnaire**, I/9-3/83.

[50]Annie Roberto's **Preliminary Survey Questionnaire**, I/10-3/83.

[51]Annie Roberto Transcription, p. 38.

[52]Annie Roberto Transcription, p. 39.

[53]Annie Roberto's **Preliminary Survey Questionnaire**, I/8-3/83.

[54]Annie Roberto Transcription, pp. 17-18.

[55]Annie Roberto Transcription, p. 18.

[56]Annie Roberto's **Preliminary Survey Questionnaire**, I/19-3/83.

[57]"*Canta, Canta*," Islander, **Pacific Daily News** (April 4, 1976), p. 6.

[58]Annie Roberto Transcription, p. 21.

[59]Annie Roberto Transcription, p. 26.

[60]"State Program Director Visits, Notes Program Success," **RSVP Quarterly** (V. 1, N. 1, May 1980), p. 5.

[61]Annie Roberto Transcription, pp. 23-33.

[62]Annie Roberto's **Preliminary Survey Questionnaire**, I/14-3/83.

[63]Annie Roberto Transcription, p. 12.

[64]Annie Roberto Transcription, p. 33.

[65]Annie Roberto Transcription, p. 16.

[66]Annie Roberto Transcription, pp. 19-20.

[67]Annie Roberto Transcription, p. 10.

[68]Annie Roberto Transcription, p. 3.

[69]Annie Roberto Transcription, p. 4.

Chapter VI

[1]**The Women's Organizations of Guam Directory** (Guam: The Women of St. John the Divine, 1983), pp. 23-35.

[2]Nancy B. Leis, "Women in Groups: Ijaw Women's Associations" in **Woman, Culture & Society**, Michelle Z. Rosaldo and Louise Lamphere (eds.) (Stanford, Calif.: Stanford University Press, 1974), p. 223.

[3]For a more detailed discussion of these concepts see: Nancy F. Cott, **The Bonds of Womanhood** (New Haven: Yale University Press, 1977); Carol Kleiman, **Women's Networks** (New York: Lippincott & Crowell, Publishers, 1980); and Michelle Z. Rosaldo and Louise Lamphere (eds.), **Woman, Culture & Society** (Stanford, Calif.: Stanford University Press, 1974).

[4]Elizabeth Perez Arriola is no stranger to me. I have known her as Isabel Arriola since my childhood. The various names Mrs. Arriola is known by reflects the propensity for nicknaming among Chamorros. In this case Isabel is the Spanish equivalent of Elizabeth. Her other nicknames include Belang, Belle, and Beck. People refer to her using any of these five first names interchangeably. Since I have always referred to her as Isabel Arriola I do so in this case study. While Mrs. Arriola and I had not worked together on a project prior to our involvement in the anti-gambling campaign, we have always been friendly towards each other. We taught at the same time at the Academy of Our Lady. These and other contacts paved the way for a relaxed interview situation. We met at Senator Arriola's legislative office for two consecutive mornings on November 1st and 2nd in 1983. Senator Arriola provided me with a campaign flyer. This supplemented her interview materials and **PSQ** responses. In addition, I consulted my own personal files on the gambling referendum as the Senator had difficulty recalling dates and the sequence of events which related to the anti-gambling campaign.

[5]Elizabeth Arriola Transcription, pp. 6-7.

[6]Elizabeth Arriola Transcription, p. 7.

[7]Elizabeth Perez Arriola Campaign Flyer.

[8]Elizabeth Arriola Transcription, pp. 18-19.

[9]Elizabeth Arriola Transcription, p. 19.

[10]Elizabeth Arriola Transcription, p. 20.

[11]Elizabeth Perez Arriola Campaign Flyer.

[12]Elizabeth Arriola Transcription, p. 20.

[13]Elizabeth Arriola Transcription, p. 6.

[14]Elizabeth Perez Arriola Campaign Flyer.

[15]Elizabeth Arriola Transcription, p. 22.

[16]Elizabeth Arriola Transcription, p. 26.

[17]Elizabeth Arriola Transcription, p. 29.

[18]Elizabeth Arriola Transcription, p. 21.

[19]Elizabeth Arriola Transcription, p. 21.

[20]Ernestina Tenorio Blas, better known as Tina, consented to be a case study subject when I explained to her what the goals of the dissertation were. We met in her office at the Department of Public Health and Social Services Mangilao facility. Between 9:00 a.m. and 2:00 p.m. on November 22, 1983, Tina shared her views on issues and particulars about her experiences and organizing work. At our meeting Tina also provided several letters and a program of the Tribute to the Religious Sisters of Mercy which she identified as the most meaningful activity she has organized so far. These materials together with her interview transcript and PSQ responses comprise the basic data for this case study. Tina and I have known each other for many years. Her older sister Bennett and I are good friends, and I have attended many Tenorio family social functions. Hence my session with Tina was comfortable and candid.

[21]Tina Blas Transcription, p. 31.

[22]Tina Blas Transcription, p. 31.

[23]Tina Blas Transcription, p. 8-9.

[24]Tina Blas Transcription, p. 33.

[25]Tina Blas Transcription, pp. 26-27.

[26] Tina Blas' **Preliminary Survey Questionnaire**, I/9-3/83.

[27] Tina Blas' **Preliminary Survey Questionnaire**, I/8-3/83.

[28] Tina Blas' **Preliminary Survey Questionnaire**, I/10-3/83.

[29] Tina Blas Transcription, pp. 3-4.

[30] Tina Blas' **Preliminary Survey Questionnaire**, I/14-3/83.

[31] Tina Blas' **Preliminary Survey Questionnaire**, 1/15-3/83.

[32] Tina Blas' **Preliminary Survey Questionnaire**, I/14-3/83.

[33] Tina Blas Transcription, p. 11.

[34] Tina Blas Transcription, p. 27.

[35] Tina Blas Transcription, p. 23.

[36] Tina Blas Transcription, p. 29.

[37] Tina Blas Transcription, pp. 28-30.

[38] Tina Blas Transcription, pp. 25-26.

[39] Tina Blas Transcription, p. 19.

[40] Tina Blas Transcription, p. 20.

[41] Tina Blas' **Preliminary Survey Questionnaire**, I/17-3/83.

[42] Tina Blas Transcription, p. 34.

[43] Of all the subjects in this study, Geraldine Joyce Chance Torres Gutierrez and I have the closest personal relationship. Geri and I are first cousins. We were reared together and have always related to each other as sisters. Due to this closeness, I have been extremely careful to include in this case study only that information which Geri directly shared on the **Preliminary Survey Questionnaire** and during our interview session, which took place in her kitchen on November 28, 1983. While much of her personal history is known to me, we agreed to focus only on material which prepared her for her role as an organizer, factors which influenced her organizing, and the process of organizing itself.

[44] Geri Gutierrez Transcription, p. 1.

[45] Don A. Farrell, **The Pictorial History of Guam: Liberation 1944** (Guam Micronesian Productions, 1984), pp. 35-37.

[46] Geri Gutierrez Transcription, p. 6.

[47] Geri Gutierrez Transcription, p. 7.

[48] Geri Gutierrez Transcription, p. 7.

[49] Geri Gutierrez Transcription, p. 7.

[50] Geri Gutierrez Transcription, p. 20.

[51] Geri Gutierrez's **Preliminary Survey Questionnaire**, I/13-3/83.

[52] Geri Gutierrez Transcription, p. 10.

[53] Geri Gutierrez Transcription, p. 20.

[54] Geri Gutierrez Transcription, pp. 1, 8, 9, 26.

[55] Geri Gutierrez's **Preliminary Survey Questionnaire**, p. I/4-3/83; I/5-3/83.

[56] Geri Gutierrez Transcription, p. 27.

[57] Geri Gutierrez Transcription, p. 22.

[58] Geri Gutierrez Transcription, p. 19.

[59] Geri Gutierrez Transcription, p. 24.

[60] Geri Gutierrez Transcription, pp. 5, 6, 12.

[61] Geri Gutierrez Transcription, p. 6.

[62] Geri Gutierrez Transcription, pp. 12-13.

[63] Geri Gutierrez Transcription, p. 14.

[64] Geri Gutierrez Transcription, pp. 14-15.

[65] Geri Gutierrez Transcription, pp. 16-18.

[66] Geri Gutierrez Transcription, p. 22.

[67] Geri Gutierrez Transcription, pp. 7-8.

[68] Geri Gutierrez Transcription, p. 9.

[69] Geri Gutierrez Transcription, p. 27.

[70] Geri Gutierrez Transcription, p. 1.

[71] Geri Gutierrez Transcription, p. 15.

[72] Geri Gutierrez Transcription, pp. 21-22.

[73] Geri Gutierrez Transcription, p. 28.

[74] Geri Gutierrez Transcription, p. 23.

[75] Geri Gutierrez Transcription, pp. 2-3.

[76] Mrs. Delgadina Hiton was recommended to me by Father

George, pastor of St. Francis parish in Yona. I did not know Mrs. Hiton personally. We communicated by telephone several times after Mrs. Hiton completed the **PSQ**. Finally our first meeting was arranged for October 26, 1983 at 1:00 p.m. Mrs. Hiton preferred being interviewed at her own home. From the moment I knocked on the door with a customary "*hoi*," I felt the warmth and sincerity of *Tan* Del's character. We sat without fanfare on her couch, and we talked and shared for the entire afternoon. *Tan* Del remarked later that she was apprehensive at first but felt as we got started that she was chatting with a close neighbor. I also felt "at home." The interview was conducted in Chamorro; so most of what *Tan* Del said is paraphrased. Short quotations in Chamorro are used to convey her manner of expression to Chamorro readers. In the course of our session *Tan* Del shared photograph albums and her handicrafts with me. This case study is based on information collected during that visit.

[77]Delgadina Hiton Transcription, p. 9.

[78]Delgadina Hiton Transcription, p. 7.

[79]Delgadina Hiton Transcription, p. 14.

[80]Delgadina Hiton Transcription, pp. 5-6.

[81]Delgadina Hiton Transcription, p. 7.

[82]Delgadina Hiton Transcription, p. 8.

[83]Delgadina Hiton's **Preliminary Survey Questionnaire**, p. I/9-3/83.

[84]Delgadina Hiton's **Preliminary Survey Questionnaire**, p. I/14-3/83 and Delgadina Hiton Transcription, p. 10.

[85]Delgadina Hiton Transcription, p. 5.

[86]Delgadina Hiton Transcription, p. 18.

[87]Delgadina Hiton's **Preliminary Survey Questionnaire**, p. I/18-3/83.

[88]Delgadina Hiton's **Preliminary Survey Questionnaire**, pp. I/18-3/83 and I/19-3/83.

[89]Delgadina Hiton Transcription, pp. 13-17.

[90]Delgadina Hiton Transcription, p. 11.

[91]Carol Kleiman, **Women's Networks** (New York: Lippincott &

Crowell, Publishers, 1980), p. 2.

[92]Personal Interview with Dr. Faye Untalan-Munoz, 7 May 1984.

[93]Carol Kleiman, **Women's Networks**, p. 2.

[94]Carol Kleiman, **Women's Networks**, pp. 5-6.

Chapter VII

[1]Etienne and Leacock, **Women and Colonization**, p. v-vi.

[2]Sherna Gluck, "What's So Special About Women? Women's Oral History", **Frontiers** 11(2):12.

[3]Manda Cesara, **Reflections of a Woman Anthropologist: No Hiding Place** (New York: Academic Press, 1982), p. 228.

[4]Ann M. Pescatello, **Power and Pawn** (Connecticut: Greenwood Press, 1976), pp. 230-231.

[5]Pescatello, p. 231.

[6]Pescatello, pp. 231-232.

[7]Laura Thompson, **Guam and Its People** (Princeton, New Jersey: Princeton University Press, 1947), p. 285.

[8]Hara Jackson in "Women Speak Out!", **A Report of the Pacific Women's Conference, October 27-November 2, 1975** (Suva, Fiji: The Pacific Women's Conference, 1976), pp. 82-83.

[9]Concepcion Cruz Barrett, "The Need for Women in Government," **Women of Guam**, p. 22.

BIBLIOGRAPHY

Agar, Michael H. **Ethnography and Cognition.** Minneapolis, Minnesota: Burgess Publishing Co., 1974.

_____. **The Professional Stranger: An Informal Introducion to Ethnography.** New York: Academic Press, Inc., 1980.

Agonito, Rosemary and Joseph Agonito. "Resurrecting History's Forgotten Women: A Case Study from the Cheyenne Indians." **Frontiers,** Vol. 6, No. 3 (1982):8-16.

Allen, Annette and Osborne Wiggins. "The Feminist Critique of Self and Society: A Phenomenological Metra-critique." **Catalyst,** Vols. 10 and 11 (Summer 1977):37-59.

"American Names for Chamorro Children." **Guam Recorder,** Vol. 2, No. 23 (1926):346.

Aquino, Sally. "Anti-Nuclear Strategy Discussed in Vanuatu." **Guam Tribune,** (29 July 1983):56.

Aragon de Valdez, Theresa. "Organizing as a Political Tool for the Chicana." **Frontiers,** Vol. 5, No. 2 (1980):7-13.

Armitage, Susan H. "The Next Step." **Frontiers,** Vol. 7, No. 1 (1983):3-8.

Armitage, Susan H., Theresa Banfield and Sarah Jacobus. "Black Women and their Communities in Colorado," **Frontiers,** Vol. 4, No.2 (1977):45-51.

Babauta, Shannon. "Guam Grabs Attention at Vanuatu." Islander, **Pacific Daily News,** (21 August 1983):5.

Bamba, Cecilia, Laura Souder, and Judy Tompkins (eds.). Women of Guam. Agana, Guam: **Guam Women's Conference,** November 1977.

"Bamba Lauds Bennett Johnston and Won Pat for Acquisition

of 6% Interest in Federal Land Claims." *Tolai Mensahi,* Quarterly Newsletter of Senator Bamba, No. 2:(n.d.):1.

Bataille, Gretchen M. and Kathleen Sands. **American Indian Women Telling Their Lives.** Lincoln, Nebraska: University of Nebraska Press, 1984.

Baum, Willa. **Oral History for the Local Historical Society.** 2nd edition. Nashville, Tennessee: American Association for State and Local History, 1975.

Beard, Mary Ritter. **Women as Force in History.** New York: Collier Books, 1946, 1962.

Beardsley, Charles. **Guam Past and Present.** Tokyo: C. E. Tuttle Co., 1964.

Bernard, Jessie. **The Female World.** New York: Free Press, 1981.

Blair, Karen J. **The Clubwoman as Feminist, True Womanhood Redefined, 1868-1914.** New York: Holmes & Meier Publishers, Inc., 1980.

Bleier, Ruth. **Science and Gender, A Critique of Biology and Its Theories on Women.** New York: Pergamon Press, 1984.

Bloch, Ruth H. "American Feminine Ideals in Transition: The Rise of the Moral Mother, 1785-1815." **Feminist Studies,** Vol. 4, No. 2 (June 1978):100-126.

Bloom, Lynn Z. "Listen! Women Speaking." **Frontiers,** Vol. 11, No. 2 (1977).

Bonney, Rachel. "The Role of Women in Indian Activism." **Western Canadian Journal of Anthropology,** Vol. 6, No. 3 (1976):243-248.

Boulding, Elsie. "Female Alternatives to Hierarchical Systems, Past and Present: A Critique of Women's NGO's in the Light of History." **International Women's Year Studies on Women,** Paper Number 3. Denver, Colorado: Program of Research on General Social and Economic Dynamics, Institute of Behavioral Sciences, University of Colorado, February 1975.

Bourque, Susan C. and Kay Barbara Warren. **Women of the Andes, Patriarchy and Social Change in Two Peruvian Towns.** Ann Arbor, Michigan: University of Michigan Press, 1981.

Bowles, Gloria and Renate Duelli-Klein. "Introduction: Trying to Find Out How to Find Out What We Know." pp. 1-10 in Gloria Bowles and Renate Duelli-Klein (eds.). **Theories of Women's Studies II.** Berkeley: Women's Studies, University of California, 1981, pp. 1-10.

_____ and Renate Duelli-Klein (eds.) **Theories of Women's Studies.** London: Routledge & Kegan Paul, 1983.

_____. **Theories of Women's Studies II.** Berkeley, California: University of California, 1981.

Branca, Patricia. "Image and Reality: the Myth of the Idle Victorian Woman," in Patricia Branca (ed.) **Class Consciousness Raised: New Perspectives on the History of Women.** New York: Harper Torchbooks, 1974.

Branca, Patricia (ed.). **Class Consciousness Raised: New Perspectives on the History of Women.** New York: Harper Torchbooks, 1974.

Brody, Ivan (ed.). "Speaking in the Name of the Real: Freeman and Mead on Samoa." **American Anthropologist,** Vol. 85, No. 4 (1983):908-947.

Building Feminist Theory: Essays from Quest, a Feminist Quarterly. New York: Longman Inc., 1981.

"*Canta, Canta.*" Islander, **Pacific Daily News,** (4 April 1976):6.

Carano, Paul and Pedro C. Sanchez. **A Complete History of Guam.** Rutland, Vermont: C. E. Tuttle Co., 1964.

Carroll, Theodora Foster. **Women, Religion, and Development in the Third World.** New York: Praeger Publishers, 1983.

Cesara, Manda. **Reflections of a Woman Anthropologist: No**

Hiding Place. New York: Academic Press, 1982.

Chai, Alice Yun. "A Picture Bride from Korea: The Life History of a Korean American Woman in Hawaii." **Bridge: An Asian American Perspective** (Winter, 1978):37-42.

_____. "Korean Women in Hawaii 1903-1945," in Hilah F. Thomas and Rosemary Skinner Keller (eds.) **Women in New Worlds**, Nashville, Tennessee: Abingdon, 1981.

_____. "The Life History of An Early Korean Immigrant Woman in Hawaii." **Working Paper Series**, Vol. 1, No. 3 (September 1978):50-60. Women's Studies Program, University of Hawaii.

_____. Toward a Holistic Paradigm for Asian American Women's Studies: A Synthesis of Feminist Scholarship and Women of Color's Feminist Scholarship. **Working Paper Number 51**. Lansing, Michigan: Women in International Development, Michigan State University, March 1984.

"Chamorro Language Year Proclaimed by Governor." **Guam Tribune**, (23 March 1984):53.

"Changing Role of Women in Society." **Pacific Daily News**, (25 November 1978).

"Characteristics of the Natives of Guam When the First Settlement was Established by the Spanish." **Guam Recorder**, (January 1930):188.

Chinas, Beverly L. **The Isthmus Zapotecs: Women's Roles in Cultural Context**. New York: Holt, Rinehart and Winston, Inc., 1973.

The Civil Code of the Territory of Guam 1970, Volume I.

_____, 1980, Volume IV.

Cohen, Cindy. "Building Multicultural and Intergenerational Networks Through Oral History." **Frontiers**, Vol. 11, No. 1 (1983): pp. 98-102.

Coles, Robert and Jane Hallowell Coles. **Women of Crisis:**

Lives of Struggle and Hope. New York: Delacorte Press, 1978.

Cott, Nancy F. **The Bonds of Womanhood, "Women's Sphere" in New England,** 1780-1835. New Haven, Connecticut: Yale University Press, 1978.

_____ and Elizabeth Pleck (eds.). **A Heritage of Her Own: Toward a New Social History of American Women.** New York: Simon and Schuster, 1979.

"Equality Focus of Women's Conference." **Guam's Shopper's Guide,** (12 November 1981):6.

Etienne, Mona and Eleanor Leacock (eds). **Women and Colonization.** New York: Praeger Publishers, 1980.

Farrell, Don A. **The Pictorial History of Guam, Liberation--1944.** Tamuning, Guam: Micronesian Productions, 1984.

Fernandez, Nani. "Nuclear Free and Independent Pacific Conference, Vanuatu-1983." **All She Wrote** (November/December 1983):11. [Honolulu, Hawaii]

Flacks, Richard. "Moral Commitment, Privatism and Activism: Notes on a Research Program." In Norma Haan, Robert N. Bellah, Paul Rabinow, and William M. Sullivan (eds.) **Social Science as Moral Inquiry,** New York: Columbia University Press, 1983.

Freeman, Jo (ed.). **Women: A Feminist Perspective.** Palo Alto, California: Mayfield Publishing Co., 1979.

Friedl, Ernestine. **Women and Men: Anthropologist's View.** New York: Holt, Rinehart and Winston, 1975.

Fry, Amelia R. "Suffragist Alice Paul's Memoirs: Pros and Cons of Oral History." **Frontiers,** Vol. 2, No. 2 (1977):82-86.

Fuge, Kenneth. "Problems of Oral History in the Pacific." Paper presented at the Third National Conference Sponsored by the National Association for Asian and Pacific American Education, April 24, 1981, Honolulu, Hawaii.

Garcia, Francisco. "Life and Martyrdom of the Venerable
     Father Diego Luis de Sanvitores, First Missionary to
     the Mariana Islands, and the Happenings in these
     Islands from the Year 1668 until the Year 1681."
     Margaret M. Higgens (trans.), **Guam Recorder** (1936-
     1939).

Gluck, Sherna. **From Parlor to Prison, Five American Suffra-
     gists Talk About Their Lives.** New York: Vintage,
     1976.

_____. "What's So Special About Women? Women's
     Oral History." **Frontiers,** Vol. 2, No. 2, (1977).

Golde, Peggy (ed.). **Women in the Field. Anthropological
     Experiences.** Chicago: Aldine Publishing Co., 1970.

Guam Annual Economic Review, 1981. Agana, Guam: De-
     partment of Commerce, August 1981.

Guam Comprehensive Development Plan. Agana, Guam:
     Bureau of Planning, 1978.

Guam Reparations Commission. **Final Report.** Agana, Guam:
     The Commission, 7 November 1983.

Guam Reparations Commission. **Status Report.** Agana,
     Guam: The Commission, December 1982.

Guam Women's Conference. **Final Report:** *Nihi ta Fandana
     Famalaona.* Agana, Guam: Guam Women's Confer-
     ence, 1977.

Guam Women's Issues Task Force. **Island Women Speak Out:
     Critical Issues of the 80's.** Agana, Guam: Guam
     Women's Issues Task Force, May 1982.

Haan, Norma, Robert N. Bellah, Paul Rabinow, and William
     M. Sullivan (eds.) **Social Science as Moral Inquiry.**
     New York: Columbia University Press, 1983.

Haechung, Cho et al. "What is Asian Feminism." **AWRAN,
     Newsletter of the Asian Women's Research and Action
     Network,** Vol. 1, No. 2 (February, 1984):17-19.

Hammond, Dorothy and Alta Jablow. **Women, Their Economic**

Role in Traditional Societies. Reading, Massachusetts: Addison-Wesley Publishing Co., 1973.

Hansen, Judith Friedman. "The Anthropologist in the Field: Scientist, Friend and Voyeur." In Michael A. Rynkiewich and James P. Spradley (eds.). **Ethics and Anthropology: Dilemmas in Fieldwork.** New York: John Wiley and Sons, Inc., 1976.

Hareven, Tamara K. (ed.). **Anonymous Americans: Explorations in Nineteenth-Century Social History.** Englewood Cliffs, New Jersey: Prentice-Hall, 1971.

_____ (ed.). **Family and Kin in Urban Communities, 1700-1930.** New York: New Viewpoints, 1977.

_____ (ed.). **Transitions: The Family and the Life Course in Historical Perspective.** New York: Academic Press, 1978.

Harrell-Bond, Barbara. "Studying Elites: Some Special Problems." In Michael A. Rynkiewich and James P. Spradley (eds.). **Ethics and Anthropology: Dilemmas in Fieldwork.** New York: John Wiley and Sons, Inc., 1976.

Hartman, Mary S. and Lois W. Banner (eds.). **Clio's Consciousness Raised: New Perspectives on the History of Women.** New York: Harper and Row, 1974.

Harvey, Youngsook Kim. **Six Korean Women: The Socialization of Shamans.** St. Paul, Minnesota: West Publishing Co., 1979.

Haswell, William. **Remarks on a Voyage in 1801 to the Island of Guam.** Historical Collections of the Essex Institute, 1917.

Hollensteiner, Mary R. **Dynamics of Power in a Philippine Municipality.** Manila: Community Development Research Council, University of the Philippines, 1963.

Hoyle, Norman. "Oral History." **Library Trends,** (July 1972):60-82.

Hsu, Francis L. K. "Cultural Problem of the Cultural Anthropologist." **American Anthropologist,** Vol. 81, No. 3 (1979):517-532.

_____. "Prejudice and the Intellectual Effect in American Anthropology: An Ethnographic Report." **American Anthropologist,** Vol. 75, No. 1 (1973):1-19.

_____. "Role, Affect, and Anthropology." **American Anthropologist,** Vol. 79, No. 4 (1977):805-808.

Hungry Wolf, Beverly. **The Ways of My Grandmothers.** New York: William Morrow and Co., Inc., 1980.

"Its Creation, *Nanajuyong.*" **Guam U.S.A. Gateway to Micronesia.** Agana, Guam: Guam Visitors Bureau, n.d.

Jain, Devaki. "Can Feminism Be a Global Ideology?" **Quest: A Feminist Quarterly,** A Special Issue on International Feminism, Vol. 4, No. 2 (Winter, 1978):9-15.

Jayaratne, Toby. "The Value of Quantitative Methodology for Feminist Research." pp. 11-24 in Gloria Bowles and Renate Duelli-Klein (eds.), **Theories of Women's Studies II.** Berkeley, California: University of California, 1981.

Jenson, Joan, Beverly Baca and Barbara Bolin. "Family History and Oral History." **Frontiers,** Vol. 2, No. 2 (1977):93-97.

Johnston, Anita. "The Ethnic Identity Experience of Chamorro Women." Ph.D. Dissertation, The California School of Professional Psychology, 1980.

Joyce, Rosemary O. **A Woman's Place: The Life History of a Rural Ohio Grandmother.** Columbus, Ohio: Ohio State University Press, 1983.

Kearney, Helen R. "Feminist Challenges to the Social Structure and Sex." **Psychology of Women Quarterly.** Vol. 4, No. 1 (Fall 1979):16-31.

Kearns, Virginia. **Women and the Ancestors: Black Carib Kinship and Ritual.** Urbana, Illinois: University of Illinois Press, 1983.

Kelly, Alison. "Feminism and Research." **Women's Studies**

International Quarterly. Vol. 1, No. 3 (1978):225-232.

Kelly, Jane Holden. **Yaqui Women, Contemporary Life Histories.** Lincoln, Nebraska: University of Nebraska Press, 1978.

Kelly, Joan. **Women, History and Theory, the Essays of Joan Kelly.** Chicago, Illinois: The University of Chicago Press, 1984.

Kessler, Evelyn S. **Women: An Anthropological View.** New York: Holt, Rinehart and Winston, 1976.

Kikumura, Akemi. **Through Harsh Winters: The Life of a Japanese Immigrant Woman.** Nevato, California: Chandler and Shart Publishers, Inc., 1981.

Kimball, Gayle (ed.). **Women's Culture, The Women's Renaissance of the Seventies.** Metuchen, New Jersey: The Scarecrow Press, Inc., 1981.

Kioshi-Nelson, Suzette. "Appraiser to Value Land Claims." **Pacific Daily News,** (31 July 1984):1.

Kleiman, Carol. **Women's Networks.** New York: Lippincott and Crowell, Publishers, 1980.

Kleinbaum, Abby Wettan. "Women's History: Old Formulas Out." **New Direction for Women,** Vol. 13, No. 2 (March/April, 1984):1.

Krause, Corrine Azen. "Grandmothers, Mothers, and Daughters: An Oral History Study of Ethnicity, Mental Health, and Continuity of Three Generations of Jewish, Italian, and Slavic-American Women." Institute on Pluralism and Group Identity of the American Jewish Committee.

Krawzcak, Jolene. "Lujan: Government Needs More Women." **Pacific Daily News,** (15 March 1983):3.

Langland, Elizabeth and Walter Gove (eds.). **A Feminist Perspective in the Academy, the Difference It Makes.** Chicago, Illinois: The University of Chicago, Press, 1983.

Langness, L. L. **Life History in Anthropological Science.** New

York: Rinehart and Winston, 1965.

_____ and Frank Gelya. Lives: **An Anthropological Approach to Biography.** Novato, California: Chandler and Sharp Publishers, Inc., 1981.

Lather, Patti. "Notes Toward An Adequate Methodology in Doing Feminist Research." Paper presented at National Women's Studies Association Conference, Bloomingdale, Indiana, June 18, 1982.

Le Gobien, Charles. **History of the Marianas.** Paris, 1700.

Michelle Rosaldo and Louise Lamphere (eds). **Women, Culture and Society.** Stanford, Ca.: Stanford University Press, 1974.

Lerner, Gerda. **The Female Experience: An American Documentary.** Indianapolis, Indiana: Bobbs-Merrill Educational Publishing, 1977.

_____. Majority Finds Its Past. **Placing Women in History.** New York: Oxford University Press, 1979.

_____. "Necessity of History and the Professional Historian." **The Journal of American History,** Vol. 69, No. 1 (June 1982):7-20.

_____ (ed.). **Black Women in White America: A Documentary History.** New York: Vintage Books, 1973.

_____ (ed.). **Teaching Women's History.** Washington, D.C.: American Historical Association, 1981.

Letter to all War Claimants from Mrs. Cecilia Bamba dba Oceania Consultants. Agana, Guam, n.d.

Lewis, Oscar. **La Vida.** New York: Vintage Books, 1966.

Linderman, Frank. **Pretty Shield: Medicine Woman of the Crows.** Lincoln, Nebraska: University of Nebraska Press, 1972.

Lind, Alice and Straughton Lynd. **Rank and File, Personal Histories by Working Class Organizers.** Boston, Massachusetts: Beacon, 1973.

MacKinnon, Catherine A. "Feminism, Marxism, Method, and the State: An Agenda for Theory." **Journal of Women in Culture and Society,** Vol. 7, No. 3 (1982):515-544.

Mander, Anica Vesel. **Bloodties, A Woman's History.** San Francisco, California: Mon Books, 1976.

Marche, Antoine-Alfred. **The Mariana Islands,** 1887-1889. Translated from the French by Sylvia E. Cheng and edited by Robert D. Craig. Agana, Guam: Micronesian Area Research Center, 1982.

Mason, Leonard E. "An Interpretation of 'Native Custom' in a Changing Oceanic Society." **Proceedings of the Seventh Pacific Science Congress,** Vol. 8 (1953):95-102.

_____. "Anthropology in American Micronesia, A Progress Report." **Clearinghouse Bulletin of Research in Human Organization.** Vol. 2, No. 3 (1953).

_____. "Characterization of American Culture in Studies of Acculturation." **American Anthropologist,** Vol. 57, No.6 (1955):1264-1279.

_____. Micronesia: Isolation or Assimilation? **IPR Notes,** Vol. 3, No. 1 (Jan. 1948). [Institute of Pacific Relations, Honolulu, Hawaii.]

_____. Proceedings of the Symposium on the Role of Anthropology in Contemporary Micronesia at the Annual Meeting of the Association for Social Anthropology in Oceania, Asilomar Conference Center. Monterey, California, Feb. 15-19, 1978; Hawaii, February 24, 1978.

_____. Research Problems and Ethics in Micronesia. A Survey Undertaken for the Committee on Research Problems and Ethics, **American Anthropological Association,** Sept. 1966, University of Hawaii.

_____. **The Role of Anthropology in Contemporary Micronesia: A Situation Report,** 1979.

McDade, Laurei. "The Interweavings of Theory and Practice: Finding the Threads for a Feminist Ethnography."

Paper presented at the National Women's Studies Association Conference, Columbus, Ohio, June 29, 1983.

McDowell, Nancy. "The Oceanic Ethnography of Margaret Mead." **American Anthropologist**, Vol. 82, No. 2 (1980):278-303.

Mead, Margaret. **Blackberry Winter: My Earlier Years.** New York: Morrow, 1972.

_____. **Letters from the Field 1925-1975.** New York: Harper and Row, Publishers, 1977.

_____. **Male and Female: A Study of the Sexes in a Changing World.** Westport, Connecticutt: Greenwood Press, 1977.

Merton, Robert K. "Insiders and Outsiders: A Chapter in Sociology of Knowledge." **American Journal of Sociology,** Vol. 78, No. 1 (1972):9-47.

Mies, Maria. "Towards a Methodology for Feminist Research." pp. 25-46, in Gloria Bowles and Renate Duelli-Klein (eds.), **Theories of Women's Studies II.** Berkeley, California: University of California, 1981.

Miles, Angela R. and Geraldine Finn (eds.). **Feminism in Canada: From Pressure to Politics.** Montreal, Canada: Black Rose Books, 1982.

Moen, Elizabeth W. "What Does 'Control Over Our Bodies' Really Mean?" **International Journal of Women's Studies,** Vol. 2 (March-April 1979):129-143.

Moubray, George Alexander. **Matriarchy in the Malay Peninsula and Neighboring Countries.** London: George Routledge and Sons, Ltd., 1931.

_____. Personal Interview, 7 May 1984.

Murphy, Yolanda and Robert F. Murphy. **Women of the Forest.** New York: Columbia University Press, 1974.

Nakane, Chie. **Garo and Khasi: A Comparative Study in Matrilineal Systems.** Paris: The Hague: Mouton,

1967.

Nash, June. "Nationalism and Field Work." **Annual Review of Anthropology,** Vol. 4 (1975):225-245.

Nelson, Frederick J. "Lieutenant William E. Safford, Guam's First Lieutenant Governor." Unpublished report, n.d.

Oakley, Ann. "Interviewing Women: A Contradiction in Terms." pp 30-61 in Helen Roberts (ed.) **Doing Feminist Research.** Boston, Massechusetts: Routledge and Kegan Paul, 1981.

O'Kelly, Charlotte G. **Women and Men in Society.** New York: D. Van Nostrand Co., 1980.

Oliver, Douglas. **The Pacific Islands.** New York: Doubleday and Co., Inc., 1961.

Paulme, Denise (ed.). **Women of Tropical Africa.** Translation by H.M. Wright. Berkeley, California: University of California Press, 1974.

Pearson, Carmen. "An Overview of the Task Force on Family Abuse and Sexual Assault." Agana, Guam, n.d.

Pescatello, Ann M. **Power and Pawn: The Female in Iberian Families, Societies, and Cultures.** Westport, Connecticut: Greenwood Press, 1976.

Pettigrew, Joyce. "Reminiscences of Fieldwork among the Sikhs." pp. 62-82 in Helen Roberts (ed.) **Doing Feminist Research.** Boston, Massachusetts: Routledge and Kegan Paul, 1981.

Pierson, Ruth and Alison Prentice. "Feminism and the Writing and Teaching of History." pp. 103-118 in Angela R. Miles and Geraldine Finn (eds.) **Feminism in Canada: From Pressure to Politics.** Montreal, Canada: Black Rose Books, 1982.

Pigafetta, Antonio. **Magellan's Voyage: A Narrative Account of the First Circumnavigation.** Translated and edited by K. A. Skelton. New Haven, Connecticut: Yale University Press, 1969. 2 Vols.

_____. **The Voyage of Magellan: The Journal of Antonio**

Pigafetta. Translated by Paula Spulin Page. Englewood Cliffs, New Jersey: Prentice-Hall, Inc.; Ann Arbor, Michigan: University of Michigan, 1969.

"Pilar Lujan." **Guam Shopper's Guide**, (5 August 1982):2.

Ploke, Genevieve. "Guam Productivity is Tops in the World." **Pacific Profile**, Vol. 2 (January 1964).

Pobutsky, Ann Marie G. "*Suruhanas*: Women Herbalists of Guam." Panorama, **Guam Tribune** (8 July 1983).

Poehlman, Sister Joanne. "Culture Change and Identity Among Chamorro Women of Guam." Ph.D. Dissertation, University of Minnesota, 1979.

"Positive Response by Air Force Command on Guam's Land Use Plan." *Tolai Mensahi*, Quarterly Newsletter of Senator Bamba, No. 2:(n.d.):1.

Preliminary Survey Questionnaire, Nos. 1-82. Agana, Guam, 1983.

"Profile of Senator Cecilia Bamba." Unpublished manuscript. Agana, Guam, n.d.

"Project Director Attends Gerontological Society Conference in California." **RSVP Quarterly**, Vol. 1, No. 1 (May 1980):2.

Quinn, Naomi. "Anthropological Studies on Women's Status." **Annual Review of Anthropology**, Vol. 6 (1977):181-225.

Ramirez, Anthony. Personal interview, 22 July 1983.

Reinharz, Shulamit. "Experiential Analysis: A Contribution to Feminist Research Methodology." pp. 68-97 in Gloria Bowles and Renate Duelli-Klein (eds.), **Theories of Women's Studies II**. Berkeley, California: University of California, 1981.

Rensberger, Boyce. "Margaret Mead. The Nature-Nurture Debate, From Samoa to Socio Biology." **Science 83** (April 1983), pp. 28-37.

Repetti, William C. "Miscelleny." **The Catholic Historical Review**, Vol. 31, No. 4 (January 1946):435.

Riley, Gresham. **Values, Objectivity and the Social Sciences.** Reading, Massachsetts: Addison-Wesley Publishing, 1974.

Roberts, Helen (ed.). **Doing Feminist Research.** Boston, Massachusetts: Routledge and Kegan Paul, 1981.

Robertson, Claire. "In Pursuit of Life Histories: The Problem of Bias." **Frontiers,** Vol. 7, No. 2 (1983):63-69.

Rogers, Susan Carol. "Woman's Place: A Critical Review of Anthropological Theory." pp. 42-55 in Sue Cox (ed.), **Female Psychology: The Emerging Self.** New York: St. Martin's Press, 1976.

Romanucci-Ross, Lola. "Anthropological Field Research: Margaret Mead, Muse of the Clinical Experience." **American Anthropologist,** Vol. 82 (1980):304-317.

Ronharr, J. H. **Women in Primitive Mother-right Societies.** The Hague: J. B. Wolters Groningen, 1931.

Rosaldo, Michelle Z. "The Use and Abuse of Anthropology: Reflections on Feminism and Cross Cultural Understanding." **Signs,** Vol. 5, No. 3 (Spring 1980):389-417.

_____ and Louise Lamphere (eds). **Women, Culture and Society.** Stanford, California: Stanford University Press, 1974.

Rubin, Barbara and Doris Friedensohn. "Daughters Interview Mothers: The Questions." **Women's Studies Quarterly,** Vol. 9, No. 2 (Summer 1981):2.

Russo, Nancy Felipe. "Overview: Sex Roles, Fertility and the Motherhood Mandate." **Psychology of Women Quarterly,** Vol. 4, No. 4 (Fall 1979):7-15.

Rutenberg, Taly (ed.). "Selected Annotated Bibliography of Articles and Theories of Women's Studies." pp. 131-151 in Gloria Bowles and Renate Duelli-Klein (eds.), **Theories of Women's Studies II.** Berkeley, California: University of California, 1981.

Ryan, Mary P. "The Power of Women's Networks: A Case

Study of Female Moral Reform in Antebellum America." **Feminist Studies,** Vol. 5, No. 1 (Spring 1979):66-86.

Rynkiewich, Michael A. and James P. Spradley (eds.). **Ethics and Anthropology: Dilemmas in Fieldwork.** New York: John Wiley and Sons, Inc., 1976.

Safford, William E. **A Year on the Island of Guam, Extracts from the Note-Book of a Naturalist on the Island of Guam [1889-1900] (TS).** This document is located in the Guam Room of the Nieves Flores Memorial Library, Agana, Guam.

"Salute to Guam's Women: Chamorro Women, a Living Tradition." Islander, **Pacific Daily News,** (13 November 1983).

Sanday, Peggy Reeves. **Female Power and Male Dominance.** London: Cambridge University Press, 1981.

_____. "Margaret Mead's View of Sex Roles in Her Own and Other Societies." **American Anthropologist,** Vol. 82, No. 2 (1980):340-340.

Schulenburg, Jane Tibbetts. "Clio's European Daughters: Myoptic Modes of Perception." pp. 33-54 in Julia A. Sherman and Evelyn Torton Beck (eds.). **The Prism of Sex: Essays in the Sociology of Knowledge.** Madison, Wisconsin: University of Wisconsin Press, 1979.

"Senator Presents UN Ambassadors with Special Report." *Tolai Mensahi,* Quarterly Newsletter of Senator Bamba, No. 2:(n.d.):4.

Shapiro, Mark. "Bamba's Puerto Rican Speech." **Guam Tribune,** (28 April 1980):4.

_____ and Janet W. Salaff (eds.) **Lives: Chinese Working Women.** Bloomington, Indiana: Indiana University Press, 1984.

Sherman, Julia A. and Evelyn Torton Beck (eds.). **The Prism of Sex: Essays in the Sociology of Knowledge.** Madison, Wisconsin: University of Wisconsin Press, 1979.

Shostak, Marjorie. *Nisa,* **The Life and Words of a Kung Woman**. Cambridge, Massachusetts: Harvard University Press, 1981.

Sicherman, Barbara et al. Recent United States Scholarship on the History of Women. A report presented at the XV International Congress of Historical Sciences, American Historical Association, 1980.

"Sisters of the Pacific Islands." *Tolai Mensahi,* Quarterly Newsletter of Senator Bamba, No. 2:(n.d.):3.

Smith, Hilda. "Feminism and the Methodology of Women's History." pp. 368-384 in (eds.) **Liberating Women's History: Theoretical and Critical Essays.** Urbana, Illinois: University of Illinois Press, 1976.

Social-Economic Impact of Modern Technology Upon a Developing Insular Region: Guam. 7 Vols in 3 parts. Agana, Guam: University of Guam Press, 1975.

Souder, Laura M. T. **ALEE Impact Study,** ALEE Spouse Abuse Program, Catholic Social Services, Guam, October 1989.

_____. **Cooperation between Government Agencies and Nongovernmental Organizations in the Delivery of Social Services for Women: Guam Report,** UN ESCAP, Bangkok, February 1988.

_____. "New Perspectives on the Chamorro Female Experience: Case Studies of Nine Comptemporary Chamorro Women Organizers," Ph.D. Dissertation, University of Hawaii at Manoa, 1985.

Spencer, Mary L. **Chamorro Language Issues and Research on Guam, A Book of Readings.** University of Guam, Mangilao Guam, 1987.

Spender, Dale (ed.). **Male Studies Modified: The Impact of Feminism on the Academic Disciplines.** New York: Pergamon Press, 1981.

Spradley, James P. **Participant Observation.** New York: Holt, Rinehart and Winston, 1980.

Stanley, Liz and Sue Wise. "Back into 'the Personal', or Our Attempt to Construct 'Feminist Research'." pp. 98-118 in Gloria Bowles and Renate Duelli-Klein (eds.), **Theories of Women's Studies II.** Berkeley, California: University of California, 1981.

_____. **Breaking Out: Feminist Consciousness and Feminist Research.** London: Routledge and Kegan Paul, 1983.

_____. "Feminist Research, Feminist Consciousness and Experiences of Sexism." **Women Studies International Quarterly.** Vol. 2. (1979):359-374.

"State Program Director Visits, Notes Program Success." **RSVP Quarterly,** Vol. 1, No. 1 (May 1980):5.

Stimpson, Catherine. "Gerda Lerner on the Future of Our Past: Interview. **Ms. Magazine,** (September 1981):51-52, 93-95.

Strobel, Margaret. "Doing Oral History as an Outsider." **Frontiers,** Vol. 2, No. 2 (1977):68-72.

Thomas, Hilah F. and Rosemary Skinner Keller (eds.) **Women in New Worlds.** Nashville, Tennessee: Abingdon, 1981.

Thomas, Sherry. "Digging Beneath the Surface: Oral History Techniques." **Frontiers,** Vol. 7, No. 1 (1983):50-55.

Thompson, Laura. "Crisis on Guam." **Far Eastern Quarterly,** Vol. 1 (November 1946):5-11.

_____. **Guam and Its People.** 3rd edition. Princeton, New Jersey: Princeton University Press, 1947.

_____. The Native Culture of the Marianas Islands. Honolulu: **Bernice P. Bishop Museum Bulletin 185.** Honolulu, Hawaii: Bernice P. Bishop Museum, 1945.

_____. "The Women of Guam." **Asia and the Americas,** (September 1944):412-415.

Tiffany, Sharon W. "Models and the Social Anthropology of Women: A Preliminary Assessment." **Man (N.S.)** Vol. 13, No. 1 (March 1978):34-51.

Tiffany, Sharon W. (ed.). **Women and Society: An Anthropological Reader.** St. Albans, Vermont: Eden Press Women's Publications, 1979.

_____. **Women, Work and Motherhood, The Power of Female Sexuality in the Workplace.** Englewood Cliffs, New Jersey: Prentice-Hall, Inc., 1982.

Transcriptions of Case Study Interviews:
> **Elizabeth Arriola Transcription,** November 1983
> **Cecilia Bamba Transcription,** Oct./Nov. 1983
> **Tina Blas Transcription,** November 1983
> **Clotilde Gould Transcription,** November 1983
> **Geri Gutierrez Transcription,** November 1983
> **Delgadina Hiton Transcription,** October 1983
> **Pilar Lujan Transcription,** November 1983
> **Carmen Pearson Transcription,** October 1983
> **Annie Roberto Transcription,** October 1983

Trask, Haunani-Kay. "Fighting the Battle of Double Colonization: The View of a Hawaiian." Unpublished manuscript, n.d.

Underwood, Jane H. "Population History of Guam: Context of Microevolution." **Micronesica,** Vol. 9, No. 1 (July 1973):11- 44.

Underwood, Robert A. "Chamorro Studies Convention: Evaluation and Summary." Unpublished Report, Agana, Guam, n.d.

_____. "The 1981 Guam Teachers Strike: A Cross Cultural Analysis," Unpublished Paper, Guam, 1984.

_____. "The Role of Mass Media in Small Pacific Societies: The Case of Guam." Panorama, **Guam Tribune,** Part 1 (19 August 1983): Part 2 (26 August 1983).

U.S. Congress. 9 [Stat. 1] 62 P1 95-134, 15 October 1977.

U.S. Bureau of the Census. 1980 Census of Population, General Population Characteristics, Guam. Washington, D.C.: Government Printing Office, April 1983.

Walkowitz, Judith R., Ellen Dubois, Mari Jo Buhle, Temma

Kaplan, Gerda Lerner, and Carroll Smith-Rosenberg. "Politics and Culture in Women's History: A Symposium." **Feminist Studies**, Vol. 6, No. 1 (Spring, 1980):26-64.

Walton, Patty. "Across Cultures." **Women**, Vol.7, No. 2 (1980):40-46.

"War Claims Responsibility of Legislative Committee." *Tolai Mensahi*, Quarterly Newsletter of Senator Bamba, No. 3:(n.d.):6.

Weaver, Juanita. "It's Always the Women: An Interview with Community Organizer Marie Nahikian." **Quest, Women in Their Communities**, Vol. 4, No. 4 (Fall 1978).

Westkott, Marcia. "Feminist Criticism of the Social Sciences." **Harvard Educational Review**, Vol. 49, No. 4 (November 1979).

_____. "Women's Studies as a Strategy for Change: Between Criticism and Vision." pp. 123-130 in Gloria Bowles and Renate Duelli-Klein (eds.), **Theories of Women's Studies II**. Berkeley, California: University of California, 1981.

"Whalers in Guam in 1850." **Guam Recorder**, (June 1925):102, 103, 121; (July 1925):140, 141.

White, Gloria. "Mary Church Terrell: Organizer of Black Women." **Integrated Education**, Vol. 17, No. 5-6 (1980):2-8.

Wilson, Amrit. **Finding a Voice, Asian Women in Britain**. London: Virago, 1978.

Women's Organizations of Guam Directory. Agana, Guam: The Women of St. John the Divine, 1983.

Women Speak Out! **A Report of the Pacific Woman's Conference, October 27-November 2, 1975**, Suva, Fiji: The Pacific Women's Conference, 1976.

GLOSSARY OF CHAMORRO TERMS

ahu (coconut sweet drink)
aniti (souls of ancestors)
antes (before)
Apostot (Apostles)
boddek, bodig (muscular disease)
chinchule' (reciprocal system of exchange and obligation)
dama di noche (woman of the night)
eskabeche (vinegar and fish dish)
Eskuelan notmat, escuelan normal (Normal School)
eskuelan pale' (Priests' school)
fiesta (party, celebration, feast day)
Fu'una (Mythical ancestress)
Guahan (Guam)
haga (daughter)
haga' (blood)
hagan-haga' (blood-daughter)
kakahna (class of sorcerers)
kanta, canta (sing)
karosa, carosa (float)
kelaguen (chicken and coconut salad)
kompadre, compadre (godfather)
kostumbren Chamorro, costumbren Chamorro (traditional
        Chamorro culture)
kuleho, colegio (college)
kumadre, comadre (godmother)
kumadren, comadren (godmother's)
litiku, litigo (muscular disease)
ma'estro (teacher)
maga'haga (oldest woman)
maga'lahi (oldest brother of maga'haga)
ma'is (corn)
makahna (class of sorcerers)
manamko' (elders)

manginge' (sign of respect)
manmaloffan na tiempo (lived experience)
manu (traditional stone implements)
matao (highest caste)
mata'pang (lackluster or immature)
mitati, metati (traditional stone implements)
nana (mother)
Nana'huyong (beginning)
nobena (novena)
Nobenan Niño (novena to the infant Jesus at Christmas)
pa'go (now)
parientes (extended families)
pueblos (village communities)
Putan (mythical ancestor)
Santa Maria Kamalin (Blessed Mother)
sasalaguan (hell)
soltera (young woman)
suruhana (traditional healer)
tan (respect term for elder)
tangantangan (a bothersome weed)
taotaomo'na (people of before)
tata (grandfather)
tataga' (unicorn fish)
techa (prayer leader)
ti'ao (small goat fish)
Uritao (associations of unmarried young men)

INDEX

Department of Public Health and Social Services, 135

Land claims, 118, 120, 123, 124, 131
Leacock, Eleanor, 226
League of Women Voters, 101, 156, 212
Lerner, Gerda, 10, 11, 234
Life history, 12, 13
Lujan, Pilar C., 17, 136, 150-152, 154, 158, 170, 181, 229

Marriage, 19, 32, 44, 47, 49, 51-54, 67, 68, 83, 126, 161, 165, 167, 170, 173, 176, 181, 197, 210, 227, 232, 233
Matrifocal, 54, 58
Matrilineal, 44, 227, 228
Modern culture (See Modernization)
Modernization, 4, 6, 8, 17, 27, 38, 41, 193, 228, 229, 232, 236, 239, 240
Mother-centered, 54

National Women's Conference, 103, 147
Naval Administration, 7, 62
Networking, 125, 128, 161, 203, 204, 213, 223, 224, 225
Nobena, 69, 175
Nurses, 72
Nursing, 135, 177

Oral history, 12-14, 20, 21

Pa'go, 7 (See also Modern culture)
Parent-Teachers' Association (PTA), 103, 157, 192, 203, 214
Pearson, Carmen L.G., 17, 136, 161, 164, 170, 181, 205, 217, 229
Pescatello, Ann M., 234, 235
Political status, 41, 95, 97, 144, 242
Postwar, 34, 35, 72, 83, 153
Precontact period, 7, 32
Prewar, 49, 69, 72, 87, 118, 153
Proverbs, 19, 55

Religious Sisters of Mercy, 202
Retired Senior Volunteer Program (RSVP), 176
Roberto, Annie P., 17, 136, 169, 170, 172, 173, 176, 178, 179, 181, 229

Social network, 186, 224, 225
Sodality of Mary, 69, 108, 137, 153-155, 170, 201, 212
Spanish period, 7, 68
Support groups, 194, 202
Support network, 16, 73, 182, 216
Support system, 15, 21, 45, 126, 128, 130, 181, 182, 185, 186, 192, 204, 223, 224
Suruhana, 58, 65, 66, 174, 175, 176

Teachers, 60, 61, 68, 72, 136, 142, 188, 192, 203, 239

About the Author

Laura Marie Torres Souder was born on Guam and received her early education at St. Francis School, Cathedral Grade School and the Academy of Our Lady. She received her undergraduate degree in Sociology from Emmanuel College (1972), her MA (1977) in Sociology and Ph.D. (1985) in American Studies from the Univeristy of Hawaii, and a Ford Foundation Post-Doctoral Fellowship for Minorities at De Paul University (1990). She has served as an Ambassador-at-Large for the island on occassions and has been a delegate or representative at meetings held beyond the shores of Guam. At home she is engaged in a variety of activities representing a wide range of professional, civic, charitable, cultural, and women-centered organizations and issues. An active organizer in her own right, she has directed political campaigns and numerous islandwide projects. She currently serves as director of the Western Pacific Women's Research Institute at the University of Guam and the Chamorro Documentary Project. Her commitment to Chamorro self-determination and the continuity of peoplehood is clearly seen in this book and in her other works. She co-edited **Women in Guam** (1972) and **Chamorro Self-Determination: The Rights of a People** (1987). Laura is an Associate Professor of Sociology in the College of Arts and Sciences at the University of Guam.